Domestic Gas Safety On

Contents: Part 1

Contents: Part 2

1. Gas Safety Legislation

1.1 The Gas Safety (Installation and Use) Regulations 1998

The major piece of legislation (law) relevant to gas engineers is "The Gas Safety (Installation and Use) Regulations 1998" [GSI&UR].

These regulations places responsibilities on a number of people carrying out their normal work activity, on gas appliances and pipework using both natural and liquefied petroleum gas on gas appliances in a variety of premises. The Gas Safety (Installation and Use) Regulations are reproduced in full within this section.

But this legislation does not stand alone, as there are number of other statutory (legally punishable) requirements that must be met whilst undertaking work, they include;

1.2 Health and Safety at Work Act 1974

This act applies to everyone concerned with work activities, every employer has a duty to ensure the health, safety and welfare of their employees while at work.

Employers and self employed people are required to carry out work in a manner which is as far as reasonably practical ensures that they do not expose people who are not their employees to risks to their health and safety.

1.3 Gas Act 1986 & 1995

The 1986 Gas Act amended in 1995 deals with a number of safety issues and duties, such as;

- To notify the connection and disconnection of service pipes and disconnection of meters in certain circumstances.
- Maintenance of service pipes.
- Duties on public gas transporter in relation to certain gas escapes.

1.4 Gas Safety (Rights of Entry) Regulations 1996

These regulations give rights where required to the gas transporter to enter premises;

- Where gas is escaping or may escape, to carry out necessary work to prevent any danger to life and property.
- Where a service pipe is connected to a gas main, inspect and test any gas fitting, flue and means of ventilation or any part of the gas system on the premises'.
- For the purpose of averting danger to life or property disconnect and seal off any gas fitting or any part of a gas system, including the disconnection of the whole premises gas supply.

1.5 Reporting of Injuries, Diseases and Dangerous Occurrences Regulations 1995 (RIDDOR)

The purpose of reporting serious accidents is to enable the Health and Safety Executive (HSE) or local authorities, to evaluate how and where risks arise and help them offer methods to reduce illness and injury within the workplace. It places a legal duty on employers, self-employed people and people in control of premises to report:

- Work-related deaths.
- Major injuries (i.e. fracture other than to fingers, thumbs or toes etc).
- Where persons are absent from work for more than 3 working days .
- Work related diseases (i.e. some skin diseases such as occupational dermatitis etc).
- Dangerous occurrences (including near miss accidents).

This regulation also includes the need to report a gas fitting and any flue or ventilation used with a gas fitting that is by reason of its:

- Design.
- Construction.
- Manner of installation.
- Modification.
- Servicing (including lack of servicing).

Is or has been likely to cause death, or any major injury by reason of:

- accidental leakage of gas;
- inadequate combustion of gas; or
- inadequate removal of the products of combustion of gas,

1.6 The Gas Appliance (Safety) Regulations 1995

This regulation requires that manufacturers shall only supply an appliance or fittings that satisfy essential requirements (constructed to operate safely and have instructions for use by installer and user), and when used under normal use is safe.

Normal use includes:

- Correctly installed and regularly serviced in accordance with manufacturer's instructions.
- Correct gas pressure.
- Intended purpose.

The appliance shall also bear CE Marking which is to be affixed to appliances (or on data plate) or fitting certificate (certificate of conformity) to be supplied with the appliance. Along with the CE marking the following details should also be clearly visible;

- Manufacturer's name (or authorized representative).
- The trade name of the appliance.
- The type of any electrical supply to be used in connection with the appliance;
- The appliance category.
- The last 2 digits of the year in which the CE marking was affixed.

1.7 The Gas Safety (Management) Regulations 1996

Requires that a gas transporter who is conveying gas through a network to have a safety case that is acceptable to the Health and Safety Executive, which must be reviewed every 3 years.

Where gas escapes from a network or from a fitting connected to a network, the company that conveys gas in that part of the network shall attend the place where the escape is, as soon as is reasonably practical after being informed and shall stop the leak within 12 hours.

The need to have a central emergency call centre number which is a direct line, and the investigation of a RIDDOR situations which involves carbon monoxide is also a requirement covered by this legislation.

Further requirements are that investigations are carried out by a persons who are competent, and the Health and Safety Executive are informed prior to the investigation and receive a copy of the report when completed.

1.8 Building Regulations (England and Wales) 2010

The aim of building regulations are to:

- Secure the health and safety, welfare and convenience of people in or about buildings and of others who may be affected by buildings or matters connected with buildings.
- Further the conservation of fuel and power.
- Prevent waste, undue consumption, misuse or contamination of water.

Anyone wanting to carry out building work which is subject to the Building Regulations is required by law to make sure the work complies with the Regulations and with some exceptions, is to use one of the two types of Building Control Service available (there will be a charge for either service), i.e.

- The Building Control Service provided by the local authority or,
- The Building Control Service provided by approved inspectors.

The exceptions mentioned above arises if the approved Competent Person Scheme is used. Competent Person Scheme are approved by the Secretary of State for specific parts of the Building Regulations. Work carried out by a registrant of such a scheme does not have to notify to building control prior to commencement and the business concerned can self-certify that the work complies with Building Regulations.

1.8.1 Approved Documents

Practical guidance on ways to comply with the functional requirements in the Building Regulations is contained in a series of 'Approved Documents' that are to be read alongside each of the 14 'parts' in schedule 1 to the Building Regulations.

England & Wales Building Regulations	
Structure	A
Fire safety	B
Ventilation	F
Sanitation, Hot Water and Water Efficiency	G
Combustion appliances and fuel storage systems	J
Conservations of fuel and power	L
Access to and use of buildings	M
Electrical safety	P

Table 1.1

1.9 Building (Scotland) Amendment Regulations 2010

The requirements of the Building (Scotland) Regulations are broadly in line with those of England and Wales, however in Scotland the functional requirements are specified in Building Standards Technical handbooks. The handbooks are subdivided into 7 sections as detailed in table 1.2. To ensure compliance specific detailed requirements are given in these standards. Where doubt exists the local building control office should be contacted prior to any works being carried out.

Scotland Building Standards	
General	0
Structure	1
Fire	2
Environment	3
Safety	4
Noise	5
Energy	6

Table 1.2

1.10 Northern Ireland and The Isle of Man

In Northern Ireland a three phased consultation process started on 6th July 2010 to introduce a completely new set of Building Regulations by 2011. Each phase of the consultation process concentrates on specific parts of the Regulations with revised formats and guidance in a number of the Technical Booklets.

Northern Ireland Technical Booklets	
Site preparation and resistance to moisture	C
Structure	D
Fire Safety	E
Conservation of Fuel and Power in Dwellings	F1
Conservation of Fuel and Power in Buildings other than Dwellings	F2
Sound	G
Ventilation	K
Combustion Appliances and Fuel Storage Systems	L
Unvented Hot water Storage Systems	P

The Isle of Man Building Regulations 2007 approved documents follow the same structure as those for England and Wales. Although working to the same regulatory documents, caution must be observed are 3 different Building Control Authorities exist, namely the Department of Infrastructure, Douglas Corporation and the Onchan District Commissioners.

1.11 Gas Cooking Appliances (Safety) Regulations 1989

Second hand appliances must comply with these regulations under normal use. Normal use includes:

- Correctly installed and regularly serviced in accordance with manufacturer's instructions.
- Correct gas pressure.
- Intended purpose.

1.12 Confined Spaces Regulations 1997

Both employers and the self employed should not enter and prevent entry by others into confined spaces unless it cannot be avoided, before anyone enters a confined space a risk assessment must be conducted and a safe procedure put into place. Any procedure must include how to enter/exit the confined space and actions are required in the event of an emergency.

Confined spaces include:

- Ductwork.
- Combustion chambers in furnaces.
- Unvented or poorly ventilated rooms.

1.13 Control of Substances Hazardous to Health Regulations (CoSHH) 2002

These regulations reinforce the HSWA requirement to not expose employees to risk to their health during work activities, work must not be carried out until the employer has assessed the risk and put measures into place to minimise any risk that are present. The measure should include:

- Inform employees of risk.
- Carry out any training required.
- Ensure risks are minimised.
- Ensure control measures required are in place and are used i.e. personnel protective equipment.

1.14 Gas Safety (Installation & Use) Regulations 1998

1998 No. 2451

HEALTH AND SAFETY

The Gas Safety (Installation and Use) Regulations 1998

Made 3rd October 1998

Laid before Parliament 9th October 1998

Coming into force 31st October 1998

ARRANGEMENT OF REGULATIONS

PART A

General

1. Citation and commencement.
2. General interpretation and application.

PART B

Gas Fittings - General Provisions

3. Qualification and supervision.
4. Duty on employer.
5. Materials and workmanship.
6. General safety precautions.
7. Protection against damage.
8. Existing gas fittings.
9. Emergency controls.
10. Maintaining electrical continuity.

PART C

Meters and Regulators

11. Interpretation of Part C.
12. Meters - general provisions.
13. Meter housings.
14. Regulators.
15. Meters - emergency notices.
16. Primary meters.
17. Secondary meters.

PART D

Installation Pipework

18. Safe use of pipes.
19. Enclosed pipes.
20. Protection of buildings.
21. Clogging precautions.
22. Testing and purging of pipes.
23. Marking of pipes.
24. Large consumers.

PART E

Gas Appliances

25. Interpretation of Part E.
26. Gas appliances - safety precautions.
27. Flues.
28. Access.
29. Manufacturer's instructions.
30. Room-sealed appliances.
31. Suspended appliances.
32. Flue dampers.
33. Testing of appliances.
34. Use of appliances.

PART F

Maintenance

35. Duties of employers and self-employed persons.
36. Duties of landlords.

PART G

Miscellaneous

37. Escape of gas.
38. Use of antifluctuators and valves.
39. Exception as to liability.
40. Exemption certificates.
41. Revocation and amendments.

The Secretary of State, in exercise of the powers conferred on him by sections 15(1), (2), (4)(a), (5), (6)(b) and 82(3)(a) of, and paragraphs 1(1), (2) and (3), 4(1), 12, 15(1) and 16 of Schedule 3 to, the Health and Safety at Work etc. Act 1974 ("the 1974 Act") and of all other powers enabling him in that behalf and for the purpose of giving effect without modifications to proposals submitted to him by the Health and Safety Commission under section 11(2)(d) of the 1974 Act after the carrying out by the said Commission of consultations in accordance with section 50(3) of that Act, hereby makes the following Regulations: -

PART A

GENERAL

Citation and commencement

1. These Regulations may be cited as the Gas Safety (Installation and Use) Regulations 1998 and shall come into force on 3rd October 1998.

General interpretation and application

2. (1) In these Regulations, unless the context otherwise requires
- "appropriate fitting" means a fitting which -

(a) has been designed for the purpose of effecting a gas tight seal in a pipe or other gasway;

(b) achieves that purpose when fitted; and

(c) is secure, so far as is reasonably practicable, against unauthorised opening or removal;

"distribution main" means any main through which a transporter is for the time being distributing gas and which is not being used only for the purpose of conveying gas in bulk;

"emergency control" means a valve for shutting off the supply of gas in an emergency, being a valve intended for use by a consumer of gas;

"flue" means a passage for conveying the products of combustion from a gas appliance to the external air and includes any part of the passage in a gas appliance duct which serves the purpose of a flue;

"gas" means any substance which is or (if it were in a gaseous state) would be gas within the meaning of the Gas Act 1986 except that it does not include gas consisting wholly or mainly of hydrogen when used in non-domestic premises;

"gas appliance" means an appliance designed for use by a consumer of gas for heating, lighting, cooking or other purposes for which gas can be used but it does not include a portable or mobile appliance suppled with gas from a cylinder, or the cylinder, pipes and other fittings used for supplying gas to that appliance, save that, for the purposes of regulations 3, 35 and 36 of these Regulations, it does include a portable or mobile space heater supplied with gas from a cylinder, and the cylinder, pipes and other fittings used for supplying gas to that heater;

"gas fittings" means gas pipework, valves (other than emergency controls), regulators and meters, and fittings, apparatus and appliances designed for use by consumers of gas for heating, lighting, cooking or other purposes for which gas can be used (other than the purpose of an industrial process carried out on industrial premises), but it does not mean -

(a) any part of a service pipe;

(b) any part of a distribution main or other pipe upstream of the service pipe;

(c) a gas storage vessel; or

(d) a gas cylinder or cartridge designed to be disposed of when empty;

"gas storage vessel" means a storage container designed to be filled or re-filled with gas at the place where it is connected for use or a re-fillable cylinder designed to store gas, and includes the vapour valve; but it does not include a cylinder or cartridge designed to be disposed of when empty;

"gas water heater" includes a gas fired central heating boiler;

"installation pipework" means any pipework for conveying gas for a particular consumer and any associated valve or other gas fitting including any pipework used to connect a gas appliance to other installation pipework and any shut off device at the inlet to the appliance, but it does not mean:

(a) a service pipe;

(b) a pipe comprised in a gas appliance;

(c) any valve attached to a storage container or cylinder; or

(d) service pipework;

"meter by pass" means any pipe and other gas fittings used in connection with it through which gas can be conveyed from a service pipe or service pipework to installation pipework without passing through the meter;

"primary meter" means the meter nearest to and downstream of a service pipe or service pipework for ascertaining the quantity of gas supplied through that pipe or pipework by a supplier;

"re-fillable cylinder" means a cylinder which is filled other than at the place where it is connected for use;

"the responsible person", in relation to any premises, means the occupier of the premises or, where there is no occupier or the occupier is away, the owner of the premises or any person with authority for the time being to take appropriate action in relation to any gas fitting therein;

"room-sealed appliance" means an appliance whose combustion system is sealed from the room in which the appliance is located and which obtains air for combustion from a ventilated uninhabited space within the premises or directly from the open air outside the premises and which vents the products of combustion directly to open air outside the premises;

"service pipe" means a pipe for distributing gas to premises from a distribution main, being any pipe between the distribution main and the outlet of the first emergency control downstream from the distribution main;

"service pipework" means a pipe for supplying gas to premises from a gas storage vessel, being any pipe between the gas storage vessel and the outlet of the emergency control;

"service valve" means a valve (other than an emergency control) for controlling a supply of gas, being a valve -

(a) incorporated in a service pipe; and

(b) intended for use by a transporter of gas; and

(c) not situated inside a building;

"supplier" in relation to gas means -

(a) a person who supplies gas to any premises through a primary meter; or

(b) a person who provides a supply of gas to a consumer by means of the filling or re-filling of a storage container designed to be filled or re-filled with gas at the place where it is connected for use whether or not such container is or remains the property of the supplier; or

(c) a person who provides gas in re-fillable cylinders for use by a consumer whether or not such cylinders are filled or re-filled directly by that person and whether or not such cylinders are or remain the property of that person, but a retailer shall not be deemed to be a supplier when he sells a brand of gas other than his own;

"transporter" in relation to gas means a person who conveys gas through a distribution main;

"work" in relation to a gas fitting includes any of the following activities carried out by any person, whether an employee or not, that is to say -

(a) installing or re-connecting the fitting;

(b) maintaining, servicing, permanently adjusting, disconnecting, repairing, altering or renewing the fitting or purging it of air or gas;

(c) where the fitting is not readily movable, changing its position; and

(d) removing the fitting;

but the expression does not include the connection or disconnection of a bayonet fitting or other self-sealing connector.

(2) For the purposes of these Regulations -

(a) any reference to installing a gas fitting includes a reference to converting any pipe, fitting, meter, apparatus or appliance to gas use; and

(b) a person to whom gas is supplied and who provides that gas for use in a flat or part of premises let by him shall not in so doing be deemed to be supplying gas.

(3) Subject to paragraphs (4) and (5) below, these Regulations shall apply to or in relation to gas fittings used in connection with -

(a) gas which has been conveyed to premises through a distribution main; or

(b) gas conveyed from a gas storage vessel.

(4) Save for regulations 37, 38 and 41 and subject to regulation 3(8), these Regulations shall not apply in relation to the supply of gas to, or anything done in respect of a gas fitting at, the following premises, that is to say -

(a) a mine or quarry within the meaning of the Mines and Quarries Act 1954 or any place deemed to form part of a mine or quarry for the purposes of that Act;

(b) a factory within the meaning of the Factories Act 1961 or any place to which any provisions of the said Act apply by virtue of sections 123 to 126 of that Act;

(c) agricultural premises, being agricultural land, including land being or forming part of a market garden, and any building thereon which is used in connection with agricultural operations;

(d) temporary installations used in connection with any construction work within the meaning assigned to that phrase by regulation 2(1) of the Construction (Design and Management) Regulations 1994;

(e) premises used for the testing of gas fittings; or

(f) premises used for the treatment of sewage,

but they shall apply in relation to such premises or part thereof used for domestic or residential purposes or as sleeping accommodation.

(5) Nothing in these Regulations shall apply in relation to the supply of gas to, or anything done in respect of a gas fitting on -

(a) a self-propelled vehicle except when such a vehicle is -

(i) hired out in the course of a business; or

(ii) made available to members of the public in the course of a business carried on from that vehicle;

(b) a sea-going ship;

(c) a vessel not requiring a national or international load line certificate except when such vessel is -

(i) hired out in the course of a business;

(ii) made available to members of the public in the course of a business carried out from that vessel; or

(iii) used primarily for domestic or residential purposes;

(d) a hovercraft; or

(e) a caravan used for touring otherwise than when hired out in the course of a business.

(6) Nothing in these Regulations shall apply in relation to -

(a) the supply of gas to the propulsion system of any vehicle or to any gas fitting forming part of such propulsion system;

(b) the supply of gas to, or anything done in respect of, a bunsen burner used in an educational establishment; or

(c) work in relation to a control device on a gas appliance if -

(i) the device is intended primarily for use by a consumer of gas; and

(ii) the work does not involve breaking into a gasway.

(7) These Regulations shall not apply in relation to a gas fitting used for the purpose of training gas fitting operatives in a college or other training establishment, except that paragraphs (1) to (5) and (7) of regulation 3 shall apply to work in relation to a gas fitting carried out by a person providing such training.

(8) These Regulations shall not apply in relation to a gas fitting used for the purpose of assessing the competence of a gas fitting operative at an assessment centre where such assessment is carried out for the purposes of a nationally accredited certification scheme, except that regulation 3(1) and (2) shall apply to work in relation to a gas fitting carried out by a person carrying out such assessment.

PART B

GAS FITTINGS - GENERAL PROVISIONS

Qualification and supervision

3. (1) No person shall carry out any work in relation to a gas fitting or gas storage vessel unless he is competent to do so.

(2) The employer of any person carrying out such work for that employer, every other employer and self-employed person who has control to any extent of such work and every employer and self-employed person who has required such work to be carried out at any place of work under his control shall ensure that paragraph (1) above is complied with in relation to such work.

(3) Without prejudice to the generality of paragraphs (1) and (2) above and subject to paragraph (4) below, no employer shall allow any of his employees to carry out any work in relation to a gas fitting or service pipework and no self-employed person shall carry out any such work, unless the employer or self-employed person, as the case may be, is a member of a class of persons approved for the time being by the Health and Safety Executive for the purposes of this paragraph.

(4) The requirements of paragraph (3) above shall not apply in respect of -

(a) the replacement of a hose or regulator on a portable or mobile space heater; or

(b) the replacement of a hose connecting a re-fillable cylinder to installation pipework.

(5) An approval given pursuant to paragraph (3) above (and any withdrawal of such approval) shall be in writing and notice of it shall be given to such persons and in such manner as the Health and Safety Executive considers appropriate.

(6) The employer of any person carrying out any work in relation to a gas fitting or gas storage vessel in the course of his employment shall ensure that such of the following provisions of these Regulations as impose duties upon that person and are for the time being in force are complied with by that person.

(7) No person shall falsely pretend to be a member of a class of persons required to be approved under paragraph (3) above.

(8) Notwithstanding sub-paragraph (b) of regulation 2(4), when a person is carrying out work in premises referred to in that sub-paragraph in relation to a gas fitting in a vehicle, vessel or caravan -

(a) paragraphs (1), (2) and (6) of this regulation shall be complied with as respects thereto; and

(b) he shall ensure, so far as is reasonably practicable, that the installation of the gas fittings and flues will not contravene the provisions of these Regulations when the gas fittings are connected to a gas supply,

except that this paragraph shall not apply where the person has reasonable grounds for believing that the vehicle, vessel or caravan will be first used for a purpose which when so used will exclude it from the application of these Regulations by virtue of sub-paragraphs (a), (c) or (e) of regulation 2(5).

Duty on employer

4. Where an employer or a self-employed person requires any work in relation to a gas fitting to be carried out at any place of work under his control or where an employer or self-employed person has control to any extent of work in relation to a gas fitting, he shall take reasonable steps to ensure that the person undertaking that work is, or is employed by, a member of a class of persons approved by the Health and Safety Executive under regulation 3(3) above.

Materials and workmanship

5. (1) No person shall install a gas fitting unless every part of it is of good construction and sound material, of adequate strength and size to secure safety and of a type appropriate for the gas with which it is to be used.

(2) Without prejudice to the generality of paragraph (1) above, no person shall install in a building any pipe or pipe fitting for use in the supply of gas which is -

(a) made of lead or lead alloy; or

(b) made of a non-metallic substance unless it is -

(i) a pipe connected to a readily movable gas appliance designed for use without a flue; or

(ii) a pipe entering the building and that part of it within the building is placed inside a metallic sheath which is so constructed and installed as to prevent, so far as is reasonably practicable, the escape of gas into the building if the pipe should fail.

(3) No person shall carry out any work in relation to a gas fitting or gas storage vessel otherwise than in accordance with appropriate standards and in such a way as to prevent danger to any person.

General safety precautions

6. (1) No person shall carry out any work in relation to a gas fitting in such a manner that gas could be released unless steps are taken to prevent the gas so released constituting a danger to any person.

(2) No person carrying out work in relation to a gas fitting shall leave the fitting unattended unless every incomplete gasway has been sealed with the appropriate fitting or the gas fitting is otherwise safe.

(3) Any person who disconnects a gas fitting shall, with the appropriate fitting, seal off every outlet of every pipe to which it was connected.

(4) No person carrying out work in relation to a gas fitting which involves exposing gasways which contain or have contained flammable gas shall smoke or use any source of ignition in such a manner as may lead to the risk of fire or explosion.

(5) No person searching for an escape of gas shall use any source of ignition.

(6) Where a person carries out any work in relation to a gas fitting which might affect the gas tightness of the gas installation he shall immediately thereafter test the installation for gas tightness at least as far as the nearest valves upstream and downstream in the installation.

(7) No person shall install a gas storage vessel unless the site where it is to be installed is such as to ensure that the gas storage vessel can be used, filled or refilled without causing a danger to any person.

(8) No person shall install in a cellar or basement -

(a) a gas storage vessel; or

(b) an appliance fuelled by liquefied petroleum gas which has an automatic ignition device or a pilot light.

(9) No person shall intentionally or recklessly interfere with a gas storage vessel or otherwise do anything which might affect a gas storage vessel so that the subsequent use of that vessel might cause a danger to any person.

(10) No person shall store or keep gas consisting wholly or mainly of methane on domestic premises, and, for the purpose of this paragraph, such gas from time to time present in pipes or in the fuel tank of any vehicle propelled by gas shall be deemed not to be so stored or kept.

Protection against damage

7. (1) Any person installing a gas fitting shall ensure that it is properly supported and so placed or protected as to avoid any undue risk of damage to the fitting.

(2) No person shall install a gas fitting if he has reason to suspect that foreign matter may block or otherwise interfere with the safe operation of the fitting unless he has fitted to the gas inlet of, and any airway in, the fitting a suitable filter or other suitable protection.

(3) No person shall install a gas fitting in a position where it is likely to be exposed to any substance which may corrode gas fittings unless the fitting is constructed of materials which are inherently resistant to being so corroded or it is suitably protected against being so corroded.

Existing gas fittings

8. (1) No person shall make any alteration to any premises in which a gas fitting or gas storage vessel is fitted if that alteration would adversely affect the safety of the fitting or vessel in such a manner that, if the fitting or the vessel had been installed after the alteration, there would have been a contravention of, or failure to comply with, these Regulations.

(2) No person shall do anything which would affect a gas fitting or any flue or means of ventilation used in connection with the fitting in such a manner that the subsequent use of the fitting might constitute a danger to any person, except that this paragraph does not apply to an alteration to premises.

(3) In relation to any place of work under his control, an employer or a self-employed person shall ensure, so far as is reasonably practicable, that the provisions of paragraphs (1) and (2) above are complied with.

Emergency controls

9. (1) No person shall for the first time enable gas to be supplied for use in any premises unless there is provided an appropriately sited emergency control to which there is adequate access.

(2) Any person installing an emergency control shall ensure that -

(a) any key, lever or hand-wheel of the control is securely attached to the operating spindle of the control;

(b) any such key or lever is attached so that -

(i) the key or lever is parallel to the axis of the pipe in which the control is installed when the control is in the open position; and

(ii) where the key or lever is not attached so as to move only horizontally, gas cannot pass beyond the control when the key or lever has been moved as far as possible downwards;

(c) either the means of operating the key or lever is clearly and permanently marked or a notice in permanent form is prominently displayed near such means so as to indicate when the control is open and when the control is shut; and

(d) any hand-wheel indicates the direction of opening or closing of the control.

(3) Where a person installs an emergency control which is not adjacent to a primary meter, he shall immediately thereafter prominently display on or near the means of operating the control a suitably worded notice in permanent form indicating the procedure to be followed in the event of an escape of gas.

(4) Where any person first supplies gas to premises where an emergency control is installed, he shall ensure that the notice required by paragraph (3) above remains suitably worded or shall, where necessary, forthwith amend or replace that notice so as to give effect to the provisions of that paragraph.

(5) This regulation shall not apply where gas is supplied in a refillable cylinder except where two or more cylinders are connected by means of an automatic change-over device.

Maintaining electrical continuity

10. In any case where it is necessary to prevent danger, no person shall carry out work in relation to a gas fitting without using a suitable bond to maintain electrical continuity until the work is completed and permanent electrical continuity has been restored.

PART C

METERS AND REGULATORS

Interpretation of Part C

11. In this Part -

"meter box" means a receptacle or compartment designed and constructed to contain a meter with its associated fittings;

"meter compound" means an area or room designed and constructed to contain one or more meters with their associated fittings;

"secondary meter" means a meter, other than a primary meter, for ascertaining the quantity of gas provided by a person for use by another person.

Meters - general provisions

12. (1) No person shall install a meter in any premises unless the site where it is to be installed is such as to ensure so far as is reasonably practicable that the means of escape from those premises in the event of fire is not adversely affected.

(2) No person shall install a meter in any premises unless it is of sound construction adequate to ensure so far as is reasonably practicable that in the event of fire gas is not able to escape in hazardous quantities, save that this paragraph shall not apply to any meter installed in non-domestic premises to which gas is supplied through a readily accessible service valve.

(3) No person shall install a meter unless the installation is so placed as to ensure that there is no risk of damage to it from electrical apparatus.

(4) No person shall install a meter except in a readily accessible position for inspection and maintenance.

(5) Where a meter has bosses or side pipes attached to the meter by a soldered joint only, no person shall make rigid pipe connections to the meter.

(6) Where a person installs a meter and the pipes and other gas fittings associated with it, he shall ensure that -

(a) immediately thereafter they are adequately tested to verify that they are gas tight and examined to verify that they have been installed in accordance with these Regulations; and

(b) immediately after such testing and examination, purging is carried out throughout the meter and every other gas fitting through which gas can then flow so as to remove safely all air and gas other than the gas to be supplied.

Meter housings

13. (1) Where a meter is housed in a meter box or meter compound attached to or built into the external face of the outside wall of any premises, the meter box or meter compound shall be so constructed and installed that any gas escaping within the box or compound cannot enter the premises or any cavity in the wall but must disperse to the external air.

(2) No person shall knowingly store readily combustible materials in any meter box or meter compound.

(3) No person shall install a meter in a meter box provided with a lock, unless the consumer has been provided with a suitably labelled key to that lock.

(4) No person shall install a meter within a meter compound which is capable of being secured unless the consumer has been provided with a suitably labelled key for that compound.

Regulators

14. (1) No person shall install a primary meter or meter by pass used in connection with a primary meter unless -

(a) there is a regulator controlling the pressure of gas supplied through the meter or the by pass, as the case may be, which provides adequate automatic means for preventing the gas fittings connected to the downstream side of the regulator from being subjected to a pressure greater than that for which they were designed;

(b) where the normal pressure of the gas supply is 75 millibars or more at the inlet to the regulator, there are also adequate automatic means for preventing, in case the regulator should fail, those gas fittings from being subjected to such a greater pressure; and

(c) where the regulator contains a relief valve or liquid seal, such valve or seal is connected to a vent pipe of adequate size and so installed that it is capable of venting safely.

(2) Without prejudice to the requirements of paragraph (1), no person shall cause gas to be supplied from a gas storage vessel (other than a re-fillable cylinder or a cylinder or cartridge designed to be disposed of when empty) to any service pipework or gas fitting unless -

(a) there is a regulator installed which controls the nominal operating pressure of the gas;

(b) there is adequate automatic means for preventing the installation pipework and gas fittings downstream of the regulator from being subjected to a pressure different from that for which they were designed; and

(c) there is an adequate alternative automatic means for preventing the service pipework from being subjected to a greater pressure than that for which it was designed should the regulator referred to in sub-paragraph (a) above fail.

(3) No person shall cause gas to be supplied through an installation consisting of one or more re-fillable cylinders unless the supply of gas passes through a regulator which controls the nominal operating pressure of the gas.

(4) Without prejudice to paragraph (3) above, no person shall cause gas to be supplied through an installation consisting of four or more re-fillable cylinders connected to an automatic change-over device unless there is an adequate alternative means for preventing the installation pipework and any gas fitting downstream of the regulator from being subjected to a greater pressure than that for which it was designed should the regulator fail.

(5) Where a person installs a regulator for controlling the pressure of gas through a primary meter, a meter by pass used in connection with a primary meter or from a gas storage vessel, or installs a gas appliance itself fitted with a regulator for controlling the pressure of gas to that appliance, he shall immediately thereafter ensure, in either case, that the regulator is adequately sealed so as to prevent its setting from being interfered with without breaking of the seal.

(6) In relation to -

(a) gas from a distribution main, no person except the transporter or a person authorised to act on his behalf;

(b) gas from a gas storage vessel, no person except the supplier or a person authorised to act on his behalf,

shall break a seal applied under paragraph (5) above other than a seal applied to a regulator for controlling the pressure of gas to the appliance to which that regulator is fitted.

(7) A person who breaks a seal applied under paragraph (5) shall apply as soon as is practicable a new seal which is adequate to prevent the setting of the regulator from being interfered with without breaking such seal.

Meters - emergency notices

15. (1) No person shall supply gas through a primary meter installed after the coming into force of these Regulations or for the first time supply gas through an existing primary meter after the coming into force of these Regulations unless he ensures that a suitably worded notice in permanent form is prominently displayed on or near the meter indicating the procedure to be followed in the event of an escape of gas.

(2) Where a meter is installed or relocated in any premises in either case at a distance of more than 2 metres from, or out of sight of, the nearest upstream emergency control in the premises, no person shall supply or provide gas for the first time through that meter unless he ensures that a suitably worded notice in permanent form is prominently displayed on or near the meter indicating the position of that control.

Primary meters

16. (1) No person shall install a prepayment meter as a primary meter through which gas passes to a secondary meter.

(2) Any person -

(a) who first provides gas through any service pipe or service pipework after the coming into force of these Regulations to more than one primary meter; or

(b) who subsequently makes any modification which affects the number of primary meters so provided,

shall ensure that a notice in permanent form is prominently displayed on or near each primary meter indicating that more than one primary meter is provided with gas through that service pipe or service pipework.

(3) Where a primary meter is removed, the person who last supplied gas through the meter before removal shall -

(a) where the meter is not forthwith re-installed or replaced by another meter -

(i) close any service valve which controlled the supply of gas to that meter and did not control the supply of gas to any other primary meter; and

(ii) seal the outlet of the emergency control with an appropriate fitting; and

(iii) clearly mark any live gas pipe in the premises in which the meter was installed to the effect that the pipe contains gas; and

(b) where the meter has not been re-installed or replaced by another meter before the expiry of the period of 12 months beginning with the date of removal of the meter and there is no such service valve as is mentioned in sub-paragraph (a)(i)above, ensure that the service pipe or service pipework for those premises is disconnected as near as is reasonably practicable to the main or storage vessel and that any part of the pipe or pipework which is not removed is sealed at both ends with the appropriate fitting.

(4) Where a person proposes to remove a primary meter he shall give sufficient notice of it to the person supplying gas through the meter to enable him to comply with paragraph (3).

Secondary meters

17. (1) Any person supplying or permitting the supply of gas through a primary meter to a secondary meter shall ensure that a line diagram in permanent form is prominently displayed on or near the primary meter or gas storage vessel and on or near all emergency controls connected to the primary meter showing the configuration of all meters, installation pipework and emergency controls.

(2) Any person who changes the configuration of any meter, installation pipework or emergency control so that the accuracy of the line diagram referred to in paragraph (1) is affected shall ensure that the line diagram is amended so as to show the altered configuration.

PART D

INSTALLATION PIPEWORK

Safe use of pipes

18. (1) No person shall install any installation pipework in any position in which it cannot be used with safety having regard to the position of other pipes, pipe supports, drains, sewers, cables, conduits and electrical apparatus and to any parts of the structure of any premises in which it is installed which might affect its safe use.

(2) Any person who connects any installation pipework to a primary meter shall, in any case where electrical equipotential bonding may be necessary, inform the responsible person that such bonding should be carried out by a competent person.

Enclosed pipes

19. (1) No person shall install any part of any installation pipework in a wall or a floor or standing of solid construction unless it is so constructed and installed as to be protected against failure caused by the movement of the wall, the floor or the standing as the case may be.

(2) No person shall install any installation pipework so as to pass through a wall or a floor or standing of solid construction (whether or not it contains any cavity) from one side to the other unless -

(a) any part of the pipe within such wall, floor or standing as the case may be takes the shortest practicable route; and

(b) adequate means are provided to prevent, so far as is reasonably practicable, any escape of gas from the pipework passing through the wall, floor or standing from entering any cavity in the wall, floor or standing.

(3) No person shall, subject to paragraph (4), install any part of any installation pipework in a cavity wall unless the pipe is to pass through the wall from one side to the other.

(4) Paragraph (3) shall not apply to the installation of installation pipework connected to a living flame effect gas fire provided that the pipework in the cavity is as short as is reasonably practicable, is enclosed in a gas tight sleeve and sealed at the joint at which the pipework enters the fire; and in this paragraph a "living flame effect gas fire" means a gas fire -

(a) designed to simulate the effect of a solid fuel fire;

(b) designed to operate with a fanned flue system; and

(c) installed within the inner leaf of a cavity wall.

(5) No person shall install any installation pipework or any service pipework under the foundations of a building or in the ground under the base of a wall or footings unless adequate steps are taken to prevent damage to the installation pipework or service pipework in the event of the movement of those structures or the ground.

(6) Where any installation pipework is not itself contained in a ventilated duct, no person shall install any installation pipework in any shaft, duct or void which is not adequately ventilated.

Protection of buildings

20. No person shall install any installation pipework in a way which would impair the structure of a building or impair the fire resistance of any part of its structure.

Clogging precautions

21. No person shall install any installation pipework in which deposition of liquid or solid matter is likely to occur unless a suitable vessel for the reception of any deposit which may form is fixed to the pipe in a conspicuous and readily accessible position and safe means are provided for the removal of the deposit.

Testing and purging of pipes

22. (1) Where a person carries out work in relation to any installation pipework which might affect the gastightness of any part of it, he shall immediately thereafter ensure that -

(a) that part is adequately tested to verify that it is gastight and examined to verify that it has been installed in accordance with these Regulations; and

(b) after such testing and examination, any necessary protective coating is applied to the joints of that part.

(2) Where gas is being supplied to any premises in which any installation pipework is installed and a person carries out work in relation to the pipework, he shall also ensure that

(a) immediately after complying with the provisions of sub-paragraphs (a) and (b) of paragraph (1) above, purging is carried out throughout all installation pipework through which gas can then flow so as to remove safely all air and gas other than the gas to be supplied;

(b) immediately after such purging, if the pipework is not to be put into immediate use, it is sealed off at every outlet with the appropriate fitting;

(c) if such purging has been carried out through a loosened connection, the connection is retested for gastightness after it has been retightened; and

(d) every seal fitted after such purging is tested for gastightness.

(3) Where gas is not being supplied to any premises in which any installation pipework is installed -

(a) no person shall permit gas to pass into the installation pipework unless he has caused such purging, testing and other work as is specified in sub-paragraphs (a) to (d) of paragraph (2)above to be carried out;

(b) a person who provides a gas supply to those premises shall, unless he complies with sub-paragraph (a)above, ensure that the supply is sealed off with an appropriate fitting.

Marking of pipes

23. (1) Any person installing, elsewhere than in any premises or part of premises used only as a dwelling or for living accommodation, a part of any installation pipework which is accessible to inspection shall permanently mark that part in such a manner that it is readily recognisable as part of a pipe for conveying gas.

(2) The responsible person for the premises in which any such part is situated shall ensure that the part continues to be so recognisable so long as it is used for conveying gas.

Large consumers

24. (1) Where the service pipe to any building having two or more floors to which gas is supplied or (whether or not it has more than one floor) a floor having areas with a separate supply of gas has an internal diameter of 50 mm or more, no person shall install any incoming installation pipework supplying gas to any of those floors or areas, as the case may be, unless -

(a) a valve is installed in the pipe in a conspicuous and readily accessible position; and

(b) a line diagram in permanent form is attached to the building in a readily accessible position as near as practicable to -

(i) the primary meter or where there is no primary meter, the emergency control, or

(ii) the gas storage vessel,

indicating the position of all installation pipework of internal diameter of 25 mm or more, meters, emergency controls, valves and pressure test points of the gas supply systems in the building.

(2) Paragraph (1) above shall apply to service pipework as it applies to a service pipe except that reference therein to “50 mm or more” is to be reference to “30 mm or more”.

(3) In paragraph (1)(b) above “pressure test point” means a gas fitting to which a pressure gauge can be connected.

PART E

GAS APPLIANCES

Interpretation of Part E

25. In this Part -

"flue pipe" means a pipe forming a flue but does not include a pipe built as a lining into either a chimney or a gas appliance ventilation duct;

"operating pressure", in relation to a gas appliance, means the pressure of gas at which it is designed to operate.

Gas appliances - safety precautions

26. (1) No person shall install a gas appliance unless it can be used without constituting a danger to any person.

(2) No person shall connect a flued domestic gas appliance to the gas supply system except by a permanently fixed rigid pipe.

(3) No person shall install a used gas appliance without verifying that it is in a safe condition for further use.

(4) No person shall install a gas appliance which does not comply with any enactment imposing a prohibition or restriction on the supply of such an appliance on grounds of safety.

(5) No person carrying out the installation of a gas appliance shall leave it connected to the gas supply unless -

(a) the appliance can be used safely; or

(b) the appliance is sealed off from the gas supply with an appropriate fitting.

(6) No person shall install a gas appliance without there being at the inlet to it means of shutting off the supply of gas to the appliance unless the provision of such means is not reasonably practicable.

(7) No person shall carry out any work in relation to a gas appliance which bears an indication that it conforms to a type approved by any person as complying with safety standards in such a manner that the appliance ceases to comply with those standards.

(8) No person carrying out work in relation to a gas appliance which bears an indication that it so conforms shall remove or deface the indication.

(9) Where a person performs work on a gas appliance he shall immediately thereafter examine -

(a) the effectiveness of any flue;

(b) the supply of combustion air;

(c) its operating pressure or heat input or, where necessary, both;

(d) its operation so as to ensure its safe functioning,

and forthwith take all reasonable practicable steps to notify any defect to the responsible person and, where different, the owner of the premises in which the appliance is situated or, where neither is reasonably practicable, in the case of an appliance supplied with liquefied petroleum gas, the supplier of gas to the appliance, or, in any other case, the transporter.

(10) Paragraph (9) shall not apply in respect of -

(a) the direct disconnection of the gas supply of a gas appliance; or

(b) the purging of gas or air from an appliance or its associated pipework or fittings in any case where that purging does not adversely affect the safety of that appliance, pipe or fitting.

Flues

27. (1) No person shall install a gas appliance to any flue unless the flue is suitable and in a proper condition for the safe operation of the appliance.

(2) No person shall install a flue pipe so that it enters a brick or masonry chimney in such a way that the seal between the flue pipe and the chimney cannot be inspected.

(3) No person shall connect a gas appliance to a flue which is surrounded by an enclosure unless that enclosure is so sealed that any spillage of products of combustion cannot pass from the enclosure to any room or internal space other than the room or internal space in which the appliance is installed.

(4) No person shall install a power operated flue system for a gas appliance unless it safely prevents the operation of the appliance if the draught fails.

(5) No person shall install a flue other than in a safe position.

Access

28. No person shall install a gas appliance except in such a manner that it is readily accessible for operation, inspection and maintenance.

Manufacturer's instructions

29. Any person who installs a gas appliance shall leave for the use of the owner or occupier of the premises in which the appliance is installed all instructions provided by the manufacturer accompanying the appliance.

Room-sealed appliances

30. (1) No person shall install a gas appliance in a room used or intended to be used as a bathroom or a shower room unless it is a room-sealed appliance.

(2) No person shall install a gas fire, other gas space heater or a gas water heater of more than 14 kilowatt gross heat input in a room used or intended to be used as sleeping accommodation unless the appliance is a room-sealed appliance.

(3) No person shall install a gas fire, other gas space heater or a gas water heater of 14 kilowatt gross heat input or less in a room used or intended to be used as sleeping accommodation and no person shall install an instantaneous water heater unless (in each case) -

(a) it is a room-sealed appliance; or

(b) it incorporates a safety control designed to shut down the appliance before there is a build up of a dangerous quantity of the products of combustion in the room concerned.

(4) The references in paragraphs (1) to (3) to a room used or intended to be used for the purpose therein referred to includes a reference to -

(a) a cupboard or compartment within such a room; or

(b) a cupboard, compartment or space adjacent to such a room if there is an air vent from the cupboard, compartment or space into such a room.

Suspended appliances

31. No person shall install a suspended gas appliance unless the installation pipework to which it is connected is so constructed and installed as to be capable of safety supporting the weight imposed on it and the appliance is designed to be so supported.

Flue dampers

32. (1) Any person who installs an automatic damper to serve a gas appliance shall -

(a) ensure that the damper is so interlocked with the gas supply to the burner that burner operation is prevented in the event of failure of the damper when not in the open position; and

(b) immediately after installation examine the appliance and the damper to verify that they can be used together safely without constituting a danger to any person.

(2) No person shall install a manually operated damper to serve a domestic gas appliance.

(3) No person shall install a domestic gas appliance to a flue which incorporates a manually operated damper unless the damper is permanently fixed in the open position.

Testing of appliances

33. (1) Where a person installs a gas appliance at a time when gas is being supplied to the premises in which the appliance is installed, he shall immediately thereafter test its connection to the installation pipework to verify that it is gastight and examine the appliance and the gas fittings and other works for the supply of gas and any flue or means of ventilation to be used in connection with the appliance for the purpose of ascertaining whether -

(a) the appliance has been installed in accordance with these Regulations;

(b) the operating pressure is as recommended by the manufacturer;

(c) the appliance has been installed with due regard to any manufacturer's instructions provided to accompany the appliance; and

(d) all gas safety controls are in proper working order.

(2) Where a person carries out such testing and examination in relation to a gas appliance and adjustments are necessary to ensure compliance with the requirements specified in sub-paragraphs (a) to (d) of paragraph (1) above, he shall either carry out those adjustments or disconnect the appliance from the gas supply or seal off the appliance from the gas supply with an appropriate fitting.

(3) Where gas is not being supplied to any premises in which any gas appliance is installed -

(a) no person shall subsequently permit gas to pass into the appliance unless he has caused such testing, examination and adjustment as is specified in paragraphs (1) and (2) above to be carried out; and

(b) a person who subsequently provides a gas supply to those premises shall, unless he complies with sub-paragraph (a)above, ensure that the appliance is sealed off from the gas supply with an appropriate fitting.

Use of appliances

34. (1) The responsible person for any premises shall not use a gas appliance or permit a gas appliance to be used if at any time he knows or has reason to suspect that it cannot be used without constituting a danger to any person.

(2) For the purposes of paragraph (1) above, the responsible person means the occupier of the premises, the owner of the premises and any person with authority for the time being to take appropriate action in relation to any gas fitting therein.

(3) Any person engaged in carrying out any work in relation to a gas main, service pipe, service pipework, gas storage vessel or gas fitting who knows or has reason to suspect that any gas appliance cannot be used without constituting a danger to any person shall forthwith take all reasonably practicable steps to inform the responsible person for the premises in which the appliance is situated and, where different, the owner of the appliance or, where neither is reasonably practicable, in the case of an appliance supplied with liquefied petroleum gas, the supplier of gas to the appliance, or, in any other case, the transporter.

(4) In paragraph (3) above the expression "work" shall be construed as if, in the definition of "work" in regulation 2(1) above, every reference to a gas fitting were a reference to a gas main, service pipe, service pipework, gas storage vessel or gas fitting.

PART F

MAINTENANCE

Duties of employers and self-employed persons

35. It shall be the duty of every employer or self-employed person to ensure that any gas appliance, installation pipework or flue installed at any place of work under his control is maintained in a safe condition so as to prevent risk of injury to any person.

Duties of Landlords

36. (1) In this regulation -

"landlord" means -

(a) in England and Wales -

(i) where the relevant premises are occupied under a lease, the person for the time being entitled to the reversion expectant on that lease or who, apart from any statutory tenancy, would be entitled to possession of the premises; and

(ii) where the relevant premises are occupied under a licence, the licensor, save that where the licensor is himself a tenant in respect of those premises, it means the person referred to in paragraph (i) above;

(b) in Scotland, the person for the time being entitled to the landlord's interest under a lease;

"lease" means -

(a) a lease for a term of less than 7 years; and

(b) a tenancy for a periodic term; and

(c) any statutory tenancy arising out of a lease or tenancy referred to in sub-paragraphs (a) or (b) above, and in determining whether a lease is one which falls within sub-paragraph (a) above -

(i) in England and Wales, any part of the term which falls before the grant shall be left out of account and the lease shall be treated as a lease for a term commencing with the grant;

(ii) a lease which is determinable at the option of the lessor before the expiration of 7 years from the commencement of the term shall be treated as a lease for a term of less than 7 years;

(iii) a lease (other than a lease to which sub-paragraph (b) above applies) shall not be treated as a lease for a term of less than 7 years if it confers on the lessee an option for renewal for a term which, together with the original term, amounts to 7 years or more; and

(iv) a "lease" does not include a mortgage term;

"relevant gas fitting" means -

(a) any gas appliance (other than an appliance which the tenant is entitled to remove from the relevant premises) or any installation pipework installed in any relevant premises; and

(b) any gas appliance or installation pipework which, directly or indirectly, serves the relevant premises and which either -

(i) is installed in any part of premises in which the landlord has an estate or interest; or

(ii) is owned by the landlord or is under his control,

except that it shall not include any gas appliance or installation pipework exclusively used in a part of premises occupied for non-residential purposes.

"relevant premises" means premises or any part of premises occupied, whether exclusively or not, for residential purposes (such occupation being in consideration of money or money's worth) under -

(a) a lease; or

(b) a licence;

"statutory tenancy" means -

(a) in England and Wales, a statutory tenancy within the meaning of the Rent Act 1977 and the Rent (Agriculture) Act 1976; and

(b) in Scotland, a statutory tenancy within the meaning of the Rent (Scotland) Act 1984, a statutory assured tenancy within the meaning of the Housing (Scotland) Act 1988 or a secure tenancy within the meaning of the Housing (Scotland) Act 1987;

"tenant" means a person who occupies relevant premises being -

(a) in England and Wales -

  (i) where the relevant premises are so occupied under a lease, the person for the time being entitled to the term of that lease; and

  (ii) where the relevant premises are so occupied under a licence, the licensee;

(b) in Scotland, the person for the time being entitled to the tenant's interest under a lease.

(2) Every landlord shall ensure that there is maintained in a safe condition -

(a) any relevant gas fitting; and

(b) any flue which serves any relevant gas fitting,

so as to prevent the risk of injury to any person in lawful occupation or relevant premises.

(3) Without prejudice to the generality of paragraph (2) above, a landlord shall -

(a) ensure that each appliance and flue to which that duty extends is checked for safety within 12 months of being installed and at intervals of not more than 12 months since it was last checked for safety (whether such check was made pursuant to these Regulations or not);

(b) in the case of a lease commencing after the coming into force of these Regulations, ensure that each appliance and flue to which the duty extends has been checked for safety within a period of 12 months before the lease commences or has been or is so checked within 12 months after the appliance or flue has been installed, whichever is later; and

(c) ensure that a record in respect of any appliance or flue so checked is made and retained for a period of 2 years from the date of that check, which record shall include the following information -

  (i) the date on which the appliance or flue was checked;

  (ii) the address of the premises at which the appliance or flue is installed;

  (iii) the name and address of the landlord of the premises (or, where appropriate, his agent) at which the appliance or flue is installed;

  (iv) a description of and the location of each appliance or flue checked;

  (v) any defect identified;

  (vi) any remedial action taken;

  (vii) confirmation that the check undertaken complies with the requirements of paragraph (9) below;

  (viii) the name and signature of the individual carrying out the check; and

  (ix) the registration number with which that individual, or his employer, is registered with a body approved by the Executive for the purposes of regulation 3(3) of these Regulations.

(4) Every landlord shall ensure that any work in relation to a relevant gas fitting or any check of a gas appliance or flue carried out pursuant to paragraphs (2) or (3) above is carried out by, or by an employee of, a member of a class of persons approved for the time being by the Health and Safety Executive for the purposes of regulation 3(3) of these Regulations.

(5) The record referred to in paragraph (3)(c) above, or a copy thereof, shall be made available upon request and upon reasonable notice for the inspection of any person in lawful occupation of relevant premises who may be affected by the use or operation of any appliance to which the record relates.

(6) Notwithstanding paragraph (5) above, every landlord shall ensure that -

(a) a copy of the record made pursuant to the requirements of paragraph (3)(c) above is given to each existing tenant of premises to which the record relates within 28 days of the date of the check; and

(b) a copy of the last record made in respect of each appliance or flue is given to any new tenant of premises to which the record relates before that tenant occupies those premises save that, in respect of a tenant whose right to occupy those premises is for a period not exceeding 28 days, a copy of the record may instead be prominently displayed within those premises.

(7) Where there is no relevant gas appliance in any room occupied or to be occupied by the tenant in relevant premises, the landlord may, instead of ensuring that a copy of the record referred to in paragraph (6) above is given to the tenant, ensure that there is displayed in a prominent position in the premises (from such time as a copy would have been required to have been given to the tenant under that paragraph), a copy of the record with a statement endorsed on it that the tenant is entitled to have his own copy of the record on request to the landlord at an address specified in the statement; and on any such request being made, the landlord shall give to the tenant a copy of the record as soon as is practicable.

(8) A copy of the record given to a tenant pursuant to paragraph (6)(b) above need not contain a copy of the signature of the individual carrying out the check if the copy of the record contains a statement that another copy containing a copy of such signature is available for inspection by the tenant on request to the landlord at an address specified in the statement, and on any such request being made the landlord shall make such a copy available for inspection as soon as is practicable.

(9) A safety check carried out pursuant to paragraph (3) above shall include, but shall not be limited to, an examination of the matters referred to in sub-paragraphs (a) to (d) of regulation 26(9)of these Regulations.

(10) Nothing done or agreed to be done by a tenant of relevant premises or by any other person in lawful occupation of them in relation to the maintenance or checking of a relevant gas fitting or flue in the premises (other than one in part of premises occupied for non-residential purposes) shall be taken into account in determining whether a landlord has discharged his obligations under this regulation (except in so far as it relates to access to that gas fitting or flue for the purposes of such maintenance or checking).

(11) Every landlord shall ensure that in any room occupied or to be occupied as sleeping accommodation by a tenant in relevant premises there is not fitted a relevant gas fitting of a type the installation of which would contravene regulation 30(2) or (3) of these Regulations.

(12) Paragraph (11) above shall not apply in relation to a room which since before the coming into force of these Regulations has been occupied or intended to be occupied as sleeping accommodation.

PART G

MISCELLANEOUS

Escape of gas

37. (1) Where any gas escapes from any pipe of a gas supplier or from any pipe, other gas fitting or gas storage vessel used by a person supplied with gas by a gas supplier, the supplier of the gas shall, within 12 hours of being so informed of the escape, prevent the gas escaping (whether by cutting off the supply of gas to any premises or otherwise).

(2) If the responsible person for any premises knows or has reason to suspect that gas is escaping into those premises, he shall immediately take all reasonable steps to cause the supply of gas to be shut off at such place as may be necessary to prevent further escape of gas.

(3) If gas continues to escape into those premises after the supply of gas has been shut off or when a smell of gas persists, the responsible person for the premises discovering such escape or smell shall immediately give notice of the escape or smell to the supplier of the gas.

(4) Where an escape of gas has been stopped by shutting off the supply, no person shall cause or permit the supply to be re-opened (other than in the course of repair) until all necessary steps have been taken to prevent a recurrence of such escape.

(5) In any proceedings for an offence under paragraph (1) above it shall be a defence for the supplier of the gas to prove that it was not reasonably practicable for him effectually to prevent the gas from escaping within the period of 12 hours referred to in that paragraph, and that he did effectually prevent the escape of gas as soon as it was reasonably practicable for him to do so.

(6) Nothing in paragraphs (1) and (5) above shall prevent the supplier of the gas appointing another person to act on his behalf to prevent an escape of gas supplied by that supplier.

(7) Nothing in paragraphs (1) to (6) above shall apply to an escape of gas from a network (within the meaning of regulation 2 of the Gas Safety (Management) Regulations 1996) or from a gas fitting supplied with gas from a network.

(8) In this regulation any reference to an escape of gas from a gas fitting includes a reference to an escape or emission of carbon monoxide gas resulting from incomplete combustion of gas in a gas fitting, but, to the extent that this regulation relates to such an escape or emission of carbon monoxide gas, the requirements imposed upon a supplier by paragraph (1) above shall, where the escape or emission is notified to the supplier by the person to whom the gas has been supplied, be limited to advising that person of the immediate action to be taken to prevent such escape or emission and the need for the examination and, where necessary, repair of the fitting by a competent person.

Use of antifluctuators and valves

38. (1) Where a consumer uses gas for the purpose of working or supplying plant which is liable to produce pressure fluctuation in the gas supply such as to cause any danger to other consumers, he shall comply with such directions as may be given to him by the transporter of the gas to prevent such danger.

(2) Where a consumer intends to use for or in connection with the consumption of gas any gaseous substance he shall -

(a) give to the transporter of the gas at least 14 days notice in writing of that intention; and

(b) during such use comply with such directions as the transporter may have given to him to prevent the admission of such substance into the gas supply;

and in this paragraph "gaseous substance" includes compressed air but does not include any gaseous substance supplied by the transporter.

(3) Where a direction under paragraphs (1) or (2) above requires the provision of any device, the consumer shall ensure that the device is adequately maintained.

(4) Any direction given pursuant to this regulation shall be in writing.

Exception as to liability

39. No person shall be guilty of an offence by reason of contravention of regulation 3(2) or (6), 5(1), 7(3), 15, 16(2)or (3), 17(1), 27(5), 30 (insofar as it relates to the installation of a gas fire, other gas space heater or a gas water heater of more than 14 kilowatt gross heat input), 33(1), 35 or 36 of these Regulations in any case in which he can show that he took all reasonable steps to prevent that contravention.

Exemption certificates

40. (1) Subject to paragraph (2), the Health and Safety Executive may, by a certificate in writing, exempt any person or class of persons from any requirement or prohibition imposed by these Regulations, and any such exemption may be granted subject to conditions and to a limit of time and may be revoked at any time by a certificate in writing.

(2) The Health and Safety Executive shall not grant any such exemption unless, having regard to the circumstances of the case and in particular to -

(a) the conditions, if any, which it proposes to attach to the exemption; and

(b) any other requirements imposed by or under any enactment which apply to the case,

it is satisfied that the health and safety of persons likely to be affected by the exemption, will not be prejudiced in consequence of it.

Revocation and amendments

41. (1) The Gas Safety (Installation and Use) Regulations 1994, the Gas Safety (Installation and Use) (Amendment) Regulations 1996 and the Gas Safety (Installation and Use) (Amendment) (No. 2) Regulations 1996 are hereby revoked.

(2) Schedule 2B to the Gas Act 1986 shall be amended as follows -

(a) In paragraph 17(1) the words "pressure fluctuation in the transporter's pipe-line system and any other" and the words "or danger" shall be deleted;

(b) In paragraph 17(2) after the words "if so required" there shall be added "other than for the purpose of preventing danger"; and

(c) In paragraph 17(5) and (6) after the words "this paragraph" there shall be added "or regulation 38 of the Gas Safety (Installation and Use) Regulations 1998[a] or directions made thereunder".

Signed by order of the Secretary of State.

Alan Meale
Parliamentary Under Secretary of State, Department of the Environment, Transport and the Regions.

3rd October 1998

EXPLANATORY NOTE

(This note is not part of the Regulations)

These Regulations re-enact, with amendments, the Gas Safety (Installation and Use) Regulations 1994, as amended by the Gas Safety (Installation and Use)(Amendment) Regulations 1996 and the Gas Safety (Installation and Use)(Amendment)(No 2) Regulations 1996 ("the 1994 Regulations"). The 1994 Regulations made provision in respect of the installation and use of gas fittings for the purpose of protecting the public from dangers arising from the distribution, supply or use of gas.

1. In addition to minor and drafting amendments, these Regulations make the following changes. The Regulations: -

(a) limit the application of the Regulations by excluding hydrogen used in non-domestic premises from the definition of "gas" *(regulation 2(1))*;

(b) add a definition of "appropriate fitting" and amend the definitions of "installation pipework", "room sealed appliance", "service pipe" and "work" *(regulation 2(1))*;

(c) are extended to vessels not requiring a national or international load line certificate when used primarily for domestic or residential purposes *(regulation 2(5)(c)(iii))*;

(d) are disapplied in respect of control devices on gas appliances in certain circumstances *(regulation 2(6)(c))*;

(e) are disapplied in part in respect of -

  (i) the formal training of gas fitters *(regulation 2(7))*; and

  (ii) the formal assessment of gas fitters for purposes of accreditation *(regulation 2(8))*;

(f) extend the duty to ensure the competence of gas fitters to employers and self-employed persons having control of the work or who require the carrying out of that work *(regulation 3(2))*;

(g) make provision for the competence of gas installers and the safe installation of fittings and flues when carrying out work in a factory in relation to vehicles, vessels or caravans *(regulation 3(8)*;

(h) extend to any employer or self-employed person who has a degree of control over work in relation to a gas fitting the duty to ensure that such work, when carried out at a place of work, is carried out by an employee of, or self-employed person who is, a member of an approved class of persons *(regulation 4)*;

(i) restrict the premises to which alterations are prohibited to those in which a gas appliance or gas storage vessel is fitted *(regulation 8(1))*;

(j) extend to cases where a meter is relocated the requirement to display a notice identifying the nearest upstream emergency control *(regulation 15(2))*;

(k) extend the duty to provide a notice where there is more than one primary meter to any person who makes a material modification *(regulation 16(2))*;

(l) require a line diagram to be displayed and, in specified cases, amended where gas is provided to a secondary meter *(regulation 17)*;

(m) modify the requirements in relation to enclosed pipes *(regulation 19(2))* and disapply the prohibition on the installation of pipework in cavity walls in respect of "living flame effect gas fires" (as defined) *(regulation 19(4))*;

(n) disapply the requirement for specified safety checks in specified circumstances *(regulation 26(10)*;

(o) extend the meaning of "room" for the purposes of regulation 30 *(regulation 30(4))*;

(p) extend the prohibition on the use of gas appliances to circumstances where they may constitute a danger to any person *(regulation 34(1))*;

(q) amend the definition of "relevant gas fitting" for the purpose of regulation 36 *(regulation 36(1))*;

(r) make further provision with regard to safety checks in rented accommodation *(regulation 36(3)(a) and (b)* and to the display and provision of records *(regulation 36(7) and (8))*;

(s) extend the duty imposed on suppliers in cases of escape of gas to the escape of carbon monoxide gas and modify the duty of suppliers in relation thereto *(regulation 37(8))*.

3. The Regulations also contain new provisions which: -

(a) require a person who breaks a regulator seal to apply a new seal *(regulation 14(7))*;

(b) require the outlet of the emergency control to be sealed when a primary meter is removed *(regulation 16(3)(a)(ii))* and notice to be given to the supplier when such removal is proposed *(regulation 16(4))*;

(c) prohibit the installation of a flue otherwise than in a safe position *(regulation 27(5))*;

(d) impose restrictions in relation to the installation of instantaneous water heaters *(regulation 30(3)*;

(e) extend to flues the employer's duty of maintenance *(regulation 35)*;

(f) provide that specified gas fittings shall not be fitted in specified accommodation *(regulation 36(11) and (12))*;

(g) impose requirements on consumers of gas in circumstances liable to cause pressure fluctuation or the introduction of extraneous substances into the gas supply *(regulation 38)*.

4. The Regulations revoke the Gas Safety (Installation and Use) Regulations 1994, the Gas Safety (Installation and Use) (Amendment) Regulations 1996 and the Gas Safety (Installation and Use) (Amendment) (No. 2) Regulations 1996; the Regulations make minor amendments to Schedule 2B of the Gas Act 1986 *(regulation 41)*.

5. These Regulations were notified in draft to the European Commission in accordance with Directive 83/189/EEC (1983 O.J. L109/8) (as amended).

6. A copy of the summary cost benefit prepared in respect of these Regulations can be obtained from the Health and Safety Executive, Economic Adviser's Unit, Rose Court, 2 Southwark Bridge, London SE1 9HS. A copy has been placed in the Library of each House of Parliament.

2. Gas Emergency

In the event of a natural gas emergency consumers should contact the relevant emergency service provider as shown below.

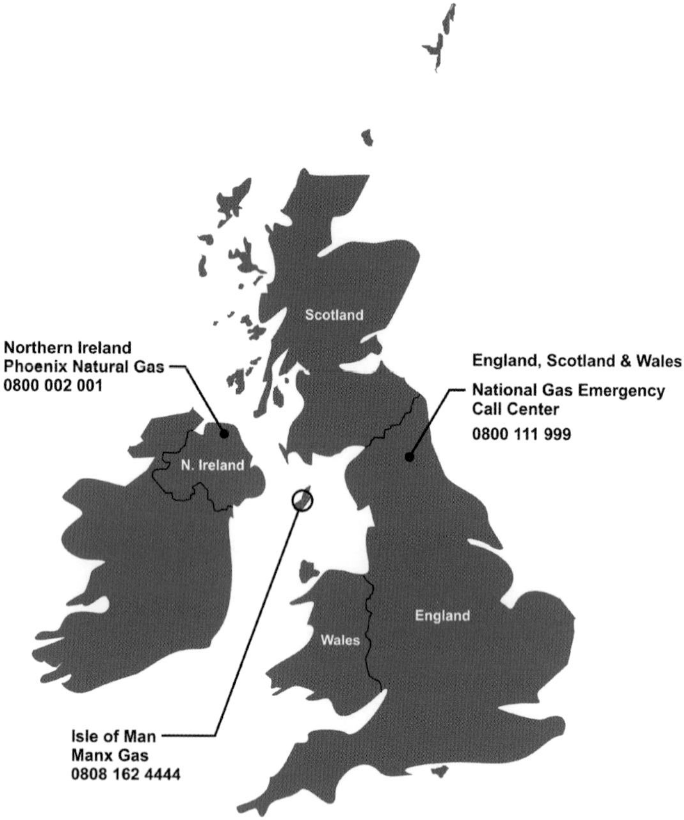

Figure 2.1

For Liquefied Petroleum Gas related emergencies, consumers should contact the gas supplier, contact details can be found on the gas storage cylinder or bulk tank.

2.0 Introduction

During the gas operative's normal working day, situations may occur where they may have to deal with gas emergencies either directly when they are on-site at the time of the emergency or indirectly where the customer has phoned, requested advice or action due to a gas emergency. The gas operative must be aware of what action must be taken, who to contact and how to deal with the emergency depending on its severity either on or off site. The correct course of action is vital to reduce any hazards which may be present and ensure our duty of care is met.

For the Natural Gas network, the National Gas Emergency Service Call Centre provides an around the clock service which provides safety related information and contact for the Emergency Service Provider (ESP). This emergency service is used in response to gas escapes and any smell of fumes from appliances.

ESP's have the relevant competencies to deal with gas escapes, identify unsafe situations, isolate any unsafe appliances and react to unsafe levels of gas within a building (evacuation procedure). They are only employed to make the installation/appliance safe.

2.1 Responsible Person

As stated in the Gas Safety (Installation & Use) Regulations GS(I&U)R 34, any responsible person for a premises must not use or permit a gas appliance to be used where it is known or suspected that it cannot be used without constituting a danger to any person. In addition where a gas escape is reported or suspected they must take all reasonable steps to isolate the gas supply to prevent further escape of gas GS(I&U)R 37 - (2). If the smell of gas persists after isolation they must contact the Supplier GS(I&U)R 37 (3).

The gas supply must not be reinstated until all remedial action has been completed GS(I&U)R 37 (4).

2.2 Advice to Gas consumer

If the gas operative is not on site and has been advised that a smell of gas exists or an escape of gas is suspected, the following actions should be performed by the gas consumer.

Clear and concise information must be provided.

- Do turn off the gas (at emergency control valve).
- Do ventilate property (open doors and windows).
- Do extinguish sources of ignition.
- Do keep away from affected area.
- Do contact the emergency service provider.
- Do ensure access into premises can be gained.
- Do Not operate electrical switches (ON or OFF).
- Do Not smoke.

2.3 Sources of ignition

A source of ignition could come from a variety of sources, some are obvious others less so.

- Naked flames - Solid fuel, Oil or Gas burning appliances, smoking and candles.
- Household electrical appliances with thermostatic, time controlled and mechanical switches (washing machines, tumble driers, central heating systems).
- Manually operated switches (electric lights, refrigerators/freezers).
- Static electricity.
- Telephones.
- Lift/elevator call buttons.
- Torches/flashlights.
- Secure entry systems/doorbells.

2.4 Gas Operative - Gas Escape

If the gas operative is in attendance on site and has been advised that an escape of gas is suspected, the following actions should be performed. Clear and concise information must be provided to the customer at all times to ensure they are fully aware of the situation:

- Turn off the gas supply at the meter control or emergency control valve.
- Extinguish and remove all sources of ignition.
- Ensure that any electrical switches are not operated either off or on.
- Ventilate the building by opening doors and windows to ensure an adequate air flow direct from outside.
- Test installation for tightness using the appropriate test method (see section 6).
- Where appropriate locate and repair the escape.
- If the escape cannot be repaired immediately, the gas industry unsafe procedure must be exercised.
- Where the smell of gas persists after isolation & ventilation, contact the National Gas Emergency Call Centre.

2.5 Reporting Gas Escapes

The following information will be required when reporting a gas escape to the National Gas Emergency Call Centre:

- Address where the gas escape has been detected.
- Name of company, contact name and telephone number of gas consumer.
- Name and contact details of person reporting the escape.
- Location of where the smell of gas is most noticeable.
- Time when the smell was fist noticed.
- Is the emergency/ meter control turned off, if not why (inaccessible, no handle, no authorisation etc).
- Does the smell of gas persist after the emergency/meter control has been turned off.
- Is there a smell of gas outside the property?

You must note down the following information and keep it on record:

- Reference number (normally the job number given to the ESP operative).
- The date and time of report.
- The name of the person whom you reported the escape to.

2.6 Gas Operative - Gas Fumes

If the gas operative is called onto site and has been advised that a smell of products of combustion exists, activation of a CO alarm or to re-establishing the gas supply following a Concern for Safety label issued by a ESP the following actions should be taken.

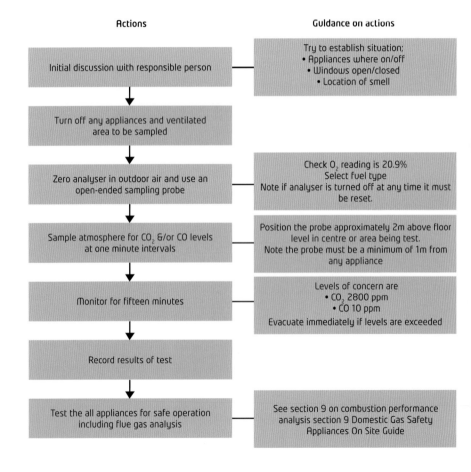

Actions	Guidance on actions
Initial discussion with responsible person	Try to establish situation; • Appliances where on/off • Windows open/closed • Location of smell
↓ Turn off any appliances and ventilated area to be sampled	
↓ Zero analyser in outdoor air and use an open-ended sampling probe	Check O_2 reading is 20.9% Select fuel type Note if analyser is turned off at any time it must be reset.
↓ Sample atmosphere for CO_2 &/or CO levels at one minute intervals	Position the probe approximately 2m above floor level in centre or area being test. Note the probe must be a minimum of 1m from any appliance
↓ Monitor for fifteen minutes	Levels of concern are • CO_2 2800 ppm • CO 10 ppm Evacuate immediately if levels are exceeded
↓ Record results of test	
↓ Test the all appliances for safe operation including flue gas analysis	See section 9 on combustion performance analysis section 9 Domestic Gas Safety Appliances On Site Guide

BS 7967 Part 1: Section 4.1 sets out the basic rules and puts them in order of priority when carrying out an investigation. These are:

(i) Protect life

(ii) Protect property

(iii) Locate all fuel burning appliances

(iv) Locate any escape of gas, fumes, smells spillage/leakage of combustion products

(v) Confirm the safe installation and operation of all suspect gas appliances

(vi) Advise the customer of any remedial actions required

(vii) Complete all necessary reports, documentation and actions as advised in the Gas Industry Unsafe Situations Procedure

i. It is important to remember while protecting life, to protect your own. BS 7967 Part 1 allows greater levels than those shown in the flow chart for CO levels for limited time periods, however BS 7967 Part 3 section 4.2 note 2 states; "Only those people with training and experience in the toxicological effects of CO who are competent are able to advice on exposure times for concentrations in excess of 10 ppm."

   Measuring the level of CO_2 in atmosphere can show problems with products of combustion leaking into the room even before the CO level begins to rise. Until recently it was not possible to ascertain accurate ambient levels of CO_2 readings using combustion performance analysers, as traditionally they would calculate the CO_2 level from the measured O_2 level. This is sufficiently accurate for calculating CO_2 levels in combustion gases in the flue but not for determining ambient room levels.

ii. Protect property by ensuring that natural gas is not leaking into property.

iii. Locate escape of gas, fumes or smells by a process of elimination working on one appliance at a time using procedures laid out in section 9 Domestic Gas Safety Appliances On Site Guide.

Problems with other fuel burning appliances can cause the room CO levels to raise, if a problem is suspected on a oil burning appliance contact the Oil Firing Technical Association 08456 585 080 and for solid fuel appliance contact the Solid Fuel Association 08456 014 406.

It is also possible to get CO from:

- Smoking
- Vehicles or generators located outside and in attached buildings
- Engines on boats

Smells can be generated from:

- Gas escapes on appliances and installation pipework
- Fibreglass log effects that have not been cured correctly
- Paint, especially on new appliances
- Cavity wall insulation that has been recently installed
- Painting and decorating
- Use of solvents and adhesives
- Damp proofing or timber treatment
- From outside, barbecues, bonfires and appliances adjacent properties
- Drains

iv. Check the installation of all appliances are in accordance with the relevant manufacturer's instructions and that they are operating safely, see sections on appliances and combustion performance analysis.

v. Advise responsible person of any required remedial work necessary to ensure the safe operation of the appliance.

vi. Complete any documentation (report of the investigation) as required and for any appliances not conforming to required standards, where remedial work has not been completed. Follow the procedure set out in the Industry Unsafe Situations Procedure, disconnect from the gas supply or turn off as necessary and issue appropriate warning notices and labels.

2.7 Gas Transporter & Supplier

The Gas Transporter/Supplier has an obligation under the GS(I&U)R to attend and make safe any installation where there has been a reported gas escape or smell of fumes within 12 hours of receipt GS(I&U)R 37-(1). Attendance on site will be by an authorised ESP operative. They will test the installation to confirm tightness down stream of the primary Emergency Control Valve/ Meter Control Valve and visually inspect any appliances for safety.

The gas operative must be aware that the ESP is only obliged to make an installation safe and may not carry out remedial works to rectify the cause of the emergency. Making safe will include turning off and/or isolating an installation/ appliance from the gas supply, and attaching a warning notice.

If whilst attendance, the ESP confirms the integrity of the installation but there has been a report of fumes, they will turn off the appliance and attach a Concern for Safety label.

Remedial work will normally be carried out by a person who is a member of a class of persons approved by the Health Safety Executive GS(I&U)R 3 (3).

Under the Gas Safety (Rights of Entry) Regulations, the Gas Transporter (GT) has the right to enter a premise where it is known or suspected that a hazardous situation exists which may threaten life and/or property and make the installation safe. It must be noted that the gas operative does not have this authorisation, so when faced with an ID situation where the customer refuses to allow disconnection, it will be necessary to contact the GT who can exercise these Regulations.

Typical labels used by the Gas Transporter are shown below:

Cause for concern Label

Figure 2.1

ID or AR Label (Installation)

Figure 2.2

2.8 Attending a Gas Incident

Where a gas operative is called to, or is in attendance at a gas related incident involving either a fatality or major injury (either loss of consciousness or an injury requiring medical treatment) they must ensure that they do not disturb anything within the incident scene and immediately contact the National Gas Emergency Call Centre. There should be minimal disturbance to the incident scene and where safe to do so, the installation must be made safe by isolating the gas supply and if necessary, ventilating the premises. In the case of a fire, explosion or ID situation, disconnect and seal the gas supply.

Record all actions taken and with full cooperation, assist relevant authorities who are in attendance and involved in any subsequent incident investigation.

Where a person or persons are suspected to be affected by carbon monoxide poisoning the relevant emergency services must be contacted. If safe to do so remove the person from the affected area and isolate/ ventilate as necessary. Make the person comfortable until the emergency services arrive.

When called to reinstate gas to premises where there has been a death or major injury, the installer should make certain that any investigations have been completed before carrying out any remedial work.

2.9 Emergency Service provider

Emergency service provider (ESP) operatives have a limited scope of duties. Specific training and qualifications limit their competence to meter related work, attending gas emergencies and re-establishing gas supplies. They are not deemed competent to "work" on gas appliances by virtue of their ESP qualifications.

The procedures detailed in further sections of this on site guide (Re-Establishing Gas Supplies & Visual Risk Assessment of Appliances) hold fast for the ESP operative but they may be required to perform this activity in commercial premises. This necessitates the ESP operative to be knowledgeable of the regulations, standards and industry guidance documents relating to commercial as well as domestic.

Commercial installations are normally categorised as:

- Commercial heating
- Commercial catering
- Commercial laundry

In order to perform a visual risk assessment of these appliance types, the ESP operative must be knowledgeable of the flueing and ventilation standards relevant to commercial appliances and premises.

There are a number of British Standards (BS) and Institution of Gas Engineers and Managers (IGE) publications which are applied.

ESP operatives must also appreciate the variety of flame pictures which may be encountered in the commercial appliance field (natural, forced or induced draught) so that they can visually identify incorrect flame pictures.

There is a huge diversity of appliance types in the commercial field and it is unreasonable to expect the ESP operative to be a "subject matter expert", however, a basic knowledge of the principle of operation and basic controls utilized will go a long way in lighting appliances e.g. knowing that there may be a canopy fan interlock mechanism controlling the gas supply to commercial catering appliances.

It is likely that installations out with the scope of IGE/UP/1B will require to be tested in accordance with IGE/UP/1 or IGE/UP/1A.

They must also recognise depending on the size and operating pressure of the gas supply (service pipe) certain valve types are unsuitable for use as A/ECVs.

3. Combustion

Combustion - the production of light and heat by a chemical reaction, in order for the reaction to take place it requires; **FUEL...OXYGEN...ENERGY**

3.1 Properties of Gases

Before we consider combustion, it is better to understand the basic properties of the gases used within the gas industry. These gases belong to a group of chemicals known as the hydrocarbons. As this name suggests, these gases contain molecules of Hydrogen and Carbon, which, given the right environment, react readily with Oxygen. This chemical reaction is commonly known as combustion.

We can split gases into three distinct groups known as families:

3.1.1 1st Family - Manufactured Gas

Manufactured gas was the generic term given to any gases produced through industrial process. Commonly known as Coke Gas, Coal Gas or Towns Gas it had high levels of impurities such as Water, Sulphur Carbon Dioxide and Carbon Monoxide giving it low heat content. Manufactured gas has been phased out of general use, most people have now converted to Natural Gas

Characteristic at Standard reference conditions	Natural Gas (Methane)	Commercial Propane	Commercial Butane
Chemical Symbol	CH_4	C_3H_8	C_4H_{10}
Specific Gravity	0.58	1.5	2.0
Boiling Point of Liquid Gas under SRC	- 162 °C	- 45 °C	- 2 °C
Gross Calorific Value (MJ/m^3)	38.72	93.1	121.8
Wobbe Number (MJ/m^3)	45.5 to 55.0	73.5 to 87.5	73.5 to 87.5
Supply Pressure (Operating Pressure)	21 mbar	37 mbar	28 mbar
Stoichiometeric air requirements. Volume/ Volume of gas (m^3)	9.76:1	23.76:1	30.00:1
Flame Speed (m/s)	0.36	0.46	0.45
Flammability Limits (gas in air)	5 to 15 %	1.7 to 10.9 %	1.4 to 9.3 %
Maximum Flame Temperature (°C)	1930	1980	1996
Ignition Temperature (°C)	704	470	372

Table 3.1 - Properties of common gases

3.1.2 2nd Family - Natural Gas

Within the gas industry we normally refer to Natural Gas as Methane, however, since it is a naturally occurring gas, Methane only represents approximately 90% of the total volume of the gas.

3.1.3 3rd Family - Liquid Petroleum Gas (LPG)

LPG is a by-product from the extraction of Natural Gas or processes within the petrochemical industry. Commercial available LPG can be either Propane or Butane.

3.1.4 Odour and Colour

Natural Gas, Propane and Butane are all colourless and odourless gases. To ensure the safe use of these gases a small amount of odorant is added prior to distribution. Odorants used within the gas industry are based on a group of chemicals called "Thiols". These pungent chemicals aid in the detection of even the smallest of gas escapes as minute traces can be detected by smell.

The most common odorants used for natural gas are methyl (methanethiol) and t-butyl mercaptan with ethyl mercaptan (ethanethoil) for both Propane and Butane. All blend well with their associated gases and in their gaseous state have similar properties

3.1.5 Toxicity

Many people still think today that Natural Gas and LPG are toxic, hence, when we hear of a person being gassed it refers to inhaling Gas. This was generally born during the days of Towns Gas, which contained Carbon Monoxide. Carbon Monoxide or CO is a very toxic gas, which readily displaces the Oxygen in the blood stream, effectively starving the body of Oxygen. Natural Gas and LPG do not contain CO, and therefore are non-toxic. However, Carbon Monoxide can be produced when we do not burn gas completely. We refer to CO as one of the products of incomplete combustion. Although Natural Gas and LPG are non-toxic there is still a risk of asphyxiation due to the gas displacing Oxygen within the atmosphere.

3.1.6 Specific Gravity (Relative Density)

From a design and safety point of view, it is important for us to understand how a gas would disperse when released into atmosphere. To help us understand this we refer to the specific gravity or relative density of the gas.

The specific gravity of a substance is its density relative to another substance, hence the term relative density. For any gas we normally use air, for liquids or solids, water. If we take air as having a specific gravity of 1 then Natural Gas is approximately 0.58. This means that it is lighter than air, hence when released into atmosphere it will rise to high level. On the other hand Propane has a specific gravity of approximately 1.5 and Butane 2.0 making them heavier than air allowing them to sink to ground level. In their liquefied state they are lighter than water.

LPG requires separate ventilation at low level, commonly known as dump holes to allow any leakage to disperse freely into outside atmosphere. This ventilation is over and above the normal appliance ventilation.

3.1.7 Calorific Value

When Natural Gas and LPG burn they give off heat, this is commonly known as an exothermic reaction. Since heat is a form of energy, we refer to the Calorific Value as the amount of energy released from a specific quantity of gas. We can specify the Calorific Value of natural gas and LPG in either the imperial (btu/ft^3) or metric (MJ/m^3) units. Today all calorific values are expressed in metric units.

The calorific value of Natural Gas is not constant and varies from region to region. This is due to the different quality of gas obtained from different sources. The approximate value for natural gas is 1040 btu's/ft^3 or 38.72 MJ/m^3. To obtain the correct CV we would refer to the customer's gas bill.

LPG has a higher heat content than Natural Gas. The calorific value of Propane is approximately 93.1 MJ/m^3 and Butane 121.8 MJ/m^3. Due to their higher calorific values we do not require to burn as much LPG to produce the same equivalent heat as Natural gas, therefore when we calculate combustion ventilation requirements the calculation method used is the same for both Natural Gas and LPG since it is based solely on the appliance heat input.

3.1.8 Wobbe Number

This number is generally used by Manufacturers for the design of burners. It is used as an indication of the heat which can be produced from a burner using a particular gas. The heat produced depends on a number of varying factors, namely:

- Gross calorific value of the gas.
- Specific gravity.
- Size and shape of injector orifice.
- Gas supply pressure to the injector.

We calculate the Wobbe number using the following formula:

$$\textbf{Wobbe Number} = \frac{\textbf{Calorific Value (MJ/m}^3\textbf{)}}{\sqrt{\textbf{Specific Gravity}}}$$

3.1.9 Flammability Limits

Gases will only burn when there is a specific concentration of gas mixed with air. The concentration required is known as the flammability limits.

Natural Gas - 5% to 15% gas in air.

Propane - 1.7% to 10.9% gas in air.

Butane - 1.4% to 9.3% gas in air.

The lower limit is known as the lower flammability limit (LFL) and the upper limit, upper flammability limit (UFL)

Since the human nose is not sensitive enough to detect the EXACT amount of gas present in atmosphere, specialised gas detection equipment has been developed to detect, measure and display the exact concentrations of specific gases in atmosphere. These instruments are invaluable when it comes to locating gas escapes, determining the safety of environments affected by gas escapes and purging gas installations.

For accuracy and safety the gas industry specifies gas detectors to measure to at least the following concentrations.

- **0 to 100% gas in air** (GIA) volume per volume.
- **0 to 100% LFL** - for natural gas this measures in the range of 0 to 5% GIA where 100% LFL is actually the 5% lower limit.
- **0 to 10% LFL** - for natural gas this measures in the range 0 to 0.5% GIA (10% of the 5% lower limit).

3.1.10 Ignition Temperature

Under normal conditions our gases would not combust, even when concentrations of the gas in air are within the flammability limits as stated above. We must introduce our mixture to an energy source normally heat. Once ignited, the heat generated by the flame is enough to maintain the combustion of the gas, we do not require to continually apply a source of ignition after the initial combustion starts.

Ignition temperatures are as follows:

Natural gas : 704 °C

Propane : 470 °C, and

Butane: 372 °C

As we can see LPG has lower ignition temperatures than Natural Gas in addition with lower flammability limits makes it a more volatile gas.

3.2 Complete Combustion

The process of complete combustion for natural gas is shown in the chemical equation below.

$$CH_4 + 2O_2 \rightarrow CO_2 + 2H_20 + Heat$$

Where;	CH_4 = 1 volume of Methane, (1 carbon atom + 4 Hydrogen atoms)
	20_2 = 2 volumes of Oxygen, (contains 4 Oxygen atoms)
	CO_2 = 1 volume of Carbon Dioxide, (1 Carbon atom + 2 Oxygen atoms)
	$2H_20$ = 2 volumes of Water Vapour, (4 Hydrogen atoms + 2 Oxygen atoms)

This shows that 1 volume of methane requires 2 volumes of Oxygen, which in turn produces 1 volume of Carbon Dioxide and 2 volumes of Water Vapour and most importantly, the release of heat.

In reality the Oxygen is not supplied neat, but is supplied by the provision of air from the atmosphere. Air is generally taken to consist of 20.9% Oxygen and 79.1% Nitrogen. Nitrogen (N_2) can be considered as an inert gas for our purposes, this means that it does not contribute to the combustion process (other than to reduce the efficiency as it enters the burner cold and is exhausted hot).

If we approximate the quantities of Oxygen (20%) and Nitrogen (80%) comprising air as being 1 and 4 respectively, then to obtain the 2 volumes of Oxygen we would need to provide 10 volumes of air to complete the chemical reaction that produces combustion.

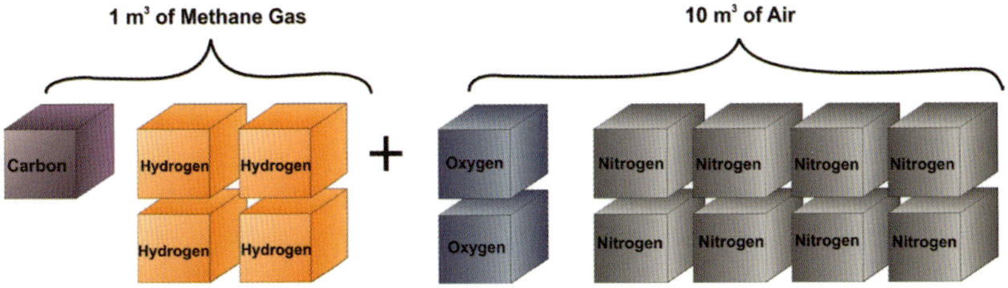

Figure 3.1

i. During the combustion process two key transformations take place. The Carbon contained within the Methane combines itself with the Oxygen taken from the supplied air and is transformed into Carbon Dioxide which gives off heat

$C + O_2 \rightarrow CO_2 + \text{Heat}$

ii. At the same time two molecules of Hydrogen contained within the Methane combines itself with Oxygen taken from the supplied air and is transformed into 2 molecules of Water which gives off heat

$2H_2 + O_2 \rightarrow 2H_2O + \text{Heat}$

This would then produce the Carbon Dioxide and Water Vapour which are products of complete combustion. Strictly speaking, Nitrogen is not a product of combustion:

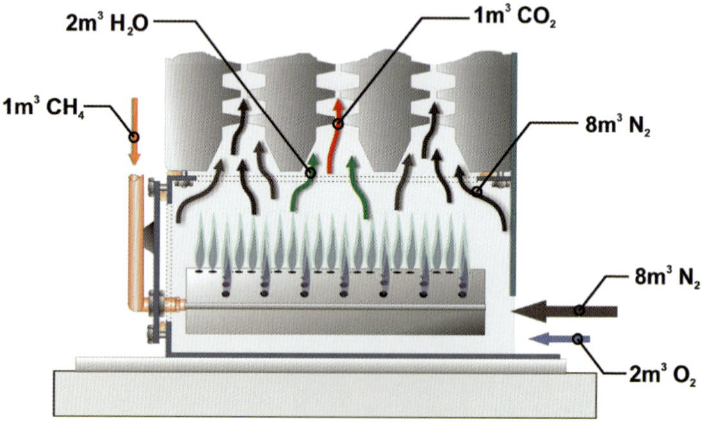

Figure 3.2

Note - in reality no atoms are consumed during the combustion process, they are just transformed.

One Carbon atom on each side of the process.
Four Hydrogen atoms on each side of the process.
Four Oxygen atoms on each side of the process.

3.3 Stoichiometric combustion

When every atom of Methane and Oxygen combine during the combustion process it is referred to as stoichiometric combustion. This is only a theoretical concept which can only be achieved under strict laboratory conditions and is not possible under normal operating conditions. It would require only the theoretical minimum volume of air, no more, no less. In practice, this state of affairs would result in incomplete combustion due to the air/gas mixing capabilities of the burner, when the supply of air is insufficient not all of the Carbon is burnt which may lead to the production of Carbon Monoxide. For this reason an excess of air has to be provided to ensure complete combustion this is one of the reasons boilers cannot achieve 100% efficiency.

3.4 Incomplete combustion

Where there is not enough air for combustion, we do not have enough Oxygen to combine fully to produce our products of complete combustion as seen above.

This is when we start to produce Carbon Monoxide (CO) which we regard as one of the products of incomplete combustion. The chemical equation for the incomplete combustion is.

$$CH_4 + XO_2 \rightarrow CO_2 + 2H_20 + CO + Heat$$

X is an unknown quantity of oxygen less than 2

With natural draught, pre-aerated burners a yellow flame does not necessarily mean incomplete combustion is taking place, account must be taken of the type of appliance/burner. A number of appliances are designed to burn with a luminous (yellow) flame e.g. flueless space heaters, Decorative Fuel Effect (DFE), Inset Live Fuel Effect (ILFE) and some oven burners.

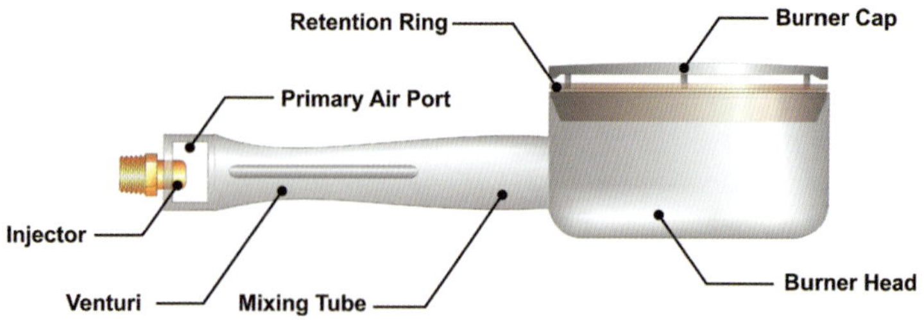

Figure 3.3

Combustion problems occur when a natural draught, pre-aerated burner is situated below a heat exchanger and the amount of primary air is compromised. This results in flame lengthening which in turn results in the flame contacting the heat exchanger causing the formation of Carbon Monoxide and Carbon (soot). The heat exchanger soon becomes blocked and spillage occurs.

With the exception of the aforementioned appliance types, generally speaking, a yellow or orange flame will mean incomplete combustion. Other tell tale signs of combustion problems may be,

- A report of a smell (spillage)
- Soot deposits or yellow/brown marks in and around the burner or appliance draught diverter or fire canopy
- Soot deposits on the heat exchanger
- Signs of heat damage around the draught diverter or fire canopy
- Excessive condensation in the room especially inside windows
- Flame lift (excessive gas rate, blocked retention ports or vitiation)
- Pilot lights that frequently blow out

Good Flame Pictures

Decorative Fuel Effect Gas

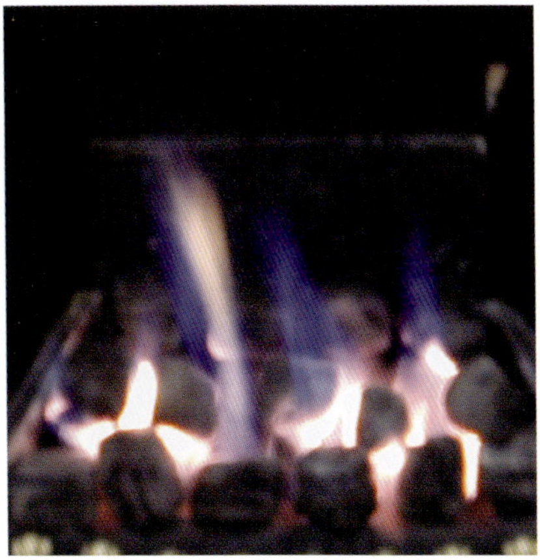

Figure 3.4

Cooker Hob

Figure 3.5

Poor Flame Pictures

Radiant Gas Fire

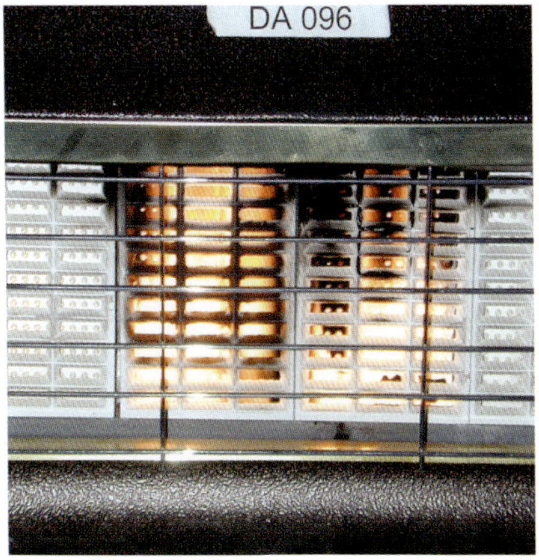

Figure 3.6

Cooker Hob

Figure 3.7

3.5 Causes of Incomplete Combustion

There are many factors that can affect the combustion of appliances, these factors being dependant on the type of burner installed within the appliance and the environment in which the appliance is installed.

- **Inadequate Ventilation** - This is where the supply of air for combustion to the appliance is restricted or contaminated. This can be through inadequately sized ventilation grilles.
- **Vitiation of atmosphere** - Vitiation of the atmosphere is where the air used to supply the appliance becomes deficient in Oxygen. This can be through products of combustion being released into atmosphere from a defective flue system.
- **Contamination of burner** - Combustion air for the appliance is entrained into the burner through either natural (natural draught burner) or mechanical means (forced/ induced draught burner). This air contains air born dusts and other contaminants which are drawn into the burner to mix with the gas, for example the primary air ports on a natural draught burner. As the air enters these apertures it deposits debris. This eventually builds up creating a restriction to the air flow into the burner.
- **Poor Flueing** - Where a problem has occurred in the flue either through a blockage or poor design, it may affect the removal of the products of combustion from the appliance. Since the products are not being removed they may re-enter the area in which the appliance has been installed or, where a forced draught burner is installed, back into the appliance combustion chamber. As the air has already been burnt its Oxygen content is reduced and will no longer support complete combustion. We call this contaminated air vitiated. In addition to poor combustion, for forced draught appliances, flame displacement may take place.
- **Blocked Flueways** - The flueways of an appliance are basically the path that the products of combustion pass through whilst dispersing their heat. When this path becomes restricted, the products of combustion re-enter the combustion chamber affecting the appliance combustion.

- **Flame Chilling** - When a flame hits a surface cooler than the temperature of ignition (approximately 704°C) It can no longer support complete combustion. This can happen when the flame touches a heat exchanger or other cool surface.
- **Flame Impingement** - This is when one flame touches another, or a cold surface. Incomplete combustion is created by one flame robbing the other of secondary air or by chilling.
- **Over Gassing** - Each type of burner has been designed by the manufacturer to ensure correct entrainment of combustion air and flame stability under specific load conditions. When we go outside these parameters by introducing more gas than that designed by the manufacturer we can cause incomplete combustion through lack of combustion air and flame instability.
- **Under Gassing** - This is normally associated more with forced and induced draught burners. These types of burners usually introduce air to be mixed with the gas at a high velocity. When we inject the correct amount of gas into the air stream the size and ferocity of the flame creates a back pressure generated from the hot products of combustion hitting off the back of the combustion chamber. This back pressure creates our flame retention on the burner. If the burner is under gassed, the flame is pushed off the burner head by the force of the combustion air creating turbulence at the burner head reducing the back pressure effect. Since the flame is unstable we can create incomplete combustion through flame chilling and impingement.

3.6 Carbon Monoxide

Carbon Monoxide (CO) is a colourless and odourless poisonous gas. It readily displaces Oxygen in the blood stream to produce Carboxyhaemoglobin (HbCO and COHb), the more it is absorbed into the blood stream through the haemoglobin the greater the affects on the body. The poisoning process is as follows:

- When we inhale contaminated air, our lungs transfer the CO to the haemoglobin in the red blood cells.
- This contaminated blood is then circulated by our arteries to our vital organs and muscles.
- The function of our organs and muscles is dramatically affected and victims are incapacitated to a greater or lesser extent depending on the level of contamination.

Effects of Carboxyhaemoglobin on the body			
% CO	Parts Per Million (PPM)	Effects	% saturation of CO in blood stream
0.01	100	Slight headache in 2 - 3 Hours	13
0.02	200	Mild Headache, dizziness, nausea and tiredness after 2 to 3 hours	20-30
0.04	400	Frontal headache and nausea after 1 to 2 hours; risk to life if exposure over 3 hours	36
0.08	800	Severe headache, dizziness, convulsions within 45 minutes; unconsciousness and death possible after 2 - 3 hours.	50
0.16	1600	Headache, dizziness, nausea within 20 minutes; collapse, unconsciousness and death possible after 1 to 2 hours.	68
0.32	3200	Headache, dizziness, nausea within 5 to 10 minutes; death possible after 15 minutes.	70-75
0.64	6400	Severe symptoms within 1 to 2 minutes; death within 15 minutes	80
1.28	12800	Immediate symptoms; death within 1 to 3 minutes	85-90

Table 3.2

If CO poisoning is suspected, the victim must be removed from the contaminated area to open air immediately, if safe to do so.

Physical exertion should be avoided and medical advice sought, The only way to be sure CO poisoning has taken place is for the person(s) concerned to have a blood or breath test taken by either a GP or an accident and emergency department. This must be completed within 4 hours as the CO leaves the blood quickly.

The safety of life is paramount; once this has been assured the cause of any incident may have to be preserved in case of an HSE investigation.

3.7 Carbon Dioxide

Carbon dioxide (CO_2) is produced when carbon containing fossil fuels are burned in air, present in the products of complete combustion. CO_2 is all around us, we exhale CO_2 with every breath.

CO_2 is a colourless, tasteless and odourless gas and when produced as a part of the combustion process it has a density similar to that of air. When cooled, CO_2 is one and one half times as heavy as air and tends to 'pool' at low levels where it can displace the air that includes Oxygen, causing pilot lights on gas appliances to go out.

The use of flue gas analysers that determine CO_2 levels by calculation are no longer acceptable as the reading can be inaccurate. The direct measurement of CO_2 using infrared sensors now means that accurate and reliable measurement of ambient CO_2 levels can now be achieved.

Because CO_2 displaces O_2, it is a health risk in its own right since we need the Oxygen in air to live. CO_2 is an asphyxiant. It can cause headaches, drowsiness and loss of ability to maintain concentration.

Because it displaces O_2, badly installed flues on gas appliances that allow leaks of products of combustion into the room can affect the amount of O_2 reaching the gas appliance and in extreme circumstances causing the production of CO.

- Normal outside levels are between 350 - 400 ppm,
- Rising in built up areas or near roads to 600 ppm.
- Typical levels found indoors are 350 - 1000 ppm.
- Maximum levels set by World Health Organisation (WHO) and Health and Safety Executive over a weighted 8 hour day - 5000 ppm.
- Maximum levels set by the gas industry during with appliances under normal operational conditions - 2800 ppm

Effects of Carbon Dioxide on the body		
% CO	**Parts Per Million (PPM)**	**Effects**
0.1 - 0.2	1 000 - 2 000	Complaints of drowsiness and poor air quality
0.2 - 0.5	2 000 - 5 000	Headache, sleepiness and stagnant stale, stuffy air. Poor concentration, loss of attention, increase heart rate and slight nausea
0.04 Greater than 4.00	Greater than 40 000	Potential for serious oxygen deprivation resulting in permanent brain damage, coma and eventually death

Table 3.2

3.8 Carbon Monoxide Detectors

Owners of gas appliances are responsible for maintaining them in a safe condition, they can ensure this by having them regularly checked by a suitably qualified competent person. Additional protection can be achieved by the installation of Carbon Monoxide detectors, especially where open flued and flueless appliances are installed.

This should not be taken as a replacement to regular checks but as an additional level of safety.

3.8.1 CO indicator card (spot/colour change)

These types indicate the presence of CO by the orange spot turning grey/black. Once opened their life span is in the order of 3 months.

BS 7967 Part 1 does not recommend their use in sleeping accommodation, because they do not have an audible alarm.

Figure 3.8

They do not require a power source but can be rendered inoperative by certain household chemicals/aerosol sprays.

Use an electronic combustion analyser in accordance with BS 7967 Part 2 to verify CO levels, when an indicator card has changed colour.

3.8.2 Electronic detectors

Can be either battery or mains powered (inc. hard wired). These types must be manufactured to BS EN 50291 (previously BS 7860, expired November 2006).

Figure 3.9

The sensors can be either;

Reagent Gel: Also referred to as "colourimetric", this system relies on a colour change affecting the passage of a light beam. It is claimed to mimic the action of the human body in terms of taking in and expelling CO, and hence is sometimes called "biomimetic". However, the main drawback in terms of the CO alarm application is the very slow recovery time.

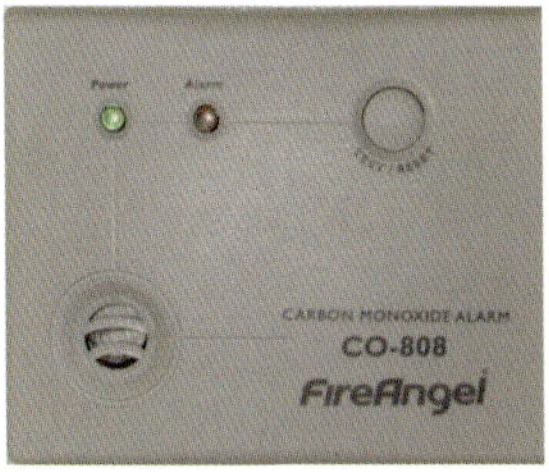

Figure 3.10

Semiconductor: Usually based on a metallic oxide, with various catalysts added to improve sensitivity and selectivity. The sensing material normally needs to be heated to a working temperature of 300°C to 400°C, which often necessitates mains voltage supplies to provide the power requirements. Semiconductors have been used in this application for many years and, whilst by no means ideal, they have previously been well characterised and are relatively inexpensive. New sources of semiconductor sensors are becoming available, especially from the Far East, which are claimed to give improved long-term stability.

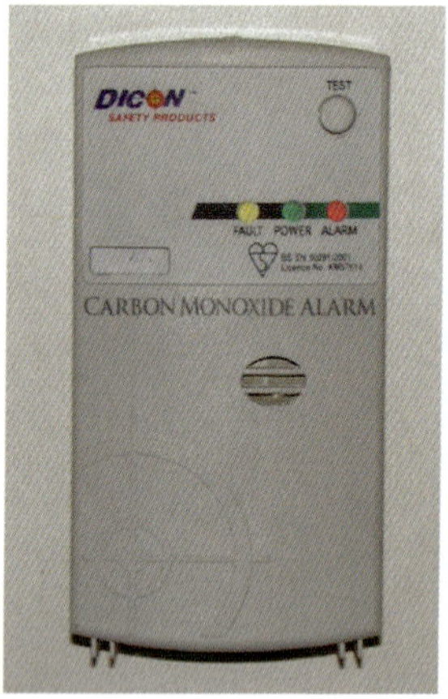

Figure 3.11

Electrochemical Cell: Well-established technology, low contamination from environmental and humidity effects.

Cell life span of circa 5 years.

Generally assumed to be the best type.

Figure 3.12

Note: An atmosphere sensing device as required by regulation 30(3)(b) of the GSIUR 1998 is NOT a CO detector. See Controls section for details on the types of atmospheric sensing devices commonly in use on domestic appliances.

3.8.3 Installation

The detector should be:

- located in the same room as the appliance
- be at a height of 1.5 metres from floor level but above the top of any opening windows.
- at least 1.85 metres from the appliance.
- kept away from excessively dusty, dirty, or greasy areas such as kitchens, garages and boiler or utility rooms.
- Dust, grease and household chemicals can affect the sensor.
- Kept out of damp and humid areas such as the bathroom.
- Avoid spraying aerosols near the CO alarm

The detector should NOT be;

- installed in turbulent air from ceiling fans
- installed in dead air spaces such as peaks of vaulted ceilings, or gabled roofs.
- placed near fresh air vents or close to doors and windows that open to the outside.
- installed in areas where the temperature is below 40°F (4.4°C) or hotter than 100°F (37.8°C).
- placed behind curtains or furniture.
- CO must be able to reach the sensor for the unit to accurately detect Carbon Monoxide.
- NEVER place the CO alarm flat on a table top or similar surface.

3.8.4 Performance

BS 7860 (expired)		BS EN 50291 (current)	
CO Level	**Alarm Time**	**CO Level**	**Alarm Time**
35 to 70 ppm	4 hours	35 ppm	More than 2 hours
150 ppm	10 to 30 minutes	50 ppm	Within 90 minutes
350 ppm	Within 6 minutes	100 ppm	Within 40 minutes
600 ppm	Instant	300 ppm	Within 3 minutes

3.8.5 Activation of CO Alarm

If a customer reports that a spot card has changed colour from orange to grey/light brown/black or an electrical detector is sounding, they must be advised to turn off the appliance(s), ventilate the room and evacuate the property until as such times as an investigation can be carried out whereby the levels of CO can be measured/ascertained by a competent engineer using an appropriate analyser. The safe operation of appliances must be confirmed at this time.

If checks reveal that no CO is present the detector may be faulty, likewise if a detector is not sounding and CO is present the detector can be considered to be faulty. The manufacturer will specify what different frequency of "chirping" indicates e.g. 1 chirp per minute is battery fault, 2 chirps per minute is detector fault, 3 chirps per minute indicates sensor expired, 5 chirps per second indicates CO present.

Be aware that CO can come from a number of sources, not just faulty gas burning appliances within the property. Other fossil fuel burning appliances may be responsible or CO may be entering via pipe ducts, warm air ducts, false chimney breasts, joist spaces, stairwells, from flue terminals via wind or natural convection.

Check with the customer what circumstances prevailed at the time of activation (e.g. fossil fuel burning appliances in use, doors and windows open or closed, weather conditions, car engines left idling in adjacent areas/ buildings, engines on boats, generators, etc.).

3.9 Flue gas analysers

Analysers can be used to measure the levels of CO and CO_2 in the products of combustion of flueless (type A), open flue (type B) and room sealed appliances (type C).

Most analysers used by engineers are of the type that infers the percentage CO_2 by actually measuring the percentage of O_2 and arithmetically deriving the CO_2 figure. In other words, they have a Carbon Monoxide sensor and an Oxygen sensor. This type of analyser may be used to measure ambient CO within a premises.

These analysers should be switched on, set to measure the correct fuel type and zeroed in outside air away from any air contamination and the oxygen reading confirmed as 20.9% (± manufacturer's tolerance).

Where an analyser is used to measure CO_2 levels for indoor air quality it should conform to BS 8494. Normally this type of analyser directly measures CO_2 with a tolerance of ± 50ppm or better across a range of 0 - 5,000 ppm.

For newly installed appliances combustion/ indoor air quality analysis may be required as part of the manufacturers specific commissioning procedure. In addition it can be used as part of a maintenance/ service schedule, however this can not be regarded as a substitute for specific requirements by the appliance manufacturer.

4. Ventilation

Every gas burning appliance must be provided with a sufficient supply of clean air. This can be provided either by the air finding its way into the room by natural means through gaps around doors and windows, or by the provision of an air vent.

4.1 Supply of Clean Air

Reasons for providing a supply of clean air into a room containing a gas appliance are:

a) Occupants to breathe

Open flue and flueless gas appliances consume air from the room space when in operation. In addition flueless appliances disperse their products of combustion back into the room. If fresh clean air was not supplied into the room the levels of oxygen in atmosphere would deplete affecting the health of occupants in the room and safe operation of the appliances.

b) Complete combustion

Complete combustion as explained in section 3.2 requires 10 volumes of air for each volume of gas burnt.

c) Operation of the flue

The operation of a natural draught flue system relies on the flue pull created by the difference between the density of the warmer products of combustion in the flue and cooler outside air.

There is only a small amount of pressure generated by the differences (4 N/m^2 for a 8m high flue with a 12 ^{o}C difference between inside and outside temperature) between the densities inside the flue system and the outside air, this is the reason why extract fans can cause problems with the spillage of products of combustion from the flue.

The air enters the flue system via the appliance draught diverter where it dilutes the products of combustion and stabilises the flow through the primary flue. The volume of air entering via the draught diverter is approximately the same as that required for combustion. The proof of this happening can be seen during a spillage test when the smoke from the match is drawn into the draught diverter.

If an adequate quantity of air cannot enter the room, the products of combustion from within the flue may spill back into the room.
This deprives the room, and the appliance, of oxygen and will thereafter affect the combustion process. This will cause the appliance to produce carbon monoxide, CO in addition to carbon dioxide, CO_2 as explained in section 3.4 Incomplete Combustion.

d) Cooling
When an appliance is installed within a compartment, ventilation is required for cooling within the compartment and to prevent the appliance from overheating. It should be noted that some room sealed appliances do not require cooling ventilation. Unless this is stated in the appliance manufacturer's instructions cooling ventilation should always be provided.

4.2 Heat Input Values and Allowances

4.2.1 Gross Heat Input Value

This is the quantity of ALL the heat produced by the combustion of the gas. Until the implementation of BS 5440 Part 2 on 15th January 2000, the gross heat input of the gas was used for the calculation of ventilation for gas appliances. We now use the net value. It should be noted that this change was not made to change the amount of air provided to the appliance, but it was done to provide a consistent method of quoting the heat inputs value for appliances throughout Europe.

Ignoring allowances for adventitious ventilation, an open flued appliance rated at 14 kW gross, requires ventilation of 63 cm^2. The same open flued appliance would be rated at 12.72 kW net and the ventilation requirements would be 63 cm^2.

4.2.2 Net Heat Input Value

This is a measurement of the GROSS heat input minus the latent heat which is required to produce the water vapour in the products of combustion.

To convert a gross value to a net value, the ratio 1:1.1 should be used for natural gas. Basically this means divide the gross value by 1.1.

Example of conversion from gross to net values:

To convert 14 kW input gross value to a net value 14÷1.1 = 12.72 kW

12.72 would be used for calculation purposes for the appliance ventilation requirements in this example.

All examples and calculations within this book are net values unless stated otherwise.

4.2.3 Adventitious ventilation

Due to building construction some air can "leak" into a building unintentionally through structural defects around windows, doors, floorboards, walls etc or intentionally through design. This leakage of air is described as adventitious ventilation. An allowance of 35 cm^2 is used for this which equates to the necessary ventilation provision for an open-flue appliance **up to 7 kW net** and is taken into account when calculating the total ventilation provision of the installation. It should be noted that this provision can only be taken off once and cannot be used for each appliance in turn.

For each kilo Watt of heat input of an open-flue Natural Gas appliance, 5 cm^2 of ventilation is required for complete combustion. Taking adventitious ventilation into consideration, this would result in the following calculation:

Effective vent free area (cm^2) = [Maximum rated net heat input (kW) – 7 kW (adventitious allowance)] x 5 cm^2

Other factors that must be taken into account when calculating the size of vent required are:

a) **Modern building methods are now producing more "leak tight" housing.**
Weather sealing doors, cavity wall insulation, bonded flooring and double glazing all reduce the amount of adventitous ventilation, hence we must not take the allowance for adventitious ventilation for granted. As a consequence, additional ventilation over and above that calculated may be required. A spillage test will help confirm the adequate provision of ventilation.

b) **Type of appliance**
When calculating the ventilation requirements of a flueless appliance or **Decorative Fuel Effect Fire, no allowance** can be made for adventitious ventilation.

c) **Location of appliance**
When appliances are installed in **compartments, no allowance** can be made for adventitious ventilation.

4.3 Construction of Vents

Proprietary units/assemblies which are marked with the free-area shall be used wherever possible. No gauze or fly screen mesh having openings of less than 5 mm are allowed. The vent grille must be of a type that is permanently open, with no way of being able to close it, except by means of an intumescent device..

When considering using a vent grille that does not display the effective free area, it must be calculated.

4.3.1 Ducts

When a ventilation opening passes across a cavity wall, it shall have an uninterrupted duct that does not spoil the water resistance of the cavity. A duct must always be used where there is a chance of the gap becoming obstructed, i.e. within a cavity wall. The manufacturer's instructions should always be followed when installing ventilation ducts.

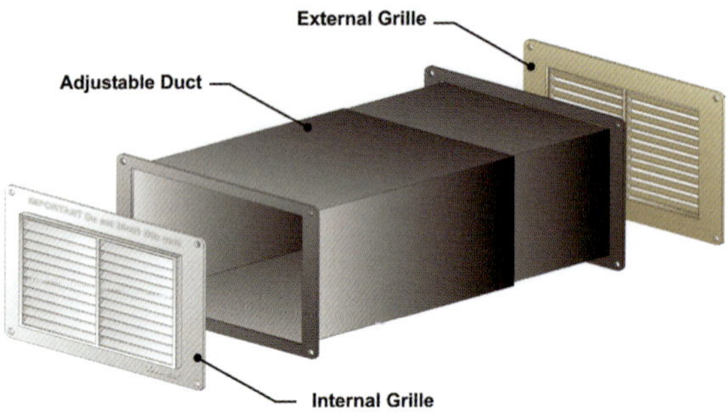

Figure 4.1 Construction of ventilator

Vent manufacturers sometimes use baffles inside the ducting to reduce draught, noise and light that passes through them. One of the disadvantages of doing this is that it may also reduce the flow of air that will pass through it. The reduction is usually between 25% and 50% of the measured vent grille free area. The manufacturer should state the equivalent free area of this type of vent.

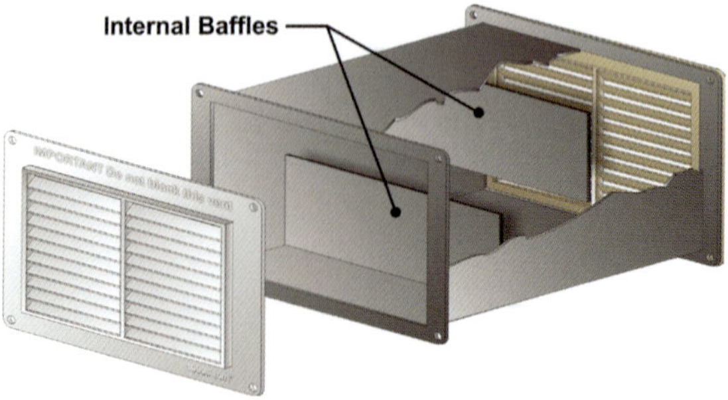

Figure 4.2 Ventilator showing internal baffles

Any ventilation duct used shall be fitted with grilles at both ends, the duct cross-sectional area shall be at least equal to the area of the grilles fitted at either end. The construction of a duct shall be such that it will allow inspection of its entire length.

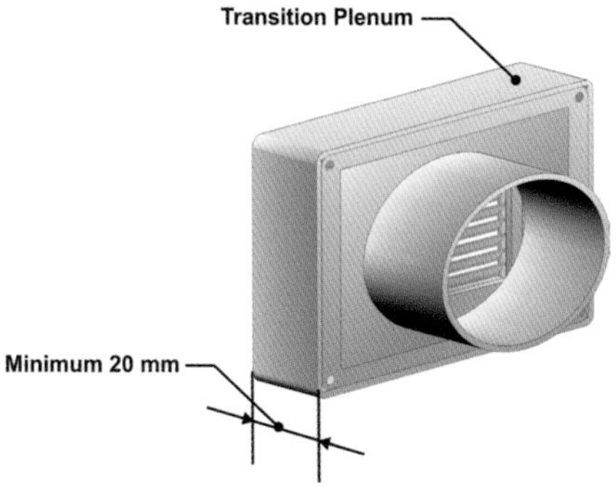

Figure 4.3 Example of transition plenum - round to square

When the shape of the cross-sectional area is different to that of the grille (a non-preferred method) for example square to round, a plenum with a 20 mm gap should be used.

Ducts from high level to low level and long horizontal runs should be avoided where possible. Where horizontal runs cannot be avoided they should be kept as short as possible. Where they are greater than 3 m and have more than 2 x 90° bends, the cross-sectional area should be increased by 50% for each 3 m or part thereof that the length exceeds the initial 3 m.

Flexible ducting should only be used where there is no other practical option, if flexible ducting is used it must be securely fixed in an extended manner.

4.3.2 Ventilated Roof and Underfloor Ventilation

It is only permissible to take air from a ventilated roof space or the space under floors, if the construction of those spaces stand alone and do not communicate with other properties. The ventilation provision into these spaces must be direct from outside air with a free area which is at least that required for the gas appliance.

Vents providing air for gas appliances from roof spaces should be positioned a minimum of 300 mm above the joists or 150 mm above the insulation, whichever is the greater, to reduce the potential obstruction caused by insulation material. It is also recommended that a terminal or bird guard be fitted to the air vent.

Where Radon gas is known to be a problem, ventilation air shall not be taken from the area under the ground floor level. One of the options available to the installer is to use ducting to take clean air from outside through the space underfloor and transfer into the property via a floor vent grille.

Advice should be sought from the local building control office to determine if the property is in area that is likely to have Radon gas.

4.3.3 Intumescent Air Vents

An intumescent air vent is a device which is specially designed to prevent the spread of fire. It is normally an insert which is placed between ventilators on a fire door or within ductwork which provides ventilation between two internal spaces. The insert consists of a metal framework which supports an open latticework of heat sensitive material. Air is free to pass through the insert, however when exposed to high temperatures, for example a fire, the material will expand sealing off the air path through the vents. It should be noted that these types of inserts may restrict the air flow through the vents and as such must be taken into consideration when measuring the effective free air of ventilation. Never remove any intumescent air vents as this will affect the fire integrity of the building or compartment.

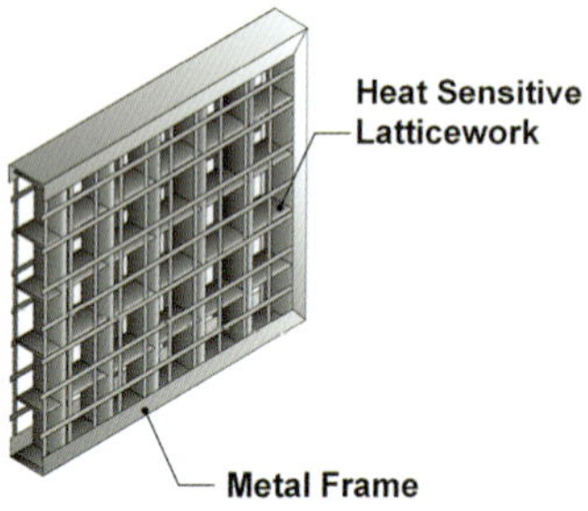

Figure 4.4 Intumescent vent Insert

Whether installing an intumescent air vent or carrying out maintenance work, the customer must be instructed that if the insert has been activated by a high temperature, for example a fire, then the gas appliance cannot be operated until the vent is replaced.

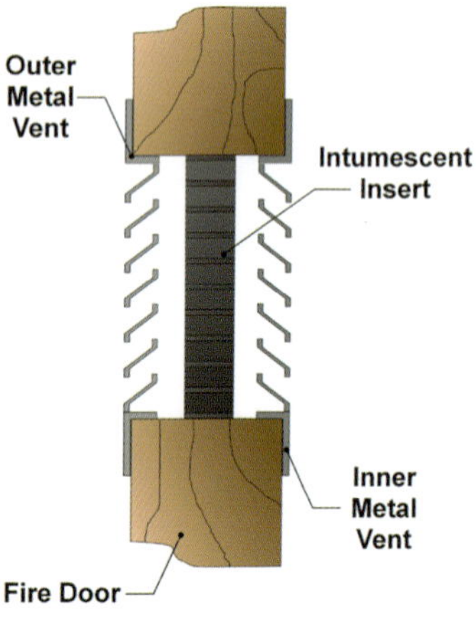

Figure 4.5 Intumescent Vent Installed In a Fire Door

4.3.4 Passive Stack Ventilation

Passive stack ventilation (PSV) is method of providing natural extract to remove odours and moisture generally from "wet" rooms, for example kitchens, bath and shower rooms. It is essentially a duct which rises vertically from the ceiling of the room to a terminal at roof level. Air movement within the duct is created due to the pressure and temperature differences between the top and bottom of the duct, similar to that of a natural draught chimney system. Any ventilation provision for gas appliances must be considered over and above that of the PSV. Consideration must be given to the location of the PSV termination to that of any open flue appliance such that it does not adversley affect the safe operation of the appliance. It is advisable to locate the open flue terminal either at the same height or above that of the PSV terminal with both terminations on the same face of the building. This will minimise pressure differences between the two terminals reducing the likleyhood of spillage.

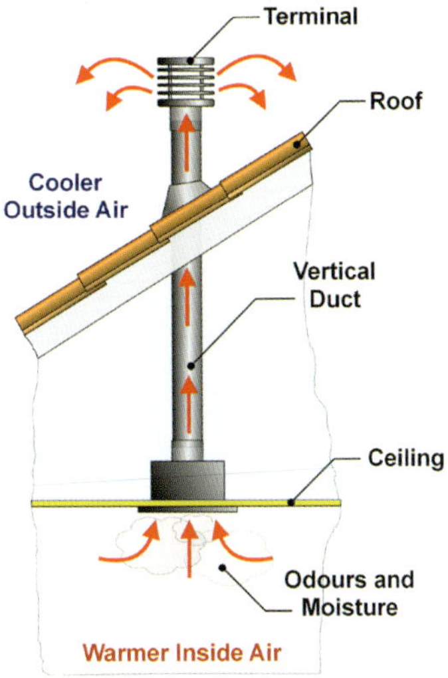

Figure 4.6 Passive Stack Ventilation

4.4 Calculating vent grilles sizes

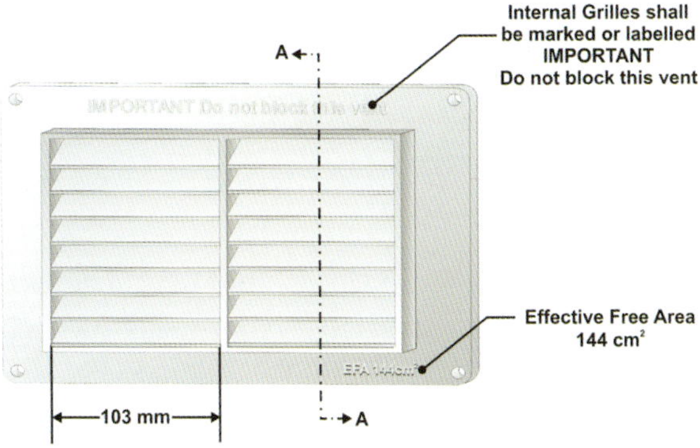

Figure 4.7 Typical Internal air vent grille

The design width of a vent grille opening shall be such that it permits entry of a ball of 5 mm diameter and prevents the entry of a 10 mm diameter ball. It has been found that vermin can find its way into openings slightly larger than 10 mm and dust/lint can block smaller openings than 5 mm.

The construction of the grille with a lip on the back of the vane prevents a 10 mm diameter ball passing right through it.

When measured correctly at **right angles** *to the louvre it is actually*
103 x 10 mm = 1030 mm²

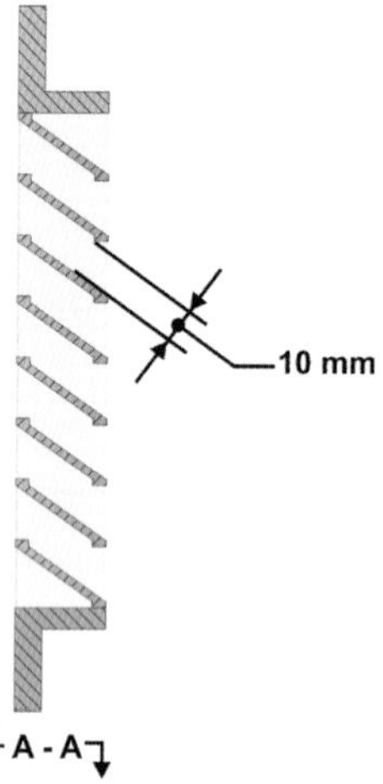

Figure 4.8 Cross section of grille

Using the example of a vent grille (figures 4.4 and 4.5), from the front it appears that the opening is:

Length of opening x width of opening

103 mm x 14 mm

When measured correctly at right angles to the louver it is actually:

103 mm x 10 mm = 1030 mm²

There are 14 openings in total

14 x 1030 mm² = 14420 mm²

Ventilation grilles are usually expressed in cm², to convert mm² into cm² divide the total by 100. Always round down when calculating ventilation.

14420 ÷100 = 144.2 cm² rounding down gives a ***total of 144 cm²***

Terracotta type vents

Terracotta type vents are constructed with wider openings at the front that taper down to give a smaller opening at the rear of the air brick.

The air brick forms part of the brick wall of the premises and it can prove difficult obtaining the smaller dimension.

Perhaps the easiest method to establish its dimensions is to use a set of twist drills and finding the largest one able to pass through the rear of the hole. Usually this is 8 or 9 mm^2.

Where the holes on the rear face measure 9mm,
the free area = 9 x 9 mm x 36 (number of holes) = 29.16 cm^2 or 2916 mm^2.

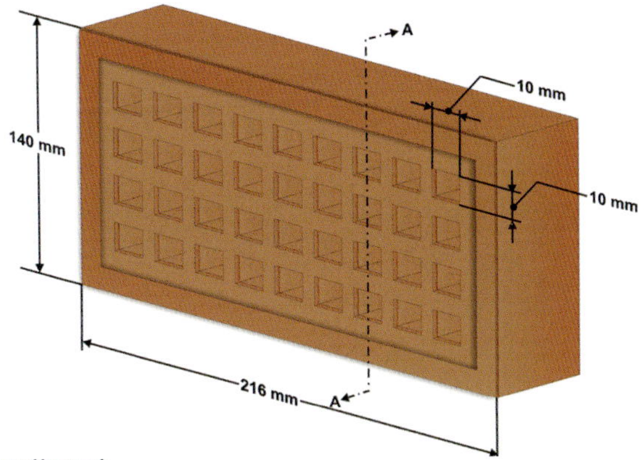

Figure 4.9 Typical Terracotta vent

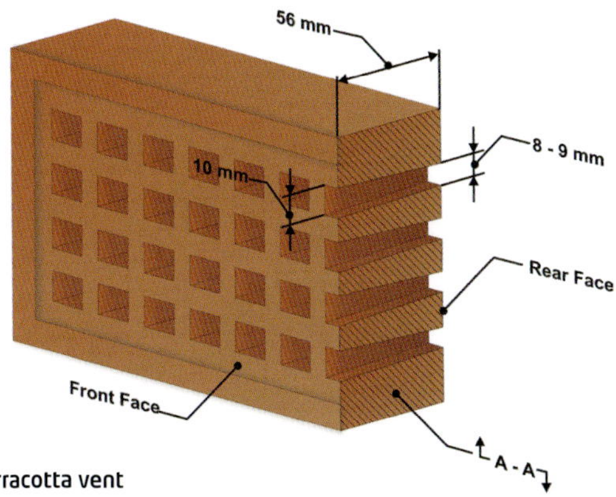

Figure 4.10 Cross section of Terracotta vent

4.5 Location of vents

4.5.1 Vents communicating direct to outside air

Air vents should have a minimum separation distance from any appliance flue terminal, see table 4.1.

The purpose of the separation distance is to reduce the chances of products of combustion entering the property.

These distances also apply to mechanical ventilation openings and any vents in roof spaces.

When deciding where to locate air vents;

- **DO** follow appliance manufacturer instructions when locating and sizing vents.
- **DO** install air vents adjacent to the appliance.
- **DO** install air vents at a high level with the vanes directing the flow of air away from sitting Areas.
- **DO** take the shortest route through a cavity wall with an air vent sleeve.
- **DO** install flueless gas fires 1 m away from any vent supplying it with combustion air or a ventilator installed in a redundant chimney unless the appliance manufacturer specifies otherwise.
- **DO** treat Oil or Solid Fuel appliances as if they are gas appliances. Normally they do not state an input, instead the output is usually given, assume an efficiency of 60% in order to estimate the input.
- **DO NOT** locate air vents in positions where they could be obstructed by;
  - i. Plants growing nearby or leaves collecting with the autumn winds.
  - ii. Snow drifting in the winter.
  - iii. Water pooling following a downpour.
- **DO NOT** install an air vent into car ports or other areas where polluted air could be present.
- **DO NOT** install an air vent within a builders opening to supply air for a fire, with or without a backboiler unit or circulator connected to it.
- **DO NOT** install an air vent into a protected shaft or stairway.

- **DO NOT** install an air vent into a room or space containing a bath or shower, or use them as part of the route to supply air to an open flued appliance.
- **DO NOT** use a bedroom or bedsitting room as a route to supply air to a room that contains an open flued appliance unless the appliance is less than 12.7 kW heat input and has a device that will shut it down before a build-up of a dangerous quantity of products of combustion.
- **DO NOT** install an air vent behind a radiator.
- **DO NOT** install an air vent sleeve with an offset.

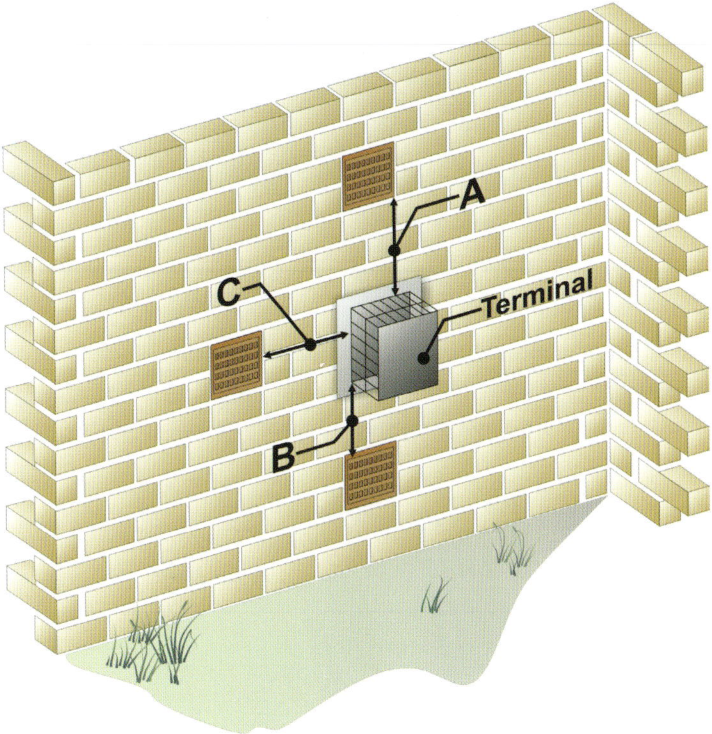

Figure 4.11 Location of air brick to flue terminal

Vent Position	Appliance Input	Balanced Flue		Open Flue	
		Natural Draught	Fanned Draught	Natural Draught	Fanned Draught
		Minimum Separation (mm)			
A (above)	0 to 7 kW > 7 to 14 kW > 14 to 32 kW > 32kW to 70kW	300 600 1500 2000	300	300 600 1500 2000	300
B (below)	0 to 7 kW > 7 to 14 kW > 14 to 32 kW > 32kW to 70kW	300 300 300 600	300	300 300 300 600	300
C (to side)	0 to 7 kW > 7 to 14 kW > 14 to 32 kW > 32kW to 70kW	300 400 600 600	300	300 400 600 600	300
Note > means greater than					

Table 4.1 Distances from openings into buildings from flue terminal

4.5.2 Vents communicating with internal space or room

Ventilation grilles in internal walls or doors shall be positioned at no greater height than 450 mm from the floor level this lessens the spread of smoke should there be a fire.

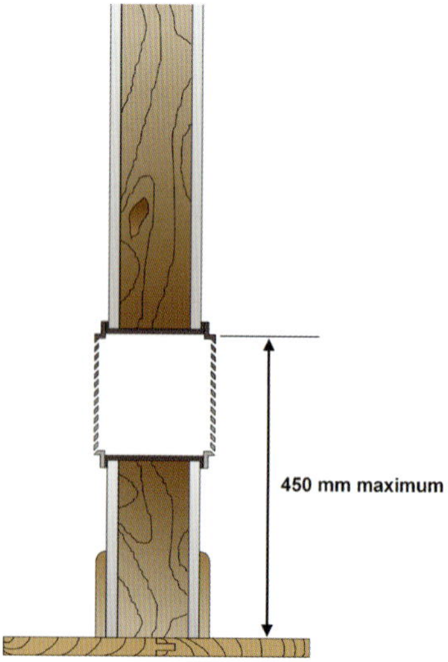

Figure 4.12 Installation of vent in internal wall or door

4.6 Flueless Appliances

The ventilation requirements for a flueless appliance can only be determined by consulting the manufacturer's instructions or the table in BS 5440 - 2, (see below). Any air vent required must be direct to outside.

Appliance Type	Maximum Input	Room Volume (m^3)	Effective Free Area of Ventilation	Openable window Required [b]
Cooker, Hotplate, Oven, Grill [a]	None	Less than 5 From 5 to 10 [c] Greater than 10	100 cm^2 50 cm^2 Zero	YES
Instantaneous Water Heater	11 kW	Less than 5 From 5 to 10 Greater than 10 up to 20 Greater than 20	Not Permitted 100 cm^2 50 cm^2 Zero	YES
Space Heater in a ROOM	45 W per m^3 of room volume		100 cm^2 plus 55 cm^2 for every kW above 2.7 kW	YES
Space Heater in an INTERNAL SPACE	90 W per m^3 of space volume		100 cm^2 plus 27.5 cm^2 for every kW above 5.4 kW	YES
Tumble Dryer	6 kW	Less than 3.7 m^3 of room volume per kW	100 cm^2	YES
		Equal to or greater than 3.7 m^3 of room volume per kW	Zero	
Refrigerator	None		Zero	NO
Single boiling ring	None		Zero	NO

Note all input values are net

a) Not allowed in a bedroom. Unless it is a single boiling ring, not allowed in bed-sitting rooms less than 20 m^3 volume

b) Openings other than windows which open directly to outside may be acceptable e.g. cooker extraction system, see local building regulations

c) If this room has a door which opens directly to outside, no ventilation is required

Table 4.2 Sizing flueless vents

4.6.1 Determining Ventilation Requirements of a Space Heater in a Room

Prior to any ventilation calculation we must determine if the room volume is large enough to allow the installation of the appliance. Firstly convert kW to watts by multiplying the net heat input by 1000, then divide by the volume of the room. The answer must be 45 w/m^3 (figure from table 4.2, is a maximum value) or less.

NOTE if value is over 45 w/m^3 the appliance cannot be installed.

NOTE LPG space heaters conforming to BS EN 449: 1997 have their own specific requirements.

Example Flueless space heater in a room

The combustion air requirements for a flueless space heater with an input of 2.8 kW fitted in a room used as a lounge measuring 6m x 4.2m x 2.5m is:

Room volume = Length x Width x Height

Room volume; 6 x 4.2 x 2.5 = 63m^3

2 800 watts ÷ 63 = 44.44 w/m^3

100 (given minimum) + 5.5 (because over 2.7) = 100 + 5.5

(55 ÷ 10 = 5.5) because (1 ÷ 0.1 = 10)

= 100 + 5.5 = 105.5 cm^2

This is the minimum required by BS 5440 Part 2, NICEIC suggest that because 2.8 kW is over 2.7 kW then the full 55 cm^2 is added to the 100 cm^2 making the requirement:

155 cm^2

4.6.2 Internal Kitchens

BS 5440 part 2 specifies that when we install a gas-fired cooking appliance into a kitchen we must have the provision of an openable window or equivalent opening direct to outside air over an above the ventilation requirement for the gas appliance(s). Where this additional ventilation is not provided, the standard indicates that the appliance(s) cannot be installed. Taking this into account industry has recognised that there are occasions where an extension or conservatory has been or may be built over the window or equivalent opening. This would result in nonconformance with both the British standard and the relevant Building Regulations. It is essential that additional ventilation is provided to ensure compliance. Further advice can be found in the Building Regulations Approved Document F (England and Wales) or the Scottish Building Standards Technical Handbook Section 3 (formally Technical Standard K).

These documents specify a general requirement for the provision of "purge ventilation" which is designed to allow rapid dilution of contaminants and/or water vapour from the kitchen. This may be provided by mechanical means (extract fans and hoods) or natural means (openable door or window, passive stack). Extract ventilation to outside air may be operated either continuously or intermittently. Intermittent operation can be either automatic (by operation of a sensor or light switch) or manual (pull cord). Where the extract is automatic a manual override should be provided to allow the occupants to turn the extract on when required. The fans should also have a 15 minute over-run.

Where an extension or conservatory have been added and no intermittent extraction has been provided the ventilation may be achieved by means of purge ventilation via an openable door, window or similar opening direct to outside air equivalent to 1/20th of the combined floor area of the kitchen and extension/conservatory and, in addition, background ventilation by means of closable trickle vents located at least 1.7m above the floor with a minimum free area of 8000 mm^2.

In some occasions passive stack ventilation provided through open flue chimney systems when an appliance is not in operation may be sufficient to provide the necessary extract. For gas fired appliances a minimum flue diameter of 125 mm is required. In all instances the ventilation requirements of the open flue appliance must be met.

4.7 Open Flue Appliances

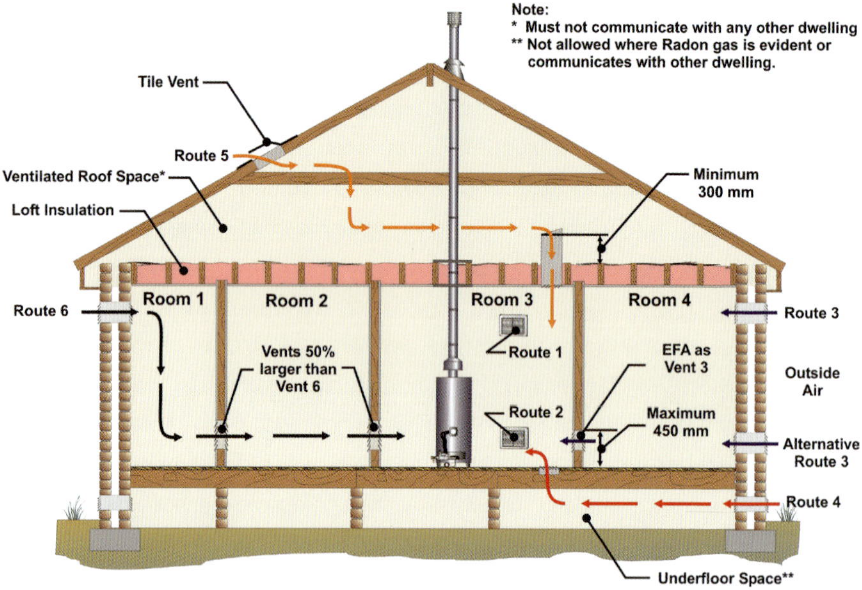

Figure 4.13 Ventilation routes into building

4.7.1 Determining Ventilation Requirements of Appliance in a Room

The size of the air vent required is determined from:

The maximum rated heat input of the appliance (kW) - adventitious air (7 kW) x 5 cm^2.

Example, open flue boiler in a room

The ventilation requirement for an open flued boiler with a heat input of 19 kW is:

19 - 7=12

Maximum appliance heat input - adventitious air = value of heat input used to determine size of ventilation grille free area required:

12 x 5 = 60 cm^2

Calculated value x constant = free area of vent required.

4.7.2 Determining series ventilation requirements

4.7.2.1 (i) Routes 1 to 5 – Figure 4.13

When vents are used in series different rules apply depending on the number of rooms (vents) involved.

Two rooms, both vents will be sized in accordance with 4.7.1.

Example, where 2 vents are in series

The ventilation requirement for an open flued boiler with a heat input of 15 kW is:

$$15 - 7 = 8$$

Maximum appliance heat input – adventitious air = the value of heat input used to determine the ventilation grille free area

$$8 \times 5 = 40 \text{ cm}^2$$

Calculated value x constant = free area of vent required

(ii) Route 6 – Figure 4.13

When 3 rooms are ventilated in series, room 1 will be sized in accordance with 4.7.1, and vents 2 & 3 will be increase by 50%. Note any additional room vents would also require a 50% increase in size.

Example, where there are 3 vents in series

The ventilation requirement for an open flued boiler with a heat input of 25 kW is:

$$25 - 7 = 18$$

Maximum appliance heat input – adventitious air = the value of heat input used to determine the ventilation grille free area

$$18 \times 5 = 90 \text{ cm}^2$$

Room 1

Using calculation above, 90 cm^2 is required

Rooms 2 & 3

A vent 50% greater than that which is calculated for room 1:

To calculate 50% of 90

$$90 \div 100 \times 50 = 45$$

The 45 + 90 = 135

The requirement for rooms 2 & 3 is 135 cm^2

Note *any addition vents would also require a 50% increase in size on the value calculated for room 1.*

(iii) Route B & C – Figure 4.14

When a room is supplying air in series into a compartment containing an open flued appliance, room 1 (or room 2) will be sized in accordance 4.7.1, vents B & C will be sized in accordance with Table 4.3 section 4.7.3.

Example, 3 vents in series supplying air to a compartment

The ventilation requirement for an open flued boiler with a heat input of 16 kW is:

$$16 - 7 \times 5 = 45 \text{ cm}^2$$

Room Vent Route C

Using calculation above, 45 cm^2 is required for the boiler from outside into the room

Compartment Vents Route C

High level compartment vent 16 = 160 cm^2 (see table 4.3)

Low level compartment vent 16 x 320 cm^2 (see table 4.3)

Vents between rooms 2 & 3

A vent 50% greater than that which is calculated for room 1:

To calculate 50% of 45

$$45 \div 100 \times 50 = 22.5$$

$$22.5 + 45 = 67.5\ cm^2$$

4.7.3 Determining Ventilation Requirements of Appliance in a Compartment

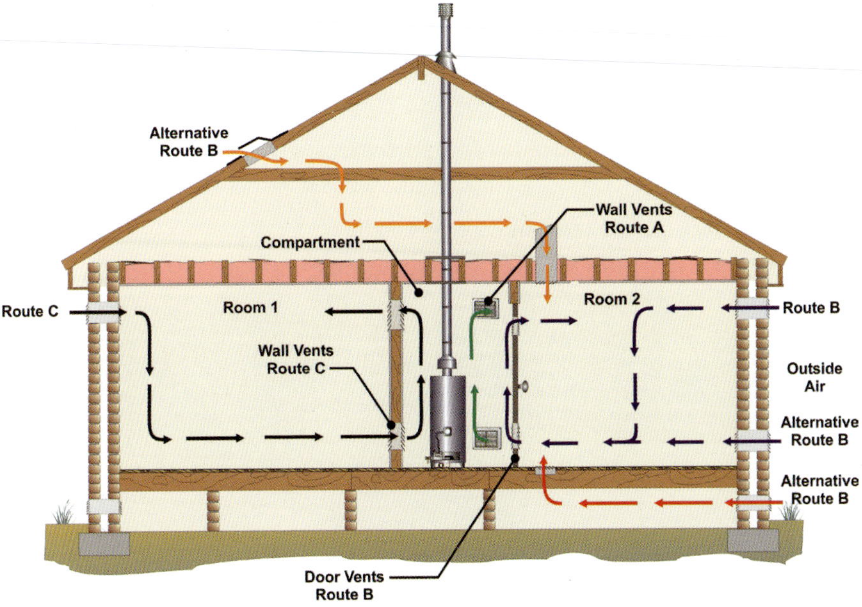

Figure 4.14 Ventilation routes into building for Compartment

Compartment ventilation can be taken from within the premises or directly from outside. Vents shall be positioned at the highest and lowest practical level and be from the same wall, when taking air from outside or inside via room or internal space.

Ducts from a high level are a non preferred method of providing, high and low level ventilation into a compartment for new installations.

- **DO** provide ventilation at both high and low level.
- **DO** provide ventilation direct to outside if possible.
- **DO** provide ventilation for open flued appliances.
- **DO** allow for adventitious air when calculating the ventilation requirement for a room or internal space if the compartment ventilation is provided from them.
- **DO** insulate ducts providing low level ventilation from a location above the appliance.
- **DO** position the lower end of any ducts below the appliance burner height when taken from a location above the appliance.
- **DO** display a label.
- **DO NOT** provide ducted high and low ventilation from the same duct.
- **DO NOT** provide high level ventilation via a duct from low level.
- **DO NOT** make any allowance for adventitious ventilation within the compartment.
- **DO NOT** use the compartment for storage.

Vent Position	cm² per kW^{net} of appliance maximum heat input	
	Appliance Compartment Ventilated to ROOM or INTERNAL SPACE*	Appliance Compartment Ventilated directly to OUTSIDE AIR
High Level	10	5
Low Level	20	10
* The room or internal space requires to ventilated		

Table 4.3 Minimum air vents free area for OPEN FLUE appliances in compartments

Example, Open flue boiler in a compartment

Where an open flued boiler of 25 kW is installed inside a compartment and the only option available is to ventilate via an internal room. The total ventilation requirement is:

Compartment

High level vent 10 x 25 = 250 cm²

10 (taken from table 4.3) x 25 (maximum heat input of appliance) = 250 cm²

Low level vent 20 x 25 = 500 cm²

20 (taken from table 4.3) x 25 (maximum heat input of appliance) = 500 cm²

Internal room

The ventilation requirement for an open flued boiler with a heat input of 25 kW is;

25 – 7 = 18

Maximum appliance heat input – adventitious air = value of heat input used to determine size of ventilation grille free area required

18 x 5 = 90 cm²

4.8 Room Sealed Appliances

Determining Ventilation Requirements of an Appliance in a Room

Room sealed appliances do not require any ventilation provision within the room the appliance is installed in.

Determining Ventilation Requirements of an Appliance in a Compartment

Room sealed appliances in compartments may or may not need ventilation. Unless the appliance manufacturer states that no compartment ventilation is required, it will have to be provided.

Vent Position	cm^2 per kW^{net} of appliance maximum heat input	
	Appliance Compartment Ventilated to ROOM or INTERNAL SPACE*	Appliance Compartment Ventilated directly to OUTSIDE AIR
High Level	10	5
Low Level	10	5

Table 4.4 Minimum air vent free area for ROOM SEALED appliances in compartments

Example, Room sealed boiler in a compartment

A room sealed boiler is installed inside a compartment the maximum heat input is 22 kW, that is ventilated direct to outside. The total ventilation requirement is:

Compartment

High level vent 5 x 22 = 110 cm²

5 (taken from table 4.4) x 22 (maximum heat input of appliance) = 110 cm²

Low level vent 5 x 22 = 110 cm²

5 (taken from table 4.4) x 22 (maximum heat input of appliance) = 110 cm²

4.9 Multiple Appliance Situations

Where there is more than one appliance in a room, the ventilation required is best interpreted as the largest ventilation requirement from the following:

a) The combined maximum rated input of flueless space heating appliances,

or

b) The combined maximum rated input of open flue space heating appliances (except where the interconnecting wall between two rooms has been removed and the resultant room contains only two chimneys, each fitted with a similar gas fire with rated inputs each less than 7 kW, an air vent may not be required),

or

c) The greatest individual rated input of any other type of appliance.

4.10 Ventilation Requirements of Decorative Fuel Effect (DFE) fires

Installation Detail	Appliance Location	Ventilation Requirement
1 DFE up to 7 kW	Single room	Normally 100 cm^2 minimum but check with manufacturer some fires do no not require any
1 DFE up to 7 kW	Single room	Normally 100 cm^2 minimum or manufacturer's instructions
2 DFE's up to 20 kW	Single room	Normally 200 cm^2 minimum (or manufacturer's instructions) plus 35 for adventitious air
2 DFE's up to 20 kW	Two rooms interconnecting wall removed (through room)	Normally 200 cm^2 minimum (or manufacturer's instructions)

Table 4.5 DFE ventilation requirements

Appliance Location	Ventilation Requirement
Single Room	DFE requirement based on table above PLUS whichever is the greatest of: a) The total flueless space heating appliance requirement b) The total open flue space heating appliance requirement (5 cm^2 / kW - do not subtract 7 kW)
ONE DFE INSTALLED Through room or space with two open flues	DFE requirement based on table above PLUS whichever is the greatest of: a) the total flueless space heating appliance requirement b) the total open flue space heating appliance requirement (5 cm^2 / kW net total rating in excess of 7 kW)
TWO DFEs INSTALLED Through room or space with two open flues	DFE requirement based on table above PLUS whichever is the greatest of: a) the total flueless space heating appliance requirement b) the total open flue space heating appliance requirement (for open flue it will be 5 cm^2 / kW - do not subtract 7 kW)

Table 4.6 Ventilation Requirements of Decorative Fuel Effect fires (DFE) and Other Appliances in the Same Room

Solid fuel fires and stoves should be treated as decorative fuel effect gas appliances.

4.11 Extract Fans and Their Effect on Appliances

Extract fans and any other air moving devices can have an adverse effect on the safe operation of fuel burning appliances, especially those which are open-flue. Air turbulance and/or depressurisation of the room or internal space can disturb the passage of ventilation to the appliance having an adverse effect on combustion and/or the operation of the flue system. This can lead to unsafe situations such as spillage.

When testing the safe operation of an appliance these fans or other air moving devices must be operated in all modes. Where it is found that they do have an adverse effect on the appliance(s) it is recommended that a minimum of 50 cm^2 additional ventilation be provided. Remember this is a minimum, additional tests must be performed to ensure that it is adequate, if not it must be increase further until satisfactory results are recorded.

Examples of fans which can effect the safe operation of an appliance are:

- Room extract Fans.
- Fan assisted flue systems.
- Air Heater circulation fans (these can be of any fuel type, eg electric).
- Cooker Hoods.
- Ceiling paddle fans.

4.12 Compartment Label

Customers must be advised on the use of the compartment by a suitably worded label.

Figure 4.15 Typical Compartment Label

5. Pipework

5.1 Introduction

The Gas Safety (Installation and Use) Regulations 18 to 24 (Part D) must be complied with in respect to installation pipework. Regulations 6 to 17 are also relevant.

BS 6891 is the document that details the current standards regarding domestic, natural gas pipework installation operating at a nominal pressure of 21 mbar; document IGE/UP/ 2 details the standards regarding commercial pipework installation. The scope of BS 6891 has been extended to include 35 mm copper and 1¼ inch (32 mm) steel.

5.2 Design and Planning

It is essential that all parties interested in the gas pipework are consulted in order to ensure that the installation is in accordance with the Gas Safety (Installation and Use) Regulations and BS 6891 and that it meets the needs of the customer. Consideration should also be given to possible future extensions. Installation will be made easier if the pipe installer can be on site before the completion of the build process e.g. before flooring is laid. Other trades should be made aware of the location of pipes in order to avoid accidental damage e.g. nails through pipes.

5.3 Pipe Sizing and Pressure Loss

The gas pipe system must be sized so that it can supply all the appliances simultaneously with a maximum pressure absorption of 1 mbar from the gas meter outlet to all appliance inlet connections. Assuming the working pressure at the gas meter outlet is 21 mbar this will ensure that the appliances are supplied with their design pressure of 20 mbar. It must be stressed that this is working pressure, not standing pressure, see the section of these notes which deals with checking meter regulators.

5.3.1 Pipe Sizing Procedure

The sizing of pipes supplying a single appliance is a relatively simple procedure.

Example 1

What is the minimum pipe size for the installation shown below?

The pipework is to be steel manufactured to BS 1387.

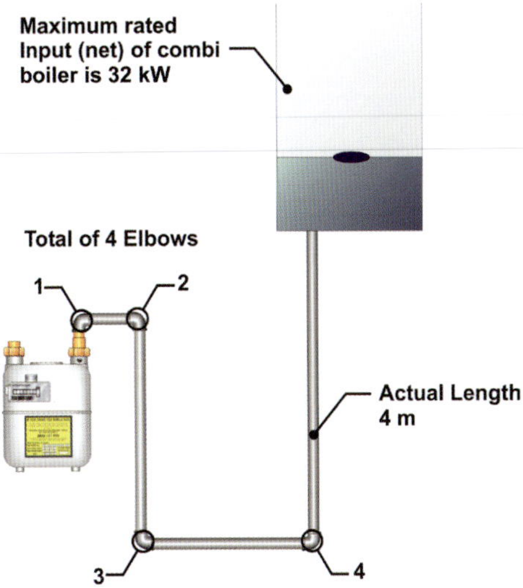

Figure 5.1 Single appliance pipe sizing exercise

Answer

The equivalent length of the pipe is the actual length plus any allowance for fittings or bends. In this case the equivalent length is 4 m + (4 x 0.5) = 6 m.

Using table 5.1 it can be seen that ½ inch steel can only supply 28.1 kW corresponding to a length of 6 m therefore ½ inch is too small.

¾ inch steel can supply 64 kW corresponding to a length of 6 m and would therefore be the size selected.

In fact, 20 metres of ¾ inch steel could supply 32 kW for a pressure absorption of 1 mbar.

In this case the equivalent length is 6 m, the actual pressure absorption would be 1 mbar x 6 ÷ 20 = 0.3 mbar.

This is based on pressure absorption being directly proportional to length, which means, if you halve the length you halve the pressure absorption, if you triple the length you triple the pressure absorption.

Pipe Type and Size				Length of Pipe (metres)							
Medium Grade Steel	Copper	Corrugated Stainless Steel	PE	Gas Rate (m^3h^{-1}) To obtain the gas rate (m^3h^{-1}) divide the net heat input by 9.7							
BS 1387	BS EN 1057	BS 7838	BS 7281	3	6	9	12	15	20	25	30
6 mm	8 mm			0.29	0.14	0.09	0.07	0.05			
8 mm				0.8	0.53	0.49	0.36	0.29	0.22	0.17	0.14
	10 mm	10 mm		0.86	0.57	0.50	0.37	0.30	0.22	0.18	0.15
10 mm				2.1	1.4	1.1	0.93	0.81	0.70	0.69	0.57
	12 mm	12 mm		1.5	1.0	0.85	0.82	0.69	0.52	0.41	0.34
	15 mm	15 mm		2.9	1.9	1.5	1.3	1.1	0.95	0.92	0.88
15 mm				4.3	2.9	2.3	2.0	1.7	1.5	1.4	1.3
			20 mm	4.0	2.7	2.1	1.8	1.6	1.3	1.2	1.05
20 mm			25 mm	9.7	6.6	5.3	4.5	3.9	3.3	2.9	2.6
	22 mm	22 mm		8.7	5.8	4.6	3.9	3.4	2.9	2.5	2.3
25 mm			32 mm	18	12	10	8.5	7.5	6.3	5.6	5.0
	28 mm	28 mm		18	12	9.4	8.0	7.0	5.9	5.2	4.7
		32 mm		29	20	15	13	12	10	8.5	7.6
32 mm	35 mm			32	22	17	15	13	11	9.5	8.5
Table based on natural gas with a relative density of 0.6 and a Gross Calorific Value of 38.76 MJ/m^3											
An addition of 0.5 m should be made to the length of the pipe for each elbow (or teepiece) and 0.3 m for a 90° bend											

Table 5.1 Gas Flow Rate in a straight length of horizontal pipe with a 1.0 mbar pressure drop between ends for gas with a relative density of 0.6

If the installation contains two or more appliances the procedure is more complicated. Consider the example shown below:

Example 2

Determine the minimum size of copper pipe required for the installation shown.

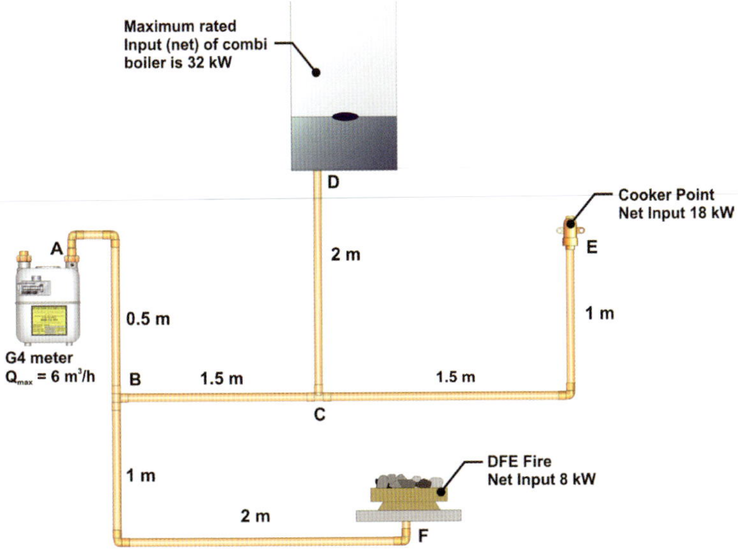

Figure 5.2 Multi-appliance pipe size exercise.

Answer

The total net heat input is 58 kW (32 + 18 + 8). The maximum gas rate is 58 ÷ 9.7 = 5.98 m^3h^{-1} (not taking the diversity factor into account which would reduce the gas rate, see section on gas meters). The gas meter is adequate to supply the appliances.

Step 1 *The pipework must be treated as separate sections determined by the gas flow. These sections are entered in column 1.*

Step 2 *The net heat input required by each section of pipework is then entered e.g. A B must supply sufficient gas flow rate for all the appliances, which is the maximum as stated above, 5.98 m^3h^{-1}.*

Step 3 *The actual length of each section is then entered.*

Step 4 *Enter the allowance for fittings or bends. Note that teepieces are only relevant to the section of pipe containing the branch.*

Step 5 *Use table 5.1 and select the pipe length column using the next column up from the equivalent length e.g. for an equivalent length of 5 m use the 6 m column, for an equivalent length of 3 m use the 3 m column.*

Step 6 *An arbitrary pipe size is then selected, although if it results in a pressure loss in that section close to the maximum of 1 mbar then it will probably require to be increased.*

Step 7 *Use table 5.1, determine the maximum length for the selected pipe size/type based on the net heat flow. Exercise common sense, e.g. for 28 mm copper, 20 m, the heat flow is 5.9 m^3h^{-1} when 5.92 m^3h^{-1} is required, enter 20 m, not 15 m.*

Step 8 *Determine the pressure absorption from the meter outlet to each appliance and ensure it does not exceed 1 mbar. If it does, the pipe section sizes will require to be increased. (Tip - divide the maximum pressure loss of 1 mbar by the number of sections, in this case 1 ÷ 5 = 0.2 mbar. Keep pressure loss for each section below this would ensure total pressure loss to each appliance does not exceed the 1 mbar)*

From the meter outlet to the combi boiler, the gas must flow through three pipe sections which are AB, BC and CD; the respective pressure absorptions are 0.075 + 0.080 + 0.167 = 0.322 mbar.

From the meter outlet to the cooker, the gas must flow through three pipe sections which are AB, BC and CE; the respective pressure absorptions are 0.075 + 0.080 + 0.500 = 0.655 mbar.

From the meter outlet to the DFE, the gas must flow through two pipe sections which are AB and BF; the respective pressure absorptions are 0.075 + 0.444 = 0.519 mbar.

Step 9 *In practice, 12 mm is not a commonly used pipe size, 15 mm would be more appropriate for pipe section BF.*

1	2	3	4	5	6	7	8
Pipe Section	Gas Flow Rate (m^3h^{-1})	Actual Length (m)	Allowance for Fittings (m)	Equivalent Length (m)	Pipe Size (mm)	Maximum Length (m)	Pressure absorption (mbar) (Col. 5 divided by Col. 7)
A B	5.92	0.5	1.0	1.5	28	20	0.075
B C	5.15	1.5	0.5	2.0	28	25	0.080
C D	3.3	2.0	0.5	2.5	22	15	0.167
C E	1.86	2.5	0.5	3.0	15	6	0.500
BF	0.82	3.0	1.0	4.0	12	9	0.444

Table 5.2 Calculation of pressure loss relative to gas flow rate and length of pipe.

5.3.2 Pressure Loss in Pipework

As stated previously we require the minimum pressure loss from the outlet of the meter to the inlet of an appliance to be no greater than 1 mbar. The calculations given provide us with enough information to make a positive judgement on new and existing installation pipework as to it's suitability to provide an adequate gas supply for the safe operation of an appliance.

Fundamentally pipework can only be proven "adequate" by pressure measurement at both the outlet of the meter and inlet to the appliance(s) under normal operating conditions. Where the pressure loss between the meter and appliance has been found unsatisfactory (greater than 1 mbar or less than manufacturers minimum) and the pipework is of adequate size, other factors must be taken into consideration as to the reason behind the excessive pressure loss.

Where the outlet pressure from the meter has been found satisfactory (21 ± 2 mbar) excessive pressure loss may be contributed to:

- Blockage in the pipework (solder, swarf, debris, sulphidation etc)
- Damaged pipe (kinks in pipe, pipe flattened, excessive bend radius causing pipe wall to collapse etc.)
- Excessive number of fittings.
- Excessive run of pipe/ tube.

- Controls partially closed such as isolation valves etc.
- Blocked filters.
- Additional appliances added to installation with a heat input greater than that of the existing appliance therefore increasing the "load".

The full installation must be examined and investigated to identify any faults which may result in excessive pressure loss within the installation.

5.4 Materials

Pipe and Fittings must conform to the standards detailed in tables:

Material	Standard of Manufacture
Steel Pipe and Fittings	BS 1387 BS 3604-2:1991 BS EN 10255:2004 BS EN 10216-1:2002 BS EN 10216-2:2002 BS EN 10217-1:2002 BS EN 10217-2:2002
Malleable Iron Fittings	BS 143 and 1256:2000 BS EN 10242:1995
Threads (Taper external and Parallel internal)	BS EN 10226-1:2004
Thread Sealing	BS EN 751-1:1997 (anaerobic) BS EN 751-2:1997 (non-hardening) BS EN 751-3:1997 (unsintered PTFE tapes) BS 6956-5:1992
BS 1387 was withdrawn on 01/06/2006	

Rigid Stainless Steel	BS EN 10216-5:2004 BS EN 10217-7:2005 BS EN 10312:2002
BS 3605-2:1992 was withdrawn on 25/02/2005	
Corrugated Stainless Steel and Fittings	BS 7837:1996 (AMD 13206, September 2001) BS EN 15266:2007
BS 7837 replaced by BS EN 15266:2007 but remains current.	

Copper	BS EN 1057:2006
Capillary Fittings (Soldered or Brazed)	BS EN 1254-1:1998 (replace BS 864-2:1983)
Soft Solder	BS EN 29453:1994
Compression Fittings	BS EN 1254-2:1998 (replace BS 864-2:1983)
Copper to PE Adaptors	BS EN 1254-3:1998 (replace BS 864-5:1990)
Fittings combining other end connections with capillary or compression ends	BS EN 1254-4:1998
Fittings with short ends for capillary brazing to copper tubes	BS EN 1254-5:1998
Fittings with press ends for metallic tubes	BS EN 1254-7: (currently in draft)

Polyethylene Pipe	BS EN 1555-1:2002 BS EN 1555-2:2002
Polyethylene Fittings	BS EN 1555-3:2002 BS 5114:1975 (Obsolescent)

Manual Valves	BS EN 331:199 (ball and taper plug valves) BS 1552:1995 (taper plug valves)
Quick Release Valves	BS 669-1:1989

Table 5.2 Pipe and Fittings Standard

Pushfit type fittings are generally not permitted for use in any gas installation, however BS 6891 uses this term to describe quick release fittings (e.g a cooker bayonet) conforming to BS 669 part 1 and push type fittings used for corrugated stainless steel tubing which conform to BS 7838.

Many factors will affect the choice of material e.g. cost, appearance, corrosion resistance. Consideration must also be given to mechanical strength i.e. accidental or malicious damage.

5.5 Installation

5.5.1 Making an End Feed Capillary Joint

Step 1

Cut the pipe to the desired length. Remove the internal pipe burr (pipe cutters) or any swarf (hacksaw). Ensure the pipe end and fitting are not malformed or damaged. Clean the pipe end (beyond the insertion depth) and the inside of the fitting with wire wool or abrasive pad.

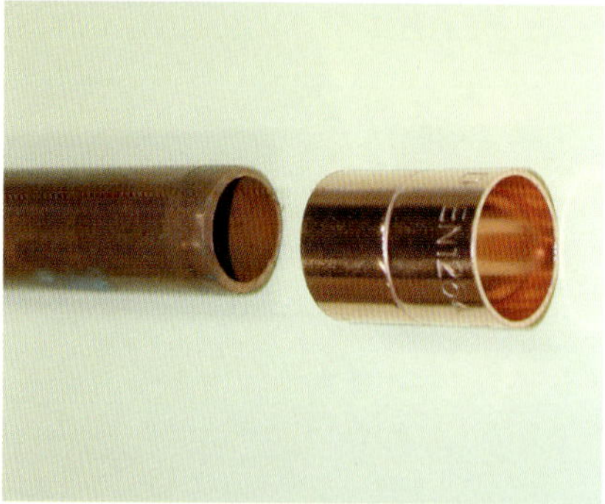

Figure 5.3 Copper tube & socket prior to assembly

Figure 5.4 Removal of internal pipe burr

Step 2

Apply a smear of flux to the pipe end only, covering the entire section of pipe which will be inserted into the fitting. Apply the flux using a brush or wear protective gloves so as to avoid skin contact.

Figure 5.5 Application of flux to copper tube end

Assemble the joint ensuring the pipe is fully inserted into the fitting.

Figure 5.6 Joint assembled prior to heating and application of solder

Step 3

Heat the assembled joint and pipe end using a propane torch. Use a heat resistant mat to avoid damage to adjacent fabric.

Figure 5.7 Heating joint with a propane torch

When the flux begins to bubble and smoke apply the solder wire to the circumference/s of the fitting. Do not apply excessive solder as it will form a blockage inside the fitting. If the fitting/pipe is hot enough the solder will melt and run around and through the joint, examine the joint to ensure the solder has run fully around the circumference. If the joint is not hot enough apply more heat but do not overheat the joint as this will incinerate the flux preventing proper adhesion of the solder to the copper/brass surfaces.

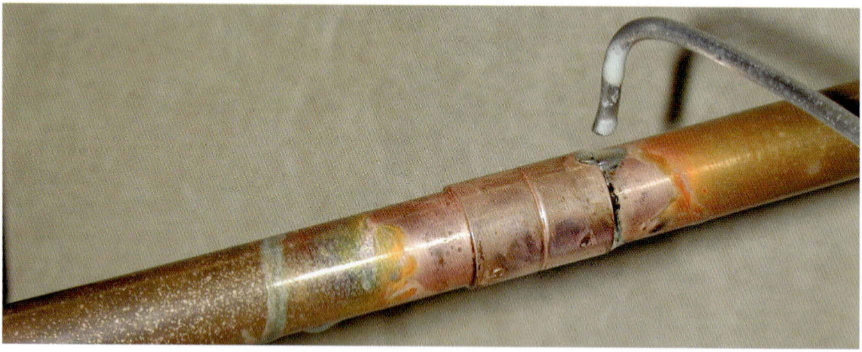

Figure 5.8 Applying solder to heated joint

Step 4

Allow the fitting to cool and remove any excess flux using a damp cloth. Never immerse the joint in water to cool it whilst the solder remains molten as this may fracture the joint.

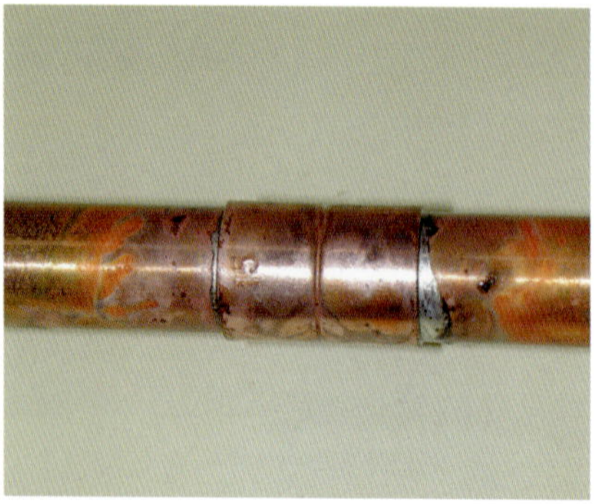

Figure 5.9 Joint after soldering

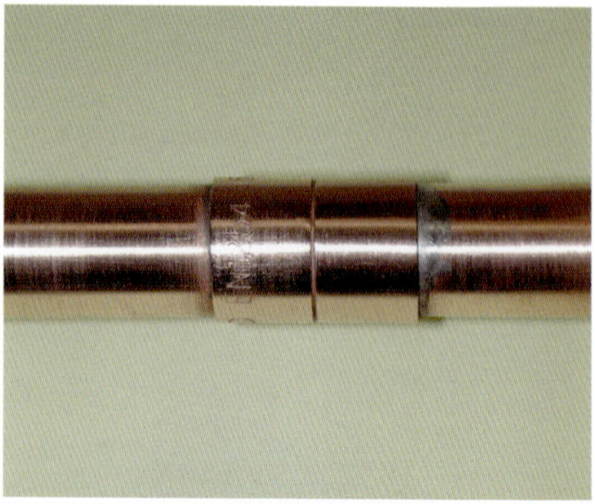

Figure 5.10 finished clean solder joint

Flux must not come into contact with stainless steel.
The flux used must be of the type that only remains active during the heating process. Lead free or solder containing lead is suitable for making a capillary joint on a gas pipe.

Copper pipe can be soldered directly into lead composition pipe or by a brass union soldered into the lead pipe provided the lead pipe is in an acceptable condition. A blown joint or cup joint is required but this needs more practice than a capillary joint. Lead solder should be used.

5.5.2 Making a Compression Joint

Step 1
Cut the pipe to the desired length. Remove the internal pipe burr (pipe cutters) or any swarf (hacksaw). Ensure the pipe end and compression ring (olive) are not malformed or damaged. Remove the nut from the fitting and place it onto the pipe, remove the ring from the fitting and place it onto the pipe.

Figure 5.11 Compression fitting on copper tube prior to assembly

Step 2
Put the pipe end into the fitting and assemble the nut to the fitting and hand tighten. There is no need to use PTFE thread tape or jointing compound on the end of the pipe and definitely not on the threads of the fitting.

Figure 5.12 Compression fitting assembled onto copper tube

Step 3

Hold the fitting with pliers/adjustable spanners and use another spanner take up the slack in the nut and then further tighten by $^1/_3$ to $^2/_3$ of a turn.

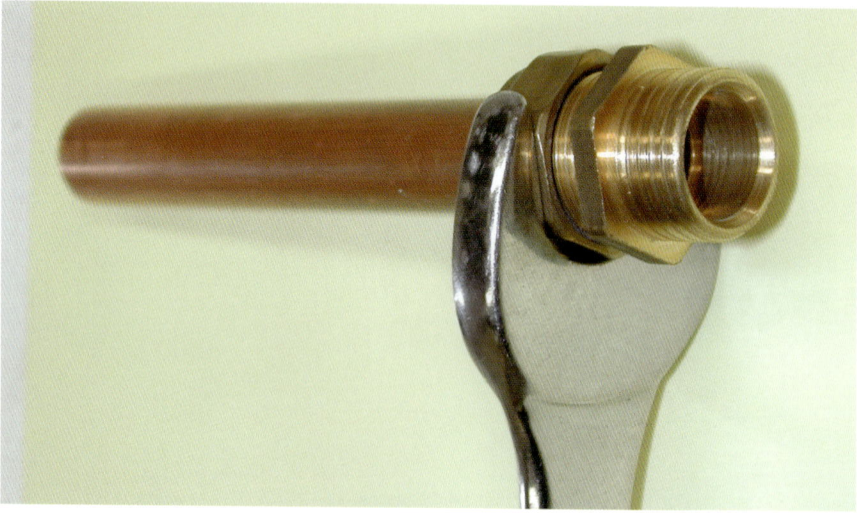

Figure 5.13 Fitting tightened to make gas tight joint

The ring will bite into and seal the copper pipe.

Figure 5.14 Fitting disassembled showing ring compressed onto copper tube wall

Compression joints on gas pipes must be accessible, that means not under floors (unless there is an access panel) and not buried in concrete screed or located within pipe sleeves.

5.5.3 Making a Threaded Joint

Pipe threads (referred to as male or external) are normally taper cut whereas female (or internal) threads are usually parallel cut. Taper male to female parallel is an acceptable combination but a better joint will be achieved by taper male to taper female. Parallel to parallel combinations are not acceptable except when assembling a long screw fitting with backnut, this fitting is seldom used nowadays.

Step 1

Assuming the thread has already been formed, remove any oil or cutting fluid and examine the thread and fitting for damage.

Figure 5.15 Factory formed taper thread on mild steel pipe

Step 2

Apply jointing compound or PTFE thread tape to the external thread only. PTFE tape should have a 50% overlap and be wound in the direction shown. PTFE tape and jointing compound must not be applied to the same joint.

Figure 5.16 Jointing Compound

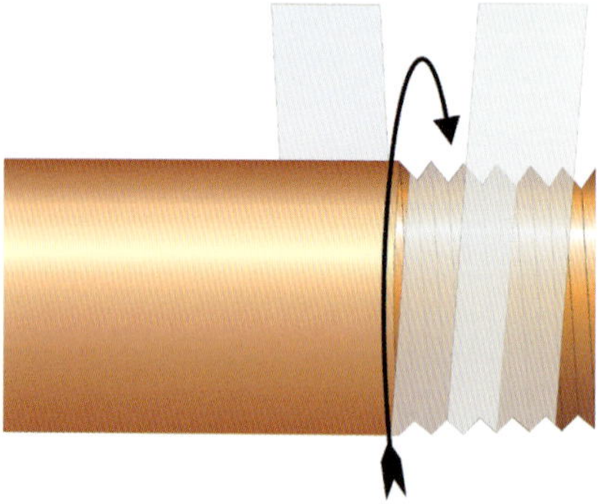

Figure 5.17 Applying PTFE Tape

Step 3

Tighten the joint using a pipe wrench or chain tongs. Remove excess tape or jointing compound.

Never loosen the joint for alignment purposes (unless joint compound manufacture allows e.g Loctite 55). Do not over tighten as this may fracture the fitting.

Hemp shall not be used except in the case of a long screw back-nut seal.

Ensure no foreign matter such as dirt, water, insulation, etc. enters the pipe or fittings during installation; this is more likely when working under an existing, suspended floor.

5.5.4 Pipe Support

Pipe must be supported in accordance with the table 5.4 below

Maximum Distance between Supports			
Pipe			
Material	**Size**	**Vertical Pipe**	**Horizontal Pipe**
Rigid Steel	Up to ½ inch (DN 15) ¾ inch (DN 20) 1 inch (DN 25) 1¼ inch (DN 32)	2.5 m 3 m 3 m 3.5 m	2 m 2.5 m 2.5 m 2.5 m
Copper & Corrugated Stainless	Up to 15 mm 22 mm and above	2 m 2.5 m	1.5 m 2 m

Table 5.4 Maximum support distances for gas pipe

5.5.5 Copper Pipe Bending

Pipes may be formed by the use of machine benders or bending springs. Bending springs (internal or external) are only suitable for small diameter pipes (6 mm to 15 mm).

Figure 5.18 External pipe bending spring 8mm

Bending machines are easier to use and form a more uniform bend.

Figure 5.19
Floor Standing

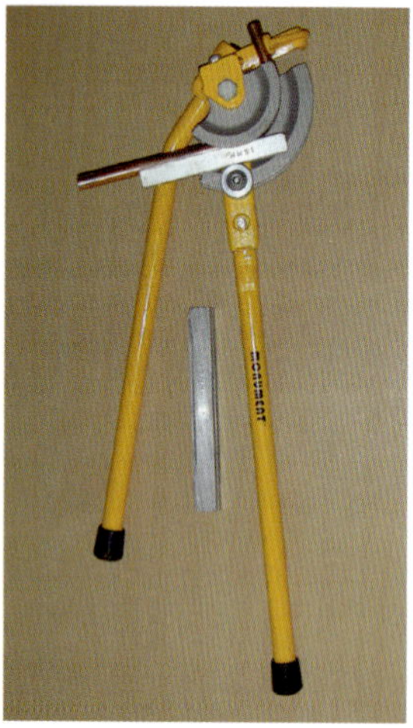

Figure 5.20 Hand Held
(15mm & 22mm)

Figure 5.21 6 mm to 10mm

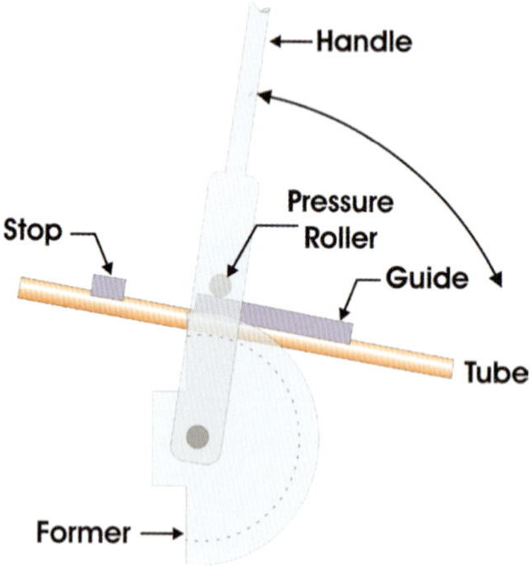

Figure 5.22 Construction of bending machine

5.5.5.1 Forming an Offset

Step 1

Measure length and make first bend at a 30° to 45° bend

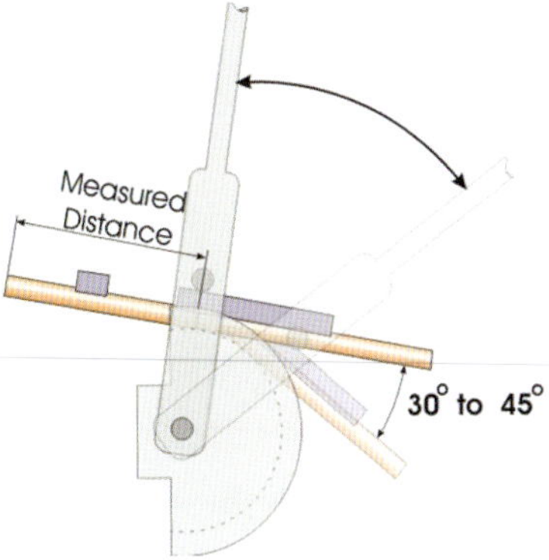

Figure 5.23 Forming first bend in machine

Step 2

Lay pipe next to obstruction. Lay a small length of copper tube (same nominal bore) on top of obstruction. Measure above and below pipe with a pencil.

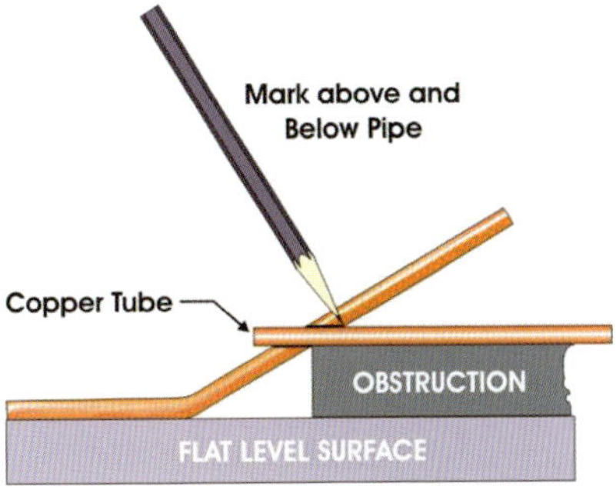

Figure 5.24 Marking height for second bend

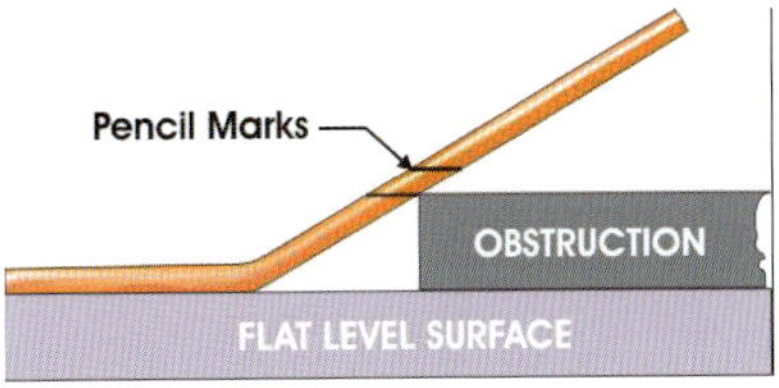

Figure 5.25 Markings on tube

Step 3

Insert pipe into former with top pencil mark running along outer edge. Ensure pipe is square by looking down pipe line.

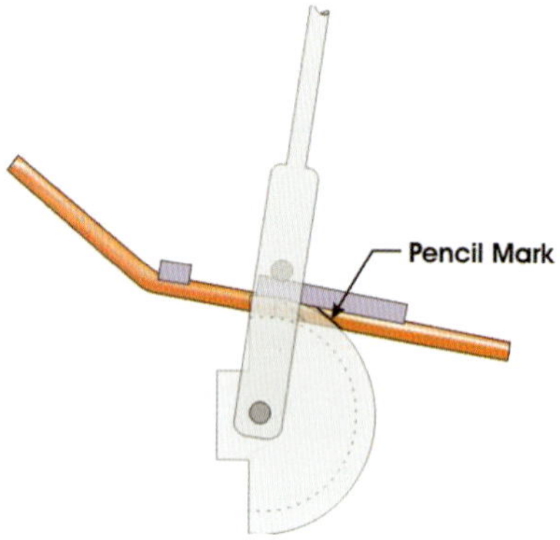

Figure 5.26 Tube placed in bending machine with markings aligned to former

Step 4

Form bend, the angle should allow both ends to run parallel with each other.

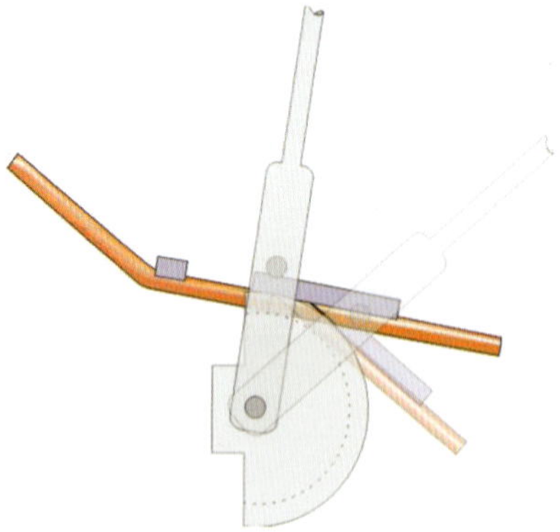

Figure 5.27 Bend formed in machine - ends aligned parallel to each other

5.5.5.1 Forming a 90⁰ Bend

Measure required length and mark around the circumference of the copper tube. Insert tube into the former. With a small cutting of the same nominal bore tubing. Insert it into the former perpendicular to the pipe. Move the pipe until the mark is level with the inserted piece of tubing. This is the outside of the bend. Form the bend until both pipes are perpendicular. It is advisable to form the bend slightly greater than 90° as the pipe will spring back after releasing the guide arm. It can always be pulled back a small amount to the correct angle.

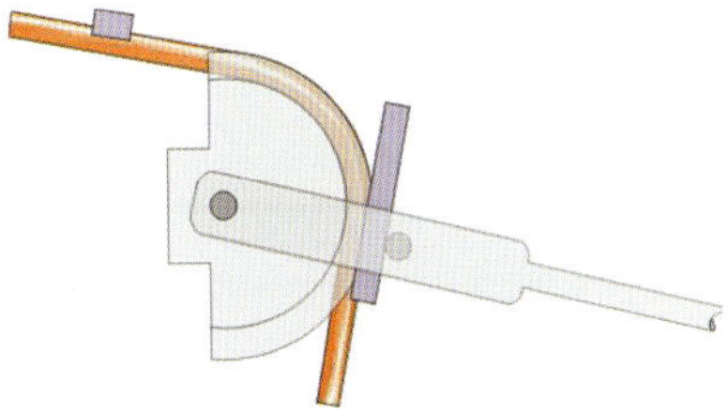

Figure 5.28 Tube marked prior to forming bend

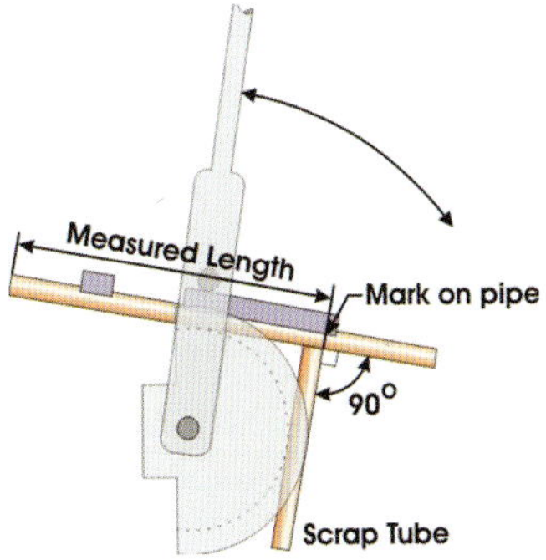

Figure 5.28 Tube marked prior to forming bend

5.5.6 Corrugated Stainless Steel Tubing (e.g Trac pipe)

Corrugated stainless steel tubing (CSST) and fittings must be manufactured to BS EN 15266 or BS 7838, as appropriate. Jointing must only be done using approved methods and fittings as specified by the manufacturer. Hot methods, such as welding or brazing, are not allowed. Fittings must not be disassembled then subsequently re-assembled unless permitted by the manufacturer.

The pipe diameter is limited 50 mm with a maximum operating pressure of 75 mbar, unless stated otherwise by the manufacturer. One manufacturer of CSST is Omega Flex who produce Trac pipe. Unique auto flare fittings are used to joint the tube, no other fitting type is permitted by the manufacturer.

Trac pipe is supplied in coils ranging in size from 12 mm to 50 mm. It has a primrose yellow coloured factory fitted protective sheath covering. It should be noted that the gas industry does not consider the sheathing to fulfil the purpose of a pipe sleeve.

The material and structure of the tubing allow it to be bent by hand without the use of bending springs or machines. Care must be taken when bending the pipe as not to exceed the manufacturers stated maximum bend radii. Too sharp a bend can result in damage and/or failure of the tube wall.

General procedure for installation of CSST (see manufacturer for specific installation requirements as fittings do vary):

a) Confirm the correct length of tube required.

b) Using a standard tube cutter cut through the sheath and pipe (it is advisable not to use a hack saw as this may not provide a square clean end on the tube). Ensure the wheel is located between the corrugations. Do not over tighten the cutter when cutting the tube as this can flatten pipe.

c) Ensure the ends of the tube are square and cleanly cut with no ragged edges.

d) Cut back the sheathing from the cut end enough to allow assembly of the fitting. Be careful at this point as the tube end is very sharp and can cause injury.

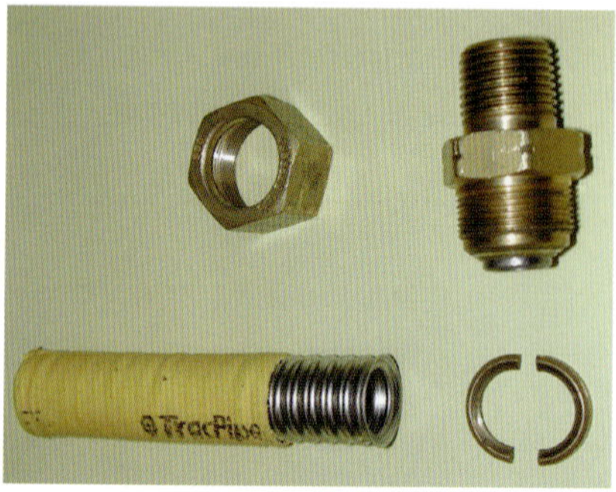

Figure 5.30 Tube and sleeving cut with split ring, nut and fitting prior to assembly.

e) Slide the back nut over the cut end and place the two split rings into the first corrugation from the cut end. Slide the nut back over the split rings to hold them in place.

f) Line the tube up with the body of the fitting and engage onto the thread. Hand tighten until the resistance to turn the nut increases.

g) Using an appropriate spanner tighten the nut until the manufacturers recommended torque is achieved. At this point the stainless steel tube will have flared and sealed onto the body of the fitting creating a gas tight joint. Do not over tighten as this can damage both the tube and fitting.

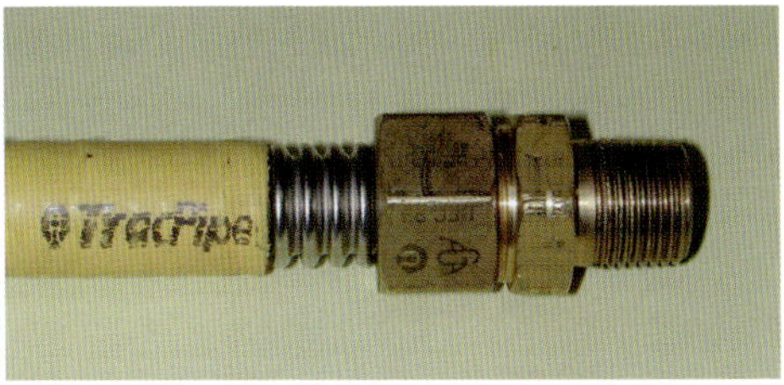

Figure 5.31 Assembled Joint prior to tightness test

h) Perform a tightness test once the installation is complete.

i) After a successful test any exposed stainless steel must be wrapped using an approved, normally self-bonding, tape to reduce the possibility of corrosion

Figure 5.32 Tape applied over Joint after the tightness test

5.5.7 Pressed Joints (e.g Xpress fittings)

Pressed joint fittings can only be used on copper and stainless steel up to a MOP of 100 mbar and 108mm nominal bore. Fittings must meet approved fire test requirements (procedure A of BS EN 1775) and standards such as DVGW VP614 for high temperature tests. In addition they must also meet approved manufacturing standards. Jointing must be made as per the Manufacturers instruction using the approved jointing tool. Demountable press fit joints must not be used.

Pressed fittings achieve a sound joint through the exertion of pressure from a press-fit tool; a purpose designed 'O' ring provides the mechanism by which a perfect seal is created. Care must be taken to ensure that the 'O'ring is of a material suitable for use with gas such as butyl or NBR. Most Manufacturers use a colour coding system to identify the use of the fitting, for example yellow/tan 'O' ring for gas and black (EPDM) for water. The fittings are slightly deformed (not a perfect rounded opening). This has been introduced as a "leak till pressed" principle. Original fittings were leak tight even though the fitting had not been made. This had dire consequences after installation.

Figure 5.33 Tan coloured 'O' ring used for gas

Figure 5.34 Tan coloured 'O' ring used for gas

All operatives making a pressed joint must be suitably trained in the specific installation requirements of the fitting and machine manufacturer. Only fitting tools which comply with the appropriate standard must be used. In all accounts the fitting tool should not be able to be extracted from the fitting until the full press cycle has been completed. Where the jointing process has been interrupted or abandoned, the joint must be discarded and the fitting process repeated in full. It is prohibited to weld, solder or braze any pressed joint.

Industry has identified a need for traceability of installation and has accepted permanent marking of slip depth and a cross on each joint to positively identify a completed installation.

All tools must be maintained as specified by the Manufacturer to ensure reliability of installation.

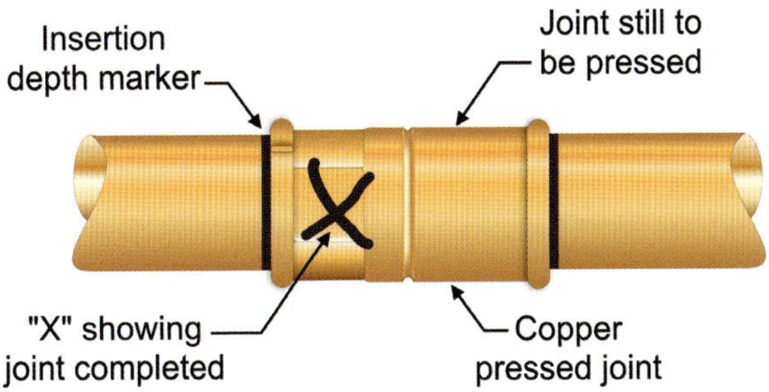

Figure 5.35 markings on fitting before and after joint is made

A general jointing procedure for pressed joints is given below (see manufacturer for specifics):

a) Visual inspection of pipe and fittings for any damage, suitability of application and cleanliness.

b) Cut and prepare pipework using methods as detailed by the Manufacturer.

c) Ensure pipe ends are deburred, square with no damage and clean.

d) Using depth guide (normally supplied by manufacturer) or tape measure, mark insertion depth using a permanent marker.

e) Choose an appropriate fitting suitable for pipe NB.

f) Check the 'o' ring is applicable for gas (tan or grey) and not for water (black).

g) Ensure the pressing tool is set up correctly (correct size of jaws) and is suitable for the fitting being made.

h) Ensure the tube is fully inserted into the fitting and the jaws of the press-fit tool are placed correctly around the collar of the fitting.

i) With the jaws at a 90° angle to the fitting, the press-fit tool is activated and the jaws compress the 'O' ring tightly onto the tube creating a strong and reliable joint.

j) Mark made joints with an "X" using a permanent marker.

5.5.8 Meter Outlet Connection

Unless the meter is securely restrained (e.g. by a meter bracket), the connection to the meter installation shall be in securely fixed rigid pipe for at least the first 600 mm.

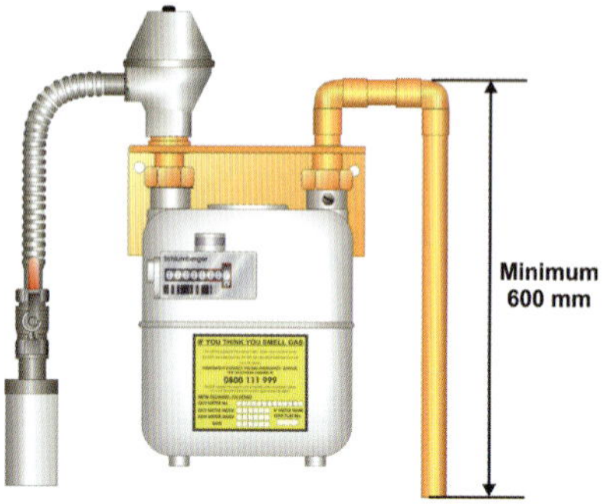

Figure 5.36 Minimum length of rigid outlet pipework for gas meter

5.6 Safety Precautions

If work is in progress and the installation is to be left unattended, then, either:

a) the meter must be temporarily disconnected and dust caps fitted to the connections and any pipework left connected to the supply sealed with an appropriate fitting, or

b) open ended pipes shall be capped or plugged with an appropriate fittings or self sealing appliance connector.

This is to prevent the gas supply being restored by a third party (other trades or the customer) when it is unsafe to do so.

When using a naked flame to solder capillary joints on pipes that contain or have contained gas, the meter shall be temporarily disconnected and its connections sealed until the flame is extinguished.

Oxy-gas cutting equipment shall not be applied to any pipe or fitting containing gas.

When connecting or disconnecting any gas fitting, a temporary continuity bond must be used to prevent the production of a spark from stray electrical currents (possible ignition source) and to protect the engineer from electrocution.

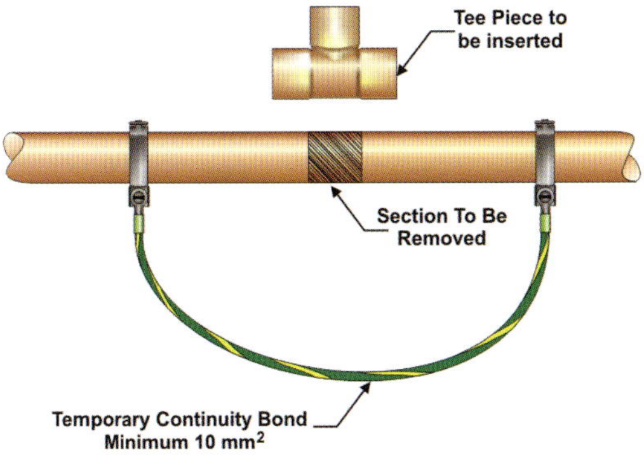

Figure 5.37 - Installation of a continuity bond prior to installing a 'T-piece'

Redundant pipework should not be left connected to the gas supply, it should be cut and sealed close to the point of connection i.e. tee-piece.

If a gas meter is being permanently disconnected and the service pipe and the installation pipe could be simultaneously touched, they shall be permanently bonded. If the ends are in excess of 2 metres apart there is no need to bond. Bonding is not necessary if the meter inlet and outlet connections remain attached to a meter bracket or if one side of the disconnection is short and not earthed i.e. a PE service or short length of outlet pipework.

5.7 PE Pipework

PE pipework is only suitable for external below ground applications. It must only be installed in it's own purpose provided duct or track. Unprotected PE pipe shall not be used within premises.

Above ground PE must be sleeved to protect it from daylight and mechanical damage. Normally above ground PE is only at the points of entry or exit from a premise. It must only be joined using compression or fusion joints, solvent welding is not permitted.

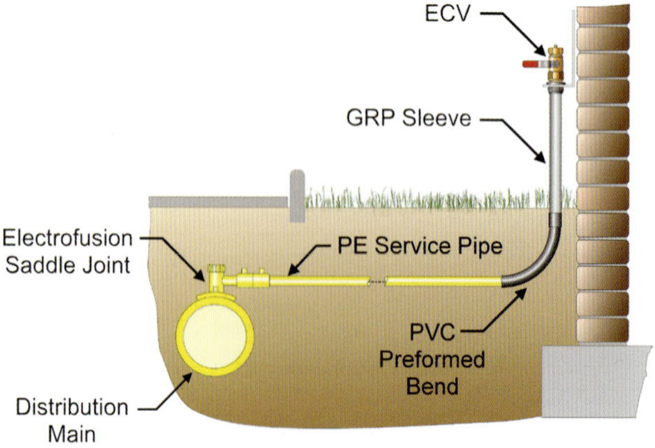

Figure 5.38 PE gas service showing electrofusion jointing and above ground protection

5.8 Pipework in Fireplace Openings

Pipework within fireplace openings must be protected against corrosion caused by soot deposits or debris.

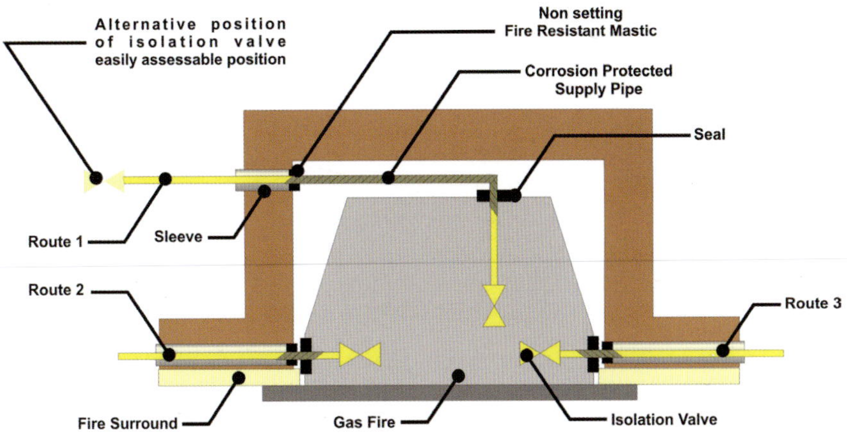

Figure 5.39 Different pipe routes to supply an ILFE gas fire showing suitable protection within fireplace

5.9 Separation from Electrical Services

When not separated by insulating material, gas meters shall be at least 150 mm from any electrical cables and/or fittings.

When not separated by insulating material, gas pipework shall be at least 25 mm from any electrical cables and/or fittings and at least 150 mm from any electrical meters, circuit breakers, switches, distribution boards or consumer units.

A main equipotential bond of cross sectional area 10 mm^2 shall be connected on the consumer's side of the meter, as close as practicable to the meter and before any branch pipework.

It must be accessible for inspection and be suitably labelled.

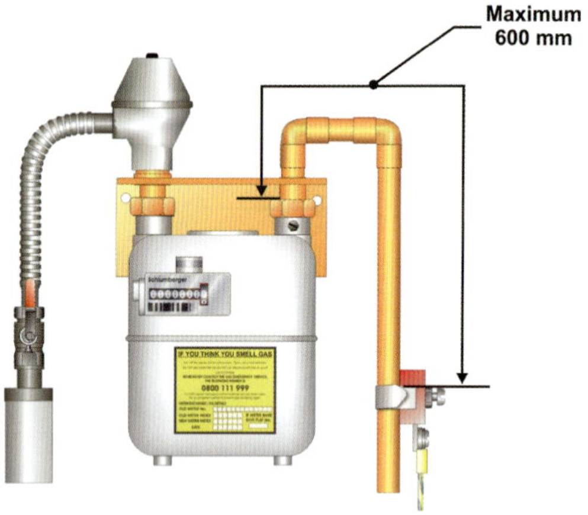

Figure 5.40 Minimum distance for main equipotential bonding at meter outlet

For internal meters the connection should be within 600 mm of the meter outlet.

For external meters the connection should preferably be internal and as near to the point of entry as practicable (connection within the meter box is acceptable but is non-preferred).

Persons performing work on the main equipotential bond must be competent to do so.

5.10 Pipework installed within joisted floors

Pipework installed between solid timber joists shall be correctly supported (see Table 5.4).

Where pipework is installed between timber engineered joists, it shall pass through the web of the joist and be correctly supported (see Table 5.4).

Where pipework is installed between metal web joists it shall pass between the metal webs with pipe supports fixed to the top or bottom of the timber flanges.

Flanges of either of these types shall not be notched.

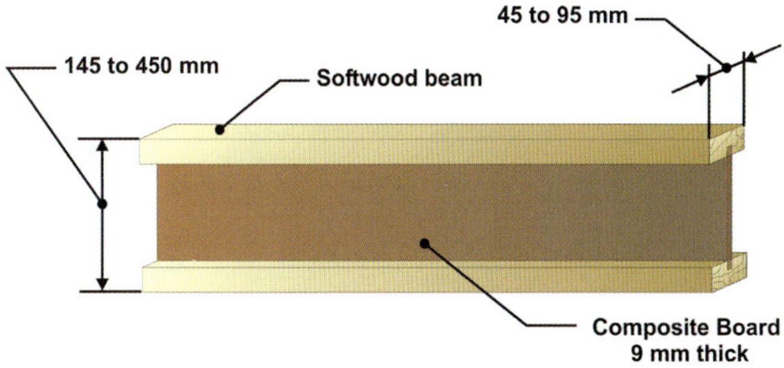

Figure 5.41 Timber Engineered joist

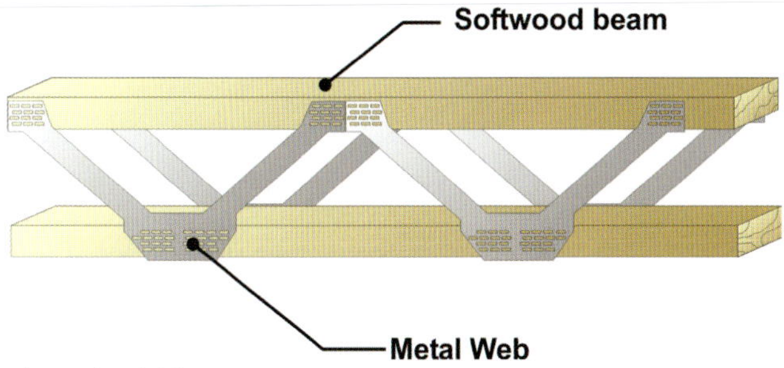

Figure 5.42 Engineered web joist

Where pipe is laid across solid timber joists it shall be located in purpose made notches or holes. See the following diagrams which detail the acceptable positions for a 200 mm deep joist, 4 metres span.

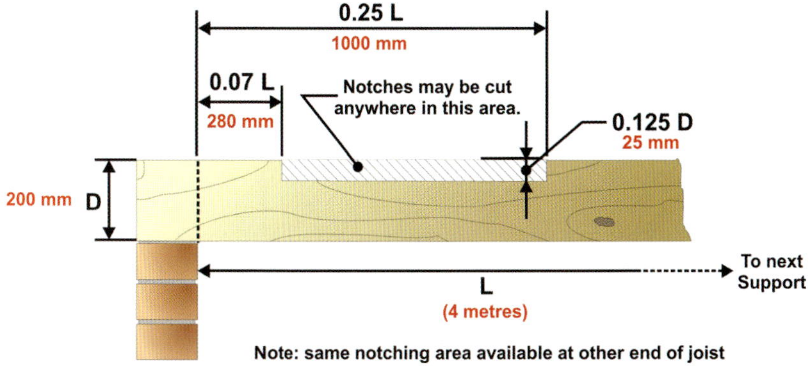

Figure 5.43 Positioning of Notches

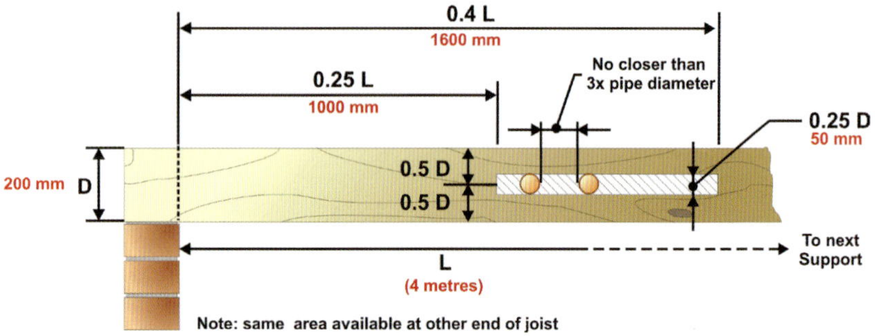

Figure 5.44 Positioning of Holes

Note: Joists less than 100mm must not be notched

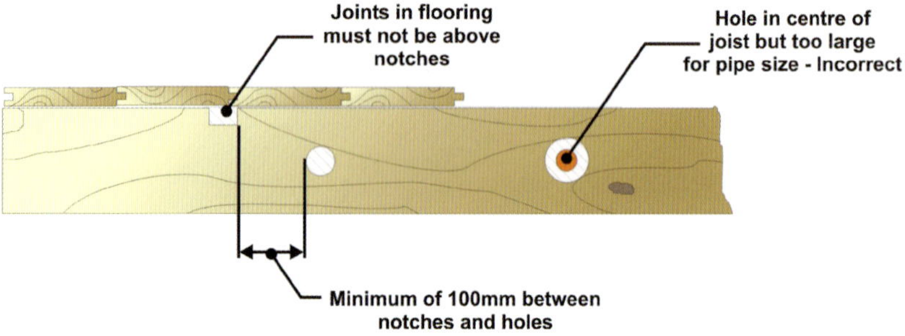

Figure 5.45 Correct and incorrect hole and notch location and sizes

5.11 Sleeves

Definition of a sleeve is a tubular case inserted in a prepared hole in a structure for the reception of an installation pipe.

Pipes passing through solid walls or solid floors shall be sleeved to protect the pipe from any structural movement.

Any pipe sleeve shall be capable of containing gas (copper, steel, PE or PVC)

Sleeves must pass through the full thickness of the floor or wall and not reduce the fire resistance of the structure. It is good practice to extend the sleeve beyond the face of the wall or floor.

The sleeve must be fixed at each end to the fabric of the building (mortar or silicone).

The annular space between the pipe and the sleeve must be sealed at one end only (inside end for external wall sleeves) with a flexible, fire resistant compound. The annular space has to allow for the insertion of the sealing material.

Only capillary joints are permitted within the sleeve but none is preferred.

5.11.1 Timber Framed Dwellings

Due to the construction of timber frame dwellings the inner leaf of the building will contract over time due to shrinkage caused by the "drying out" of the timbers after initial construction. In addition there is differing expansion and contraction between the external brick wall and inner timber frame. This movement can be enough to cause failure of any gas installation pipework as it passes through the wall. To prevent damage to the installation pipework IGE UP 7 recommends that any pipework passing through the wall should be CSST with a flexible sleeve material such as PE. The manufacturers must be consulted as to the capabilities of the materials used.

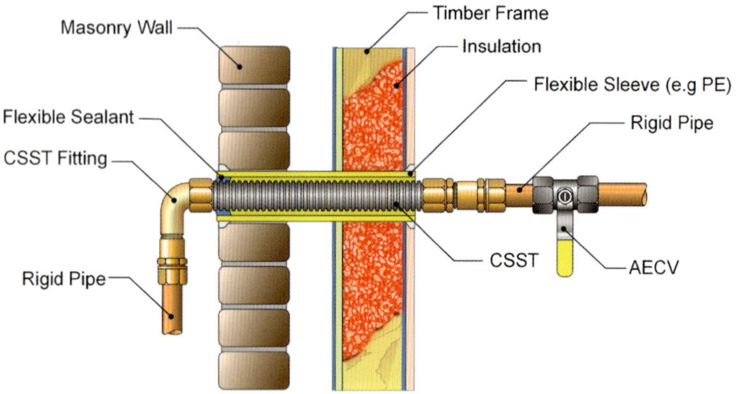

Figure 5.46 Example of a pipe and sleeve through a timber framed dwelling

5.12 Pipe in Ducts and Voids

Definition:

Duct: A purpose designed enclosure to contain gas pipes.
Void: An enclosed space through which an installation pipe may be run.

Vertical and horizontal ducts must be ventilated to ensure that minor leakage does not cause an unsafe situation (see table 5.5). Ducts of less than 0.01 m^2 and 0.01 m^3 do not require any purpose provided ventilation.

Cross Sectional Area of Duct	Minimum Free Area of Each Vent
Not exceeding 0.01m^2	Zero
0.01m^2 and not exceeding 0.05m^2	Same as C.S.A. of Duct
0.05m^2 and not exceeding 7.5m^2	0.05m^2
Exceeding 7.5m^2	1/150th of C.S.A. of Duct

Table 5.5 Minimum free area of ventilation of ducts or voids

To calculate the cross sectional area of a duct we use the following formula (see figure 5.47).

Cross Sectional Area (m^2) = Height (m) X Breadth (m)

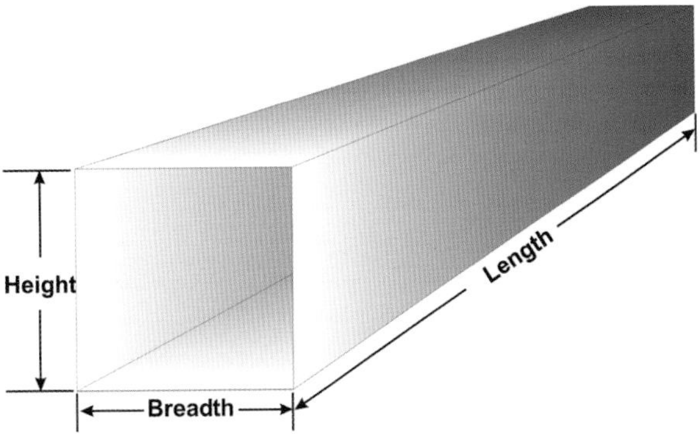

Figure 5.47 Measuring the cross sectional area of a duct - CSA = Height x Breadth

Concern has been voiced that pipework run within a modern construction joisted suspended floor having a plasterboard ceiling on the underside and sheet flooring with glued tongue and grooved joints on the topside (chipboard flooring) will be effectively contained in an unventilated void.

Following extensive research it has been found that there is enough adventitious ventilation of the floor which would safely disperse any minor escape of gas that may occur. It was concluded that there was no requirement to install additional purpose provided ventilation in this type of flooring where it is installed in conventional masonry, timber frame or light steel frame buildings.

The requirement that no ventilation is required in intermediate joisted floors only applies to floors that separate one living space from another in the same dwelling. Floors which separate dwellings are subject to the guidance in IGE/G/5 "Gas in flats and other multi-dwelling buildings" and IGE/ UP/7, "Gas installations in timber framed and light steel framed buildings".

5.13 Pipes Buried in Concrete Floors

Pipes passing through concrete floors shall be sleeved.

Pipework shall not be buried in concrete slabs, it must only be in the screed.

There must be at least 25 mm of screed cover above the pipe.

Rigid stainless steel shall not be buried (corrugated stainless to BS 7838, Trac Pipe, may be buried).

Pipe shall be protected against failure caused by movement (settlement) of the floor.

No compression joints or unions may be buried.

Tightness testing must be performed prior to the application of any corrosion protection or covering by the screed.

Acceptable methods include:

- Suitably protected pipe laid on top of slab and covered by the screed.
- Steel or copper pipe installed into preformed ducts with protective covers
- Steel or copper pipe fitted with additional soft, non-permeable covering. Gas Safe Register has issued guidance on the use of pipe insulation in this regard.

Methods of protection are:

- Factory sheathed pipe
- On site application of PVC wrapping tape or bituminous painting (wrapping tape should have a 50% overlap)
- Galvanized pipe has to be protected if it is to be buried

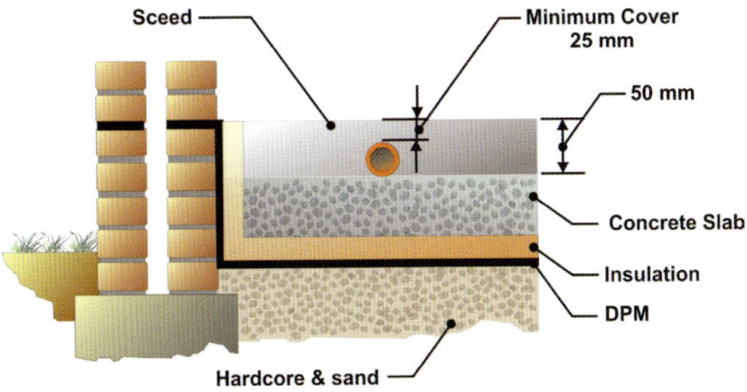

Figure 5.48 Pipework laid on concrete slab buried in screed

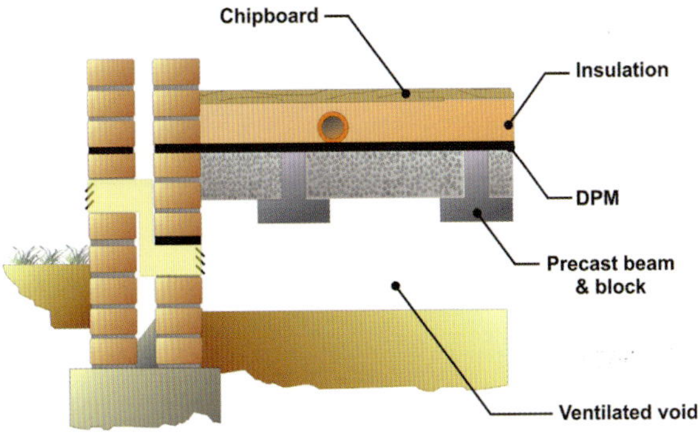

Figure 5.49 Precast beam & block with pipework in insulation layer

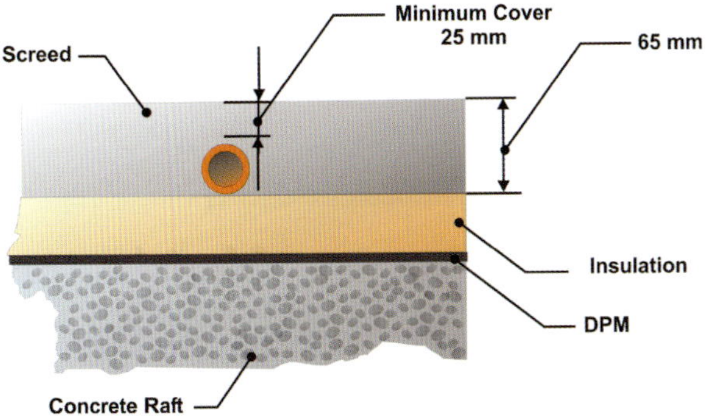

Figure 5.50 Pipe on top of insulation layer

Figure 5.51 Pipe in preformed duct

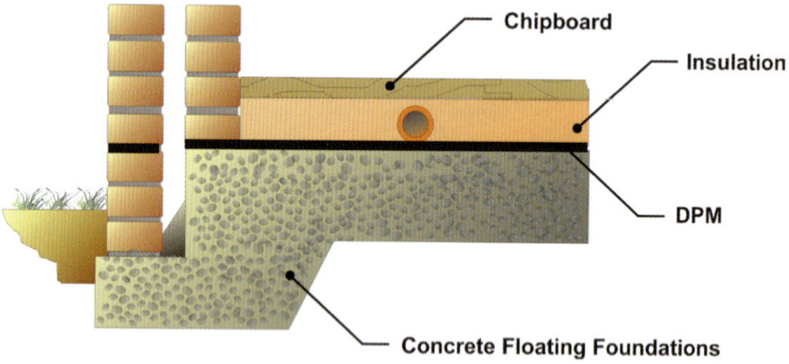

Figure 5.52 Insulation layer floating founds

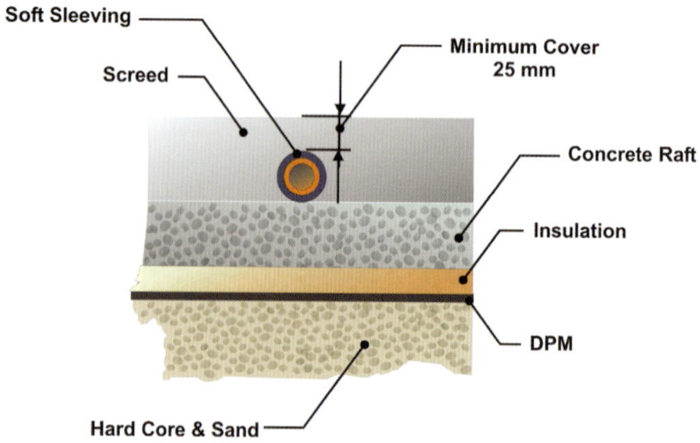

Figure 5.53 Pipework with non-permeable soft sleeve

5.14 Pipes Buried in Walls

Pipes passing through solid walls shall be sleeved

Pipes, wherever possible, should be run vertically and be in pipe chases or ducts.

It shall be secured and joints kept to a minimum.

Pipework shall not be run within cavities of cavity walls (with the exception specified in regulation 19(4) of the Gas Safety (Installation and Use) Regulations, see Figure 5.54) and shall only pass through the cavity wall by the shortest route and be sleeved.

A living flame effect gas fire means a gas fire
(a) designed to simulate the effect of a solid fuel fire:
(b) designed to operate with a fanned flue system; and
(c) installed within the inner leaf of a cavity wall.

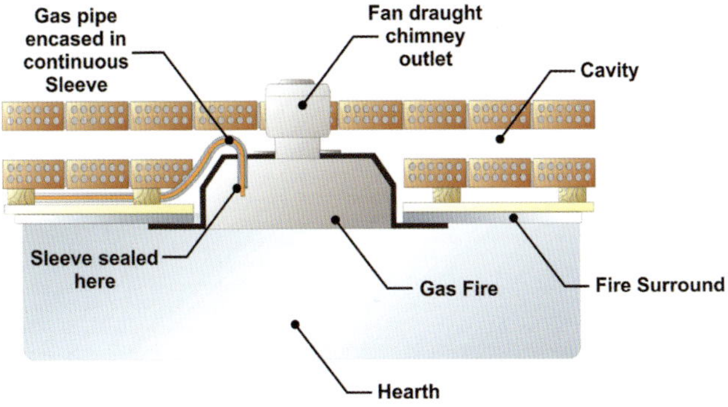

Figure 5.54 Pipework supplying a fanned draught ILFE fire

Pipework installed in dry lined walls must be encased in building material by the formation of a channel (timber or plaster).

Timber frame walls shall have purpose designed channels or ducts constructed and pipework shall be protected against corrosion. The pipe should have a metallic cover for protection

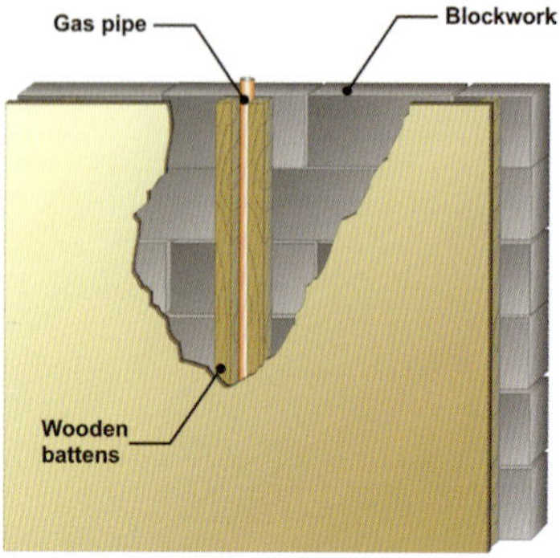

Figure 5.55 Dry Lined Wall on battens - Pipe Encased in wood Battens.

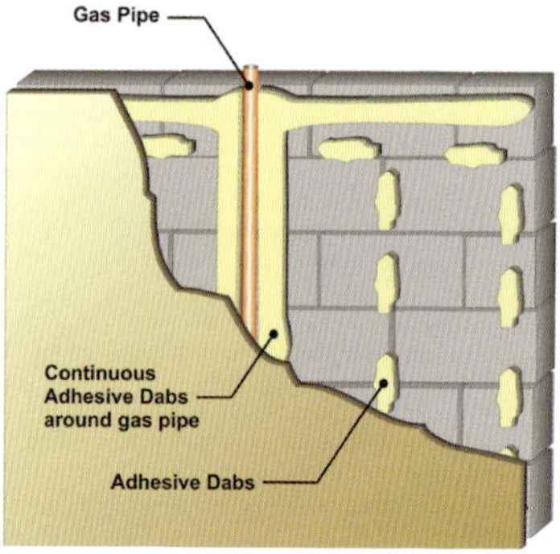

Figure 5.56 Dot and dab dry lined wall - Pipe encased in continuous adhesive dabs

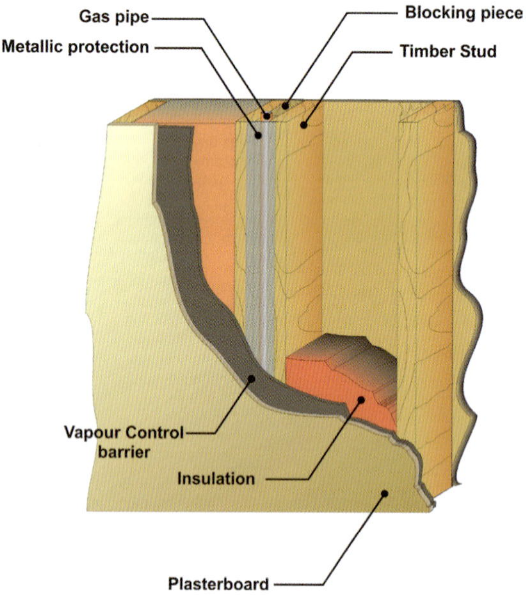

Figure 5.57 Timber Frame constructed wall

5.15 External Pipe (Buried)

Pipe shall be PE, factory sheathed copper, steel or corrugated stainless steel Covering requirements are given in the table 5.6.

Location	Pipe Material	Minimum Cover
Buried in soil	PE Copper Corrugated Stainless Rigid Steel	375 mm
Below Vehicular Traffic Areas		
Below Concrete with only Pedestrian Traffic	Copper Corrugated Stainless Rigid Steel	40 mm
Below a Building	PE	375 mm below base concrete*
*Pipework shall not pass through foundations. There shall be no joints below the building		

Table 5.6 Depth of cover for buried pipework

Pipework shall not be installed under the foundations of a building or in the ground under the base of a wall or footing unless adequate steps are taken to prevent damage due to movement. This will require design, inspection and certification by a structural engineer.

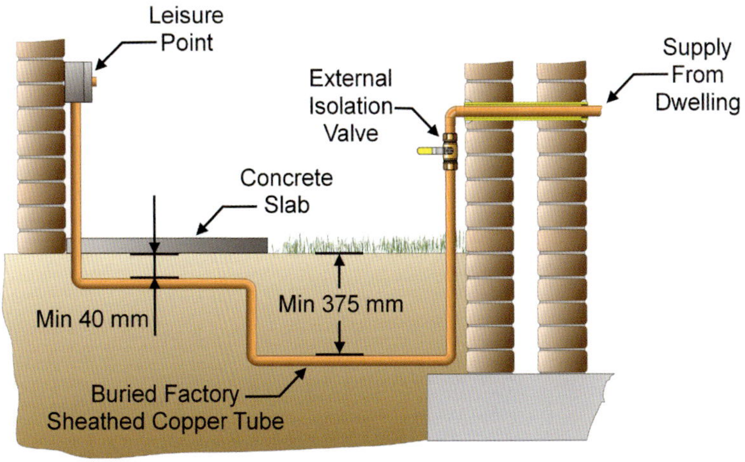

Figure 5.58 Supply of gas to an external leisure point

Where installation pipework is run from inside a premise to supply external appliances such as barbecues, patio heaters, green house heaters etc, an additional isolation valve must be installed externally as near as practicable to the point of exit from the premises.

5.16 External Pipe (Surface)

Mechanical damage and corrosion are the two main factors which can affect the safety of gas pipework installed in external above ground locations. Where no alternative is practicable, any pipe installed in a location where it is susceptible to mechanical damage must either be protected by a suitable robust covering, or alternatively, constructed of a material which has a greater resilience to damage such as steel. Corrosion protection can be provided by factory fitted sheathing, wrapping, painting or by material type which is corrosion resistant (copper or galvanized steel). Additional care must be given to ensure any corrosion protection is not damaged during installation. On site protection must only be applied after completion of a satisfactory tightness test.

Pipe clips such as saddle or nail style clips should not be used as they hold the pipe against the building fabric. Building materials such as brick and concrete contain chemicals which react with metal. This coupled with any rain and moisture being trapped between the pipe wall and the building structure can cause accelerated corrosion leading to failure. Stand-off style clips support the pipe away from the building fabric, hence reducing this problem. Clip material should not cause electrolytic corrosion. It is preferable to use like for like materials such as brass or copper clips for copper. Plastic clips may not be suitable for external locations due to their low mechanical strength and construction as some plastics degrade with exposure to UV light making them brittle.

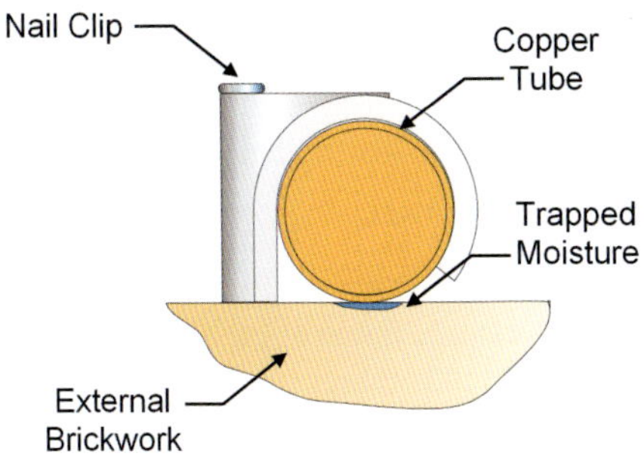

Figure 5.59 Incorrect support of external copper pipe using a nail clip

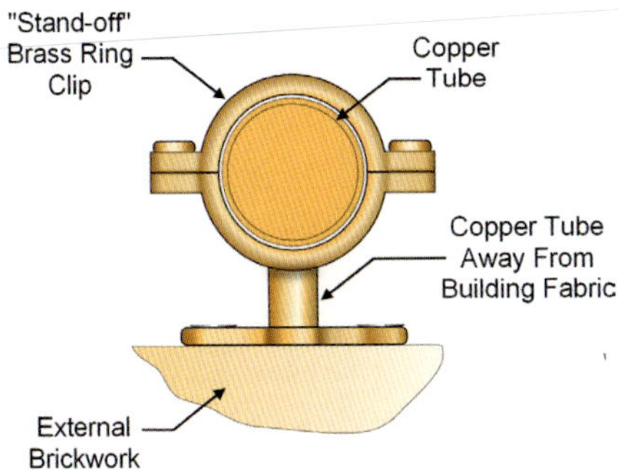

Figure 5.60 Correct support of external copper pipe using a brass stand-off bracket

5.17 Leisure Point (micro-point)

Leisure points are specifically designed termination points for a gas supply feeding moveable or mobile appliances. The pipe termination is normally within a recessed or surface mounted plastic box, similar to those used for electrical sockets. The appliance may be connected to this point by means of a rigid pipe or, in most cases, a flexible connection. Where a flexible connection is used the termination point incorporates a self-sealing socket allowing connection of a bayonet style hose suitable for the likes of tumble dryers, cookers etc.

This type of fitting is particularly suitable for the connection of outdoor leisure appliances such as barbeques allowing ease of connection and disconnection of the appliance, leaving a non-intrusive and neat termination point. For this purpose the connection point is encased in a weather tight enclosure with a chained sealing plug attached which can be fitted to the shut-off valve when the appliance is not in use. The cap prevents any contamination entering into the fitting.

Connection is normally by means of 10 mm or 12 mm copper tube, however smaller sizes are available such as 6 mm & 8 mm.

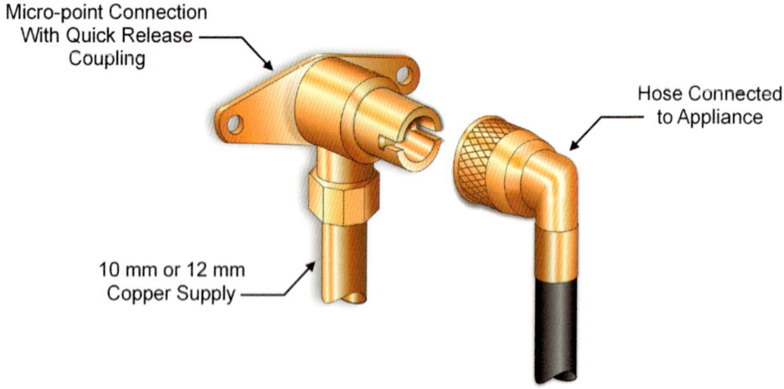

Figure 5.61 Correct support of external copper pipe using a brass stand-off bracket

5.18 Protected Shafts Containing Stairs or Fire Escape Routes

The installation of the pipe in these areas must be fire stopped and not impair the fire resistance of the structure.

Pipework in protected structures shall be of welded or screwed steel or a continuous length of copper or corrugated stainless steel.

Only screwed or welded steel pipe shall be used in or through a protected shaft. The shaft must be ventilated at high and low levels directly to outside.

5.19 Fire Stopping

For flats and maisonettes pipes shall be fire stopped as they pass from one floor to another unless they are in their own protected shaft that is ventilated top and bottom to outside air. They should also be fire stopped as they run laterally from a riser into a property.

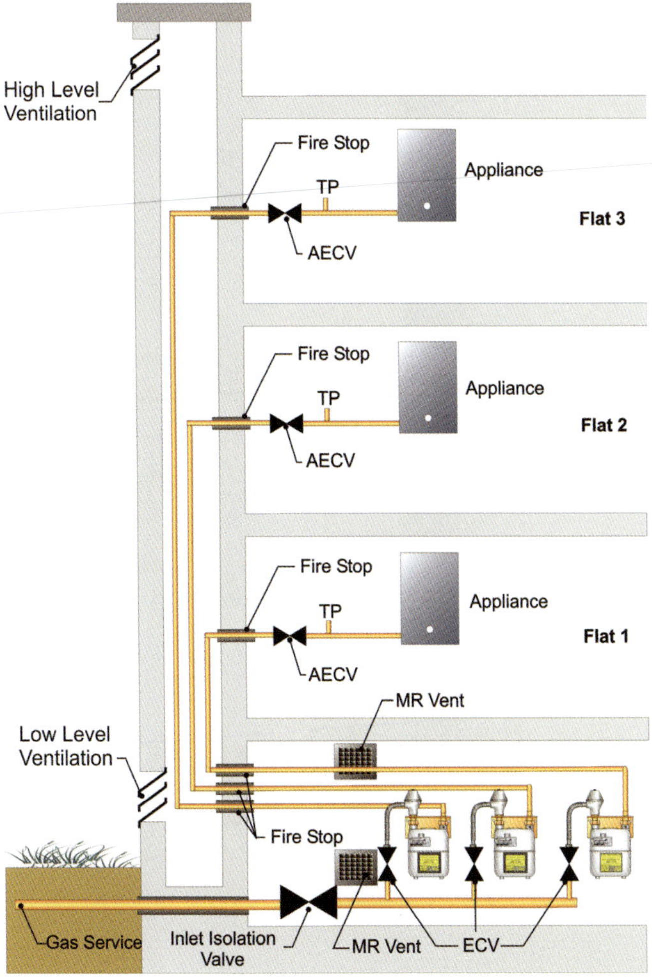

Figure 5.62 Multi-occupancy building with remote meters - Installation pipework is located within a purpose provided ventilated protected shaft

5.20 Multi-occupancy Dwellings

Pipework in multi-occupancy dwellings shall only be routed through the dwelling where the appliances are located. Other dwelling's pipework shall be in purpose provided riser shafts or ducts.

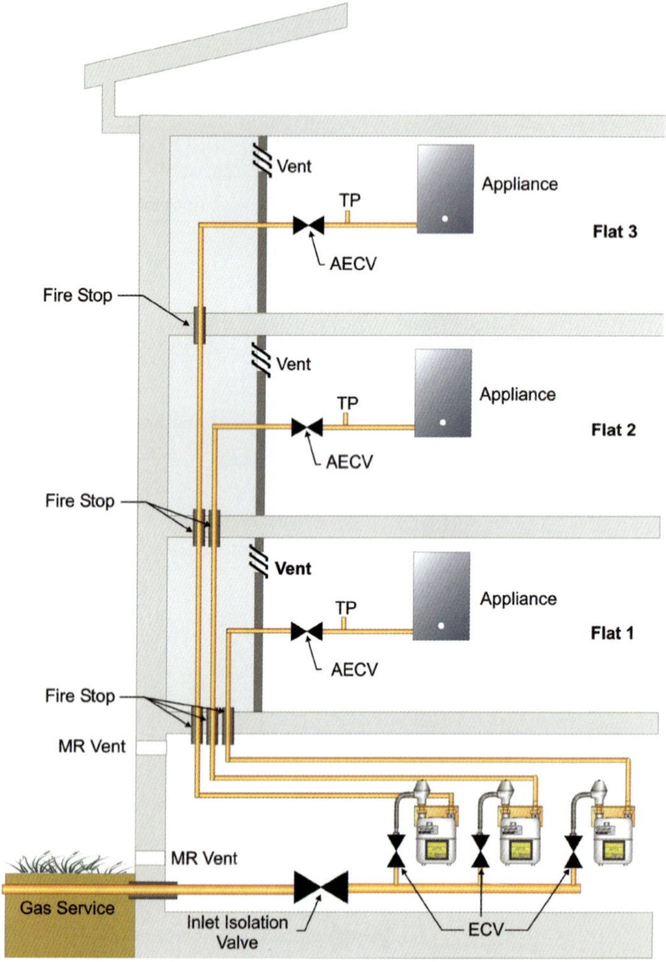

Figure 5.63 Multi-occupancy dwelling with remote meters - Installation pipework run in purpose provided ducts in each flatted property.

5.21 Emergency Control Valve Location and Operation For Single and Multi-occupancy Dwellings.

An emergency control valve (ECV) is the most important isolation valve in any gas installation. It allows for the safe isolation of the full gas supply to the premise in the event of an emergency such as a gas escape. Where the primary meter is located in an outside meter box, access to the ECV is via a locked access hatch or door which opens using a common key. This key must be supplied to the responsible person when the meter is first installed. Where a meter is installed remote from the premises, either for single or multi-occupancy dwellings, any key into the meter housing or room must be freely available at all times and clearly marked as to it's purpose. An additional emergency control (AECV) must also be installed at the point of entry into the premises to allow local isolation of the gas supply.

Regulation 9 of the Gas Safety (Installation & Use) Regulations states the criteria that must be met when installing an emergency control with further information given in BS 6891.

The ECV, or where appropriate AECV, must be installed as near as practicable to the point of entry to the building. In some instances the meter control valve (MCV) may be deemed as the emergency control. Where the ECV is located next to the primary meter, the meter itself normally has "an appropriately worded notice" attached providing the customer with the following important information:

- The action to be taken in the event of an escape
- The name of the supplier
- An emergency telephone number
- The date the label was first displayed

If the ECV is remote from the meter or an AECV is installed a further notice must be attached on or near the valve supplying the information as stated. In addition a further label must be attached stating "Gas Emergency Control". Normally both notice and label come as a composite notice (see section 13).

Any key, lever or hand wheel used to operate the valve must be securely attached to the operating spindle of the control. The key or lever must not be able to freely rotate such that it may pass beyond the closed position allowing gas to pass when the control is deemed off. When in the on position the key or lever must be running along the same axis as the pipe and must fall only to the off position when perpendicular to the pipe run.

Figure 5.64 Emergency Control in "off" position

The method of operation should be permanently marked on or near the valve. Normally this is done by the use of on-off tape applied round the pipe or anaconda, where appropriate, but may be applied to a notice near or on the valve.

5.21.1 Typical Primary Meter Installations and ECV/ AECV Locations.

The following diagrams show simplified layouts of typical metering installations which may be encountered by the domestic gas operative. They are used to illustrate the relative positions of isolations valves within a gas installation with reference to the primary meter installation and route of the service pipe. For ease of identification different colours are used to represent the different sections of the installation:

- Orange - Service pipe which is the responsibility of the gas transporter and includes the emergency control valve.

- Red - Primary meter installation which is the responsibility of the meter owner or meter asset manager (MAM).

- Blue - Installation pipework as defined in the GSIUR and is the responsibility of the customer/ responsible person

- Green - Appliance connector and appliance pipework which is again the responsibility of the customer/ responsible person. The appliance connector is defined as the pipework installed by the gas operative to connect the appliance to the gas supply, whereas the appliance pipework is supplied as part of the appliance by the manufacturer.

It should be noted that other configurations may exist depending on building layout, structure and any other building constraints. Distribution main, meter boxes, ducts and shafts are not shown for clarity. In some instances the emergency control valve may act as a meter control valve.

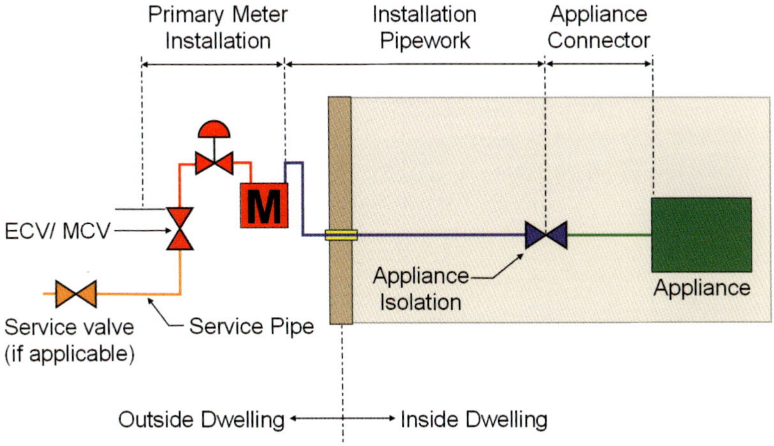

Figure 5.65 Outside meter installation within a meter box or housing attached or adjacent to a dwelling.

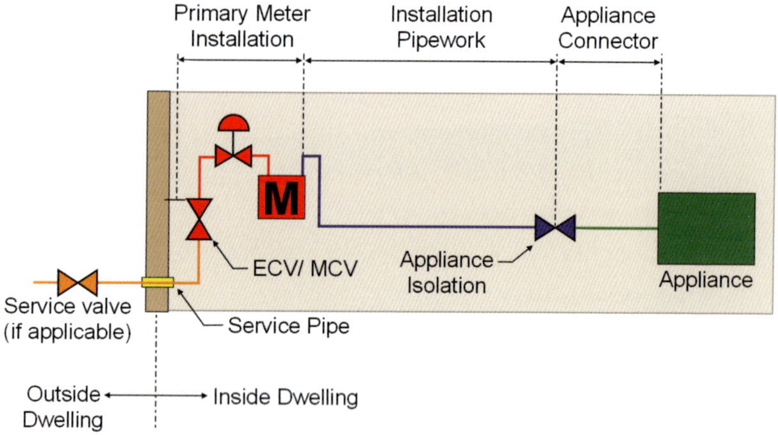

Figure 5.66 Internal meter installation.

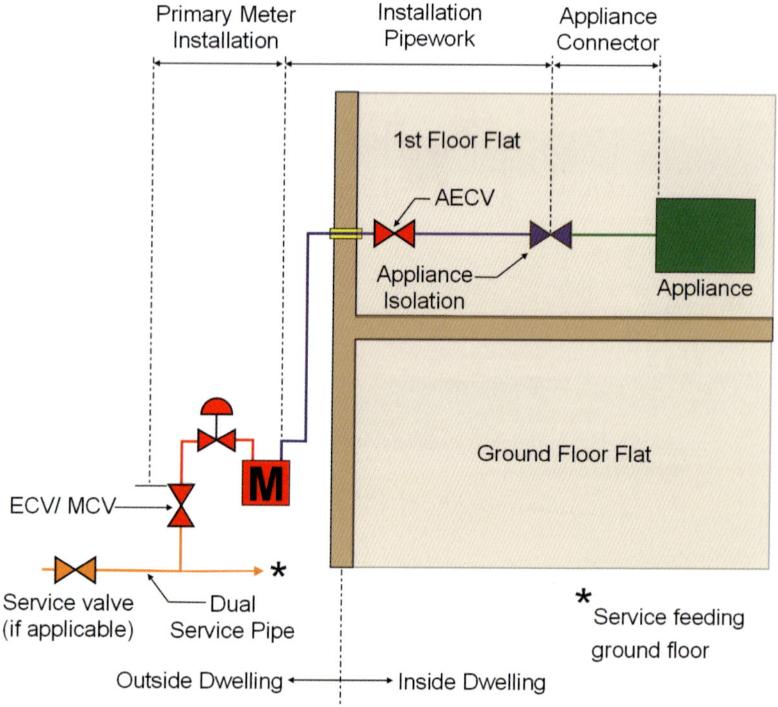

Figure 5.67 Multi-occupancy meter installation with remote meter. Ground floor flat supply removed for clarity

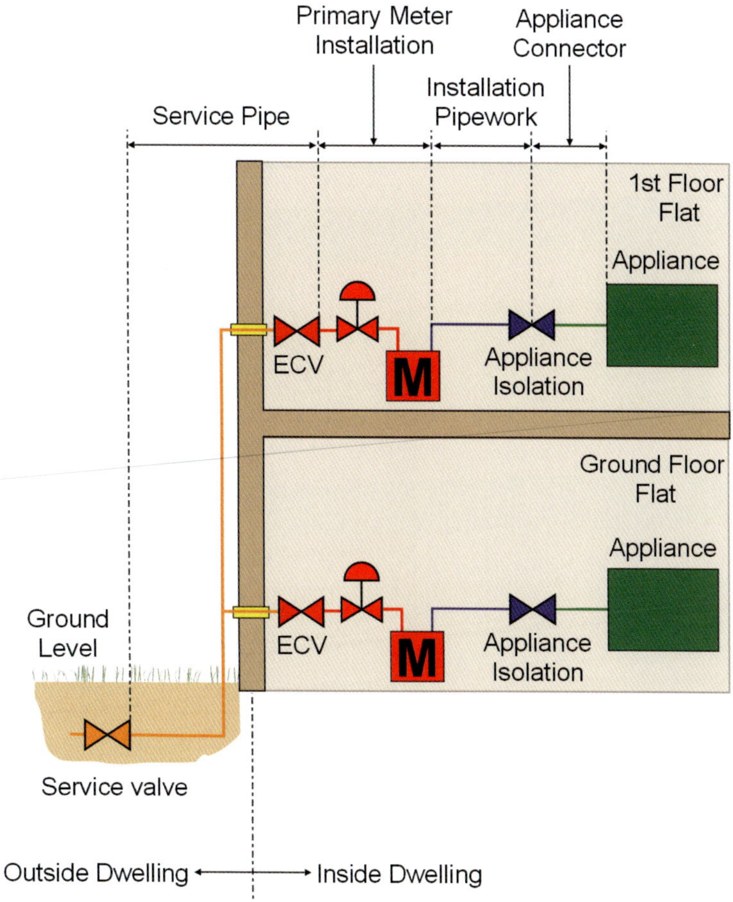

Figure 5.68 Multi-occupancy meter installation with external riser. Meters installed internally.

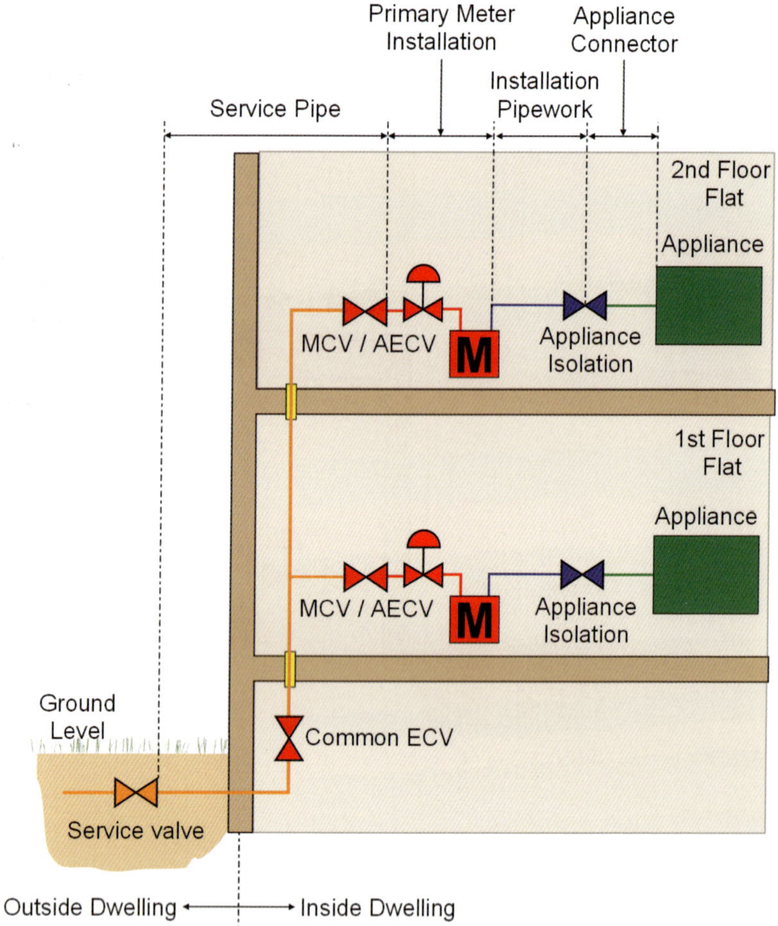

Figure 5.69 Multi-occupancy meter installation with internal riser. Meters installed internally. Common ECV generally for use by Transporter and/ or emergency services.

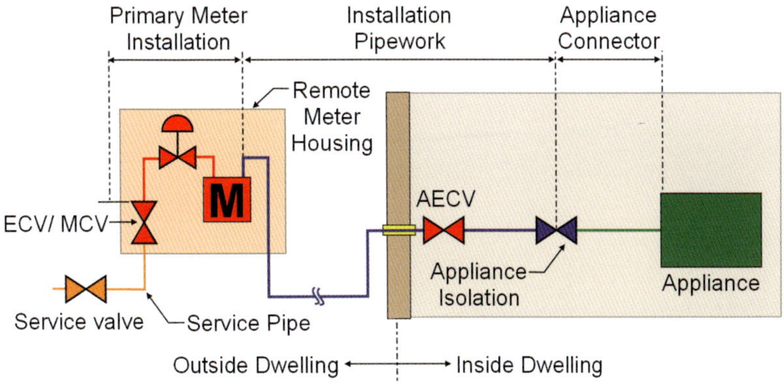

Figure 5.70 Meter within meter housing remote from dwelling.

5.22 Testing for Tightness and Purging

The procedures in document IGE/UP/1B. must be followed, see section 6. The scope of this document has been extended to include U16/ G10 meters with regard to tightness testing and purging.

6. Tightness Testing and Purging

This section is designed to cover the tightness testing and purging of smaller domestic sized gas installations including gas appliances pipework downstream of the appliance isolation valve. Installations which have a volume greater than 0.035 m^3 will fall out with the scope of UP 1B. For these larger installations we must apply either UP 1 or 1A.

6.1 What is a tightness test?

The fundamental test method for any gas installation would be to test every piece of pipe, joint and connection using either leak detection fluid or a gas detector. In most cases this would be impractical and time consuming, therefore to meet industry needs a localised test is used to prove the integrity of a gas installation from a single point on the installation, normally at the primary meter. The test is known as a tightness test. This relies on the fact that if we pressurise a gas system and isolate the pressure source, provided there is no leakage of gas from the system, the pressure will remain constant over a calculated period of time. However, if there was a leakage of gas from the system, the pressure within the system will drop. The drop in pressure over a fixed period of time is relative to the severity of the leakage

For small domestic sized installations this soundness test procedure was originally part of British Standard BS 6891 (Installation of pipework in domestic premises) and BS 6400 (Installation of domestic sized meters). Due to industry needs and European legislation a level of standardisation was required which eventually spawned IGE UP/1B. This introduced specific tightness test and purge criteria for domestic sized installations which included both domestic and non domestic installations within its scope.

6.2 Scope of UP 1B

This procedure applies to **Natural Gas** installations only, downstream of an emergency control valve where the maximum operating pressure of the upstream supply (MOP_u) does not exceed 2 bar.

It includes sections of pipework, including any meters, where the installation meets the following criteria:

- The maximum operating pressure to the outlet of the ECV does not exceed **2 bar**.
- The operating pressure at the outlet of the primary meter is **21 mbar**.
- The maximum rated capacity of the primary meter does not exceed **16 m^3/h (U16).** This equates to approx 173 kW (gross) maximum rated heat input of the installation or approx 590,000 btu/hr based on a CV of 38.76 MJ/m^3.
- The nominal bore of the installation pipework does not exceed **35 mm (1¼").**
- The installation volume does not exceed **0.035 m^3.**
- It can apply both to domestic and non-domestic premises.

6.3 Test Equipment

Equipment used during test

Equipment required for a tightness test are as follows:

- Pressure gauge, either water or electronic.
- Testing tee, if testing with air.
- Aspirator to pressurise the system with air if testing with air.

Using Testing equipment

For any electronic gauge check:

1. It is not damaged and is in good working order.
2. It is calibrated in accordance with the manufacturer and suitable for the test.
3. It is intrinsically safe.
4. The batteries are satisfactory, replace where necessary in a safe atmosphere.
5. The gauge is zeroed prior to use.

It is advisable to stabilise an electronic gauge at the ambient temperature within the area where it is being used for at least 30 to 45 minutes or as specified by the manufacturer. It must be noted that any electronic gauge used to test an installation MUST be capable of reading to at least 1 decimal place.

Any water gauge must be zeroed before use with the reading rechecked to ensure the gauge pressure is equal on the fall and rise of each limb when pressure is applied. This will remove any errors when reading the gauge.

All test equipment including gauge tubes must be checked for integrity prior to use.

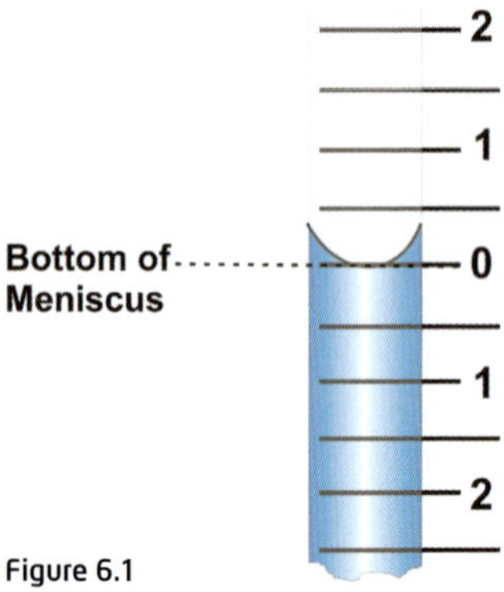

Figure 6.1

Using the Testing Tee

The testing tee is used to allow the gas engineer to introduce air into a system whilst monitoring the gauge pressure at the same time. To use the testing tee we use the following procedure:

1. Connect the aspirator to the valved inlet side of the tee.
2. The other free ends are connected to the installation and a pressure gauge as shown in figure 6.2.
3. Open the isolation valve and gently introduce air into the system, being careful not to blow the water out the gauge.
4. Once the desired pressure is reached, turn off the valve, allow the system to stabilise then monitor the gauge for the test period. Note the full test procedure is given in section 6.4.

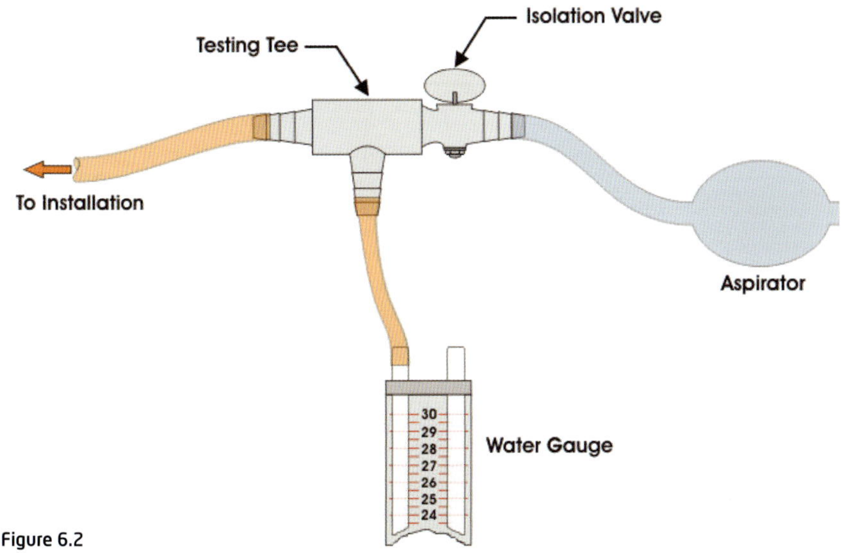

Figure 6.2

6.4 Tightness Testing Procedure UP 1B

6.4.1 Estimating Installation Volume.

A survey must be carried out on any pipework to be tested (unless it is a very simple section i.e one straight length of pipe), with the installation volume calculated to ensure the total volume of the installation to be tested does not exceed 0.035 m^3

To calculate the installation volume we must take note of the following:

- Estimated length and nominal bore of pipework sections.
- Any meters within the section to be tested.
- Fittings, including any components such as regulators etc.
- Inaccessible sections of pipework (where access is restricted to certain areas where there is different sizes of pipe, we must always use the largest nominal bore for the maximum length).

Installation Volume of meters (IV_m)

The volume of gas contained in the meter casings are given in the table below. For any other meter not stated the volume will be given by the meter Manufacturer.

Designation of meter	Case Volume (m^3)
G4/U6	0.008
U16	0.025
E6	0.0024

Installation Volume of pipework (IV_p)

The following table is used to calculate the volume of gas contained within a 1m length of a particular pipe material.

Material & Nominal Bore	Volume of 1m Length m^3
Steel	
15	.00024
20	.00046
25	.00064
32	.0011
Copper	
15	.00014
22	.00032
28	.00054
35	.00084
PE SDR 11	
20	.00019
25	.00033
32	.00053

Installation Volume of Fittings, Vessels etc (IV_f)

Additional volumes of gas contained in ancillary components, fittings, pressure vessels and accumulators etc must be included as part of the total installation volume. This specific information is normally given by the Manufacturer. However, where this information is not available **an additional allowance of 10% of the total installation pipework volume (IV_p) must be included.**

Calculating Total Installation Volume (IV).

The total installation volume is calculated using the following calculation.

$$\mathbf{IV = IV_m + IV_p + IV_f}$$

Example:

An installation comprises of the following:

A U16 primary meter.

3 m of 32 mm SDR 11 PE pipe.

6 m of 35 mm copper pipe.

4.5 m of 20 mm steel pipe

Calculation for the installation volume:

$\mathbf{IV_m}$ = U16 meter (from table) = 0.025 m^3

3 m of 32 mm PE = 3 m x 0.00053 m^3 = 0.00159 m^3

6 m of 35 mm copper = 6 m x 0.00084 m^3 = 0.00504 m^3

4.5 m of 20 mm steel = 4.5 m x 0.00046 m^3 = 0.00207 m^3

$\mathbf{IV_p}$ = 0.00159 + 0.00504 + 0.00207 = 0.0087 m^3

$\mathbf{IV_f}$ = 10% of IV_p = 10% of 0.0087 m^3 = 0.00087 m^3

$\mathbf{IV = IV_m + IV_p + IV_f}$

= 0.025 + 0.0087+ 0.00087

= 0.03457 m^3

Note: as seen from the example, relatively short lengths of the larger bore pipework can quite easily produce an installation volume in excess of 0.035 m^3.

6.4.2 New Installation Tightness Test Procedure

1. Inspect installation for compliance with relevant regulations and standards.
2. Ensure all open ends are sealed using an appropriate fitting.
3. Ensure all appliance isolation valves are turned ON, but all control taps and pilots are turned OFF. Raise any fold down cooker lids.
4. Connect a pressure gauge to an appropriate test point on the installation if testing with gas or to a suitable testing tee if air.
5. Ensure gauge is zeroed before moving on with the test.
6. If connected to the gas supply, carry out a let-by test on the upstream isolation valve or MCV/ECV as follows:

- Raise pressure to approx 10 mbar by opening the valve.
- Turn off pressure source.
- Check for any pressure rise on the gauge for 1 minute.
- **There must be no perceptible movement of the gauge (NPM for a water gauge is 0.25 mbar and for an electronic 0.2 mbar).**
- Where a rise is recorded greater than NPM the isolation valve can be confirmed as passing by first applying a temporary continuity bond between the service pipe to the valve and the meter, disconnecting the pipework downstream of the valve and applying leak detection fluid to the internal ball or barrel.
- If let by is confirmed replace or repair the valve. Where that valve is an MCV/ECV contact the National Gas Emergency Service call Centre. Where the valve cannot be repaired or replaced make the installation safe and suspend the test until an effective repair has been made.

6. Following a successful let-by test slowly raise the pressure to 20 mbar. (avoid higher pressures to prevent regulator lock-up)
7. Allow 1 minute for temperature stabilisation after which, if necessary, re-adjust pressure to 20 mbar.
8. Carry out tightness test for a further 2 minutes.
9. If there is a discernable drop or a smell of gas, the source of the leak must be traced and repaired.
10. After repair retest the installation to confirm tightness.
11. Remove gauge and reseal test point. Turn on gas supply and check test

point, ECV/AECV outlet connections, regulator connections and, where necessary, MIV connections with LDF. Remember to dry LDF from the fittings as it can be corrosive.

12. Record test results and, where appropriate, inform the responsible person.

Note: Where existing appliances are connected to a new gas supply a pressure drop may be allowed as long as it has been proved that it is not on the new pipework installation.

Note also that the pre-payment mechanism in an ETM (Quantum meter) may be closed due to there being no credit or if the tamper device has been activated. This will prevent the installation pipework and appliances from being tested for tightness with gas. Unless the valve can be opened (ESP job), an air test may have to be carried out but this then means that part of the meter installation will not have been tested and purging will be necessary.

6.4.3 Existing Installation Tightness Test Procedure

1. Inspect installation for compliance with relevant regulations and standards.
2. Ensure any open ends are sealed using the appropriate fitting.
3. Ensure all appliance isolation valves are turned ON, but all control taps and pilots are turned OFF. Raise any fold down cooker lids.
4. Connect a pressure gauge to an appropriate test point on the installation if testing with gas or to a suitable testing tee if air.
5. Ensure gauge is zeroed before moving on with the test.
6. If connected to the gas supply, carry out a let-by test on the Upstream isolation valve or MCV/ECV as follows:

- Raise pressure to approx 10 mbar by opening the valve.
- Turn off pressure source.
- Check for any pressure rise on the gauge for 1 minute.
- There must be no perceptible movement of the gauge (NPM for a water gauge is 0.25 mbar and for an electronic 0.2 mbar).
- Where a rise is recorded greater than NPM the isolation valve can be confirmed as passing by first applying a temporary continuity bond across the valve, disconnecting the pipework above the valve and applying leak detection fluid to the internal ball or barrel.

- If let by is confirmed replace or repair the valve. Where that valve is an MCV/ ECV contact the National Gas Emergency Service call Centre. Where the valve cannot be repaired or replaced make the installation safe and suspend the test until an effective repair has been made.

7. Following a successful let-by test slowly raise the pressure to 20 mbar. (avoid higher pressures to prevent regulator lock-up)
8. Allow 1 minute for temperature stabilisation after which, if necessary, re-adjust pressure to 20 mbar.
9. Carry out tightness test for a further 2 minutes.
10. With appliances connected, if the pressure drop exceeds those as given in table 6.1 or a smell of gas exists, the source of the leak must be traced and repaired.

Pipe Nominal Bore	**E6 meter ≤ 6 m^3/h or no meter**	**U6/G4 meter ≤ 6 m^3/h**	**U16/G10 > 6 m^3/h ≤ 16 m^3/h**
≤ 28mm	8 mbar	4 mbar	1 mbar
> 28mm ≤ 35mm	4.5 mbar	2.5 mbar	1 mbar

Table 6.1

11. Where no appliances are connected, the installation can only be deemed gas tight if over the 2 minute period there is no perceptible movement of the gauge.
12. After a repair retest installation to confirm tightness
13. Remove gauge and reseal test point. Turn on gas supply and check test point, ECV/AECV outlet connections, regulator connections and, where necessary, MIV connections with LDF.
14. Record test results and, where appropriate, inform the responsible person.
15. In the event that an effective repair cannot be made and the installation has failed the tightness test, the installation or appliance must be disconnected from the gas supply with a suitable label attached until as such times as a repair can be made.

6.4.4 Extensions and Alterations to Existing Installations

Existing installations must be tested prior to extending or altering the installation and its tightness assessed. If any leakage is detected then only appliance leakage is acceptable provided there is no smell of gas and the pressure drop does not exceed that specified in table 6.1. After the alteration or extension the entire installation must be tested and any pressure drop must not exceed that previously measured and there must be no smell of gas.

If a smell of gas is reported and the installation is tight, it may be due to one or more of the following which should be eliminated or confirmed as the cause;

- There may be a gas leak downstream of the appliance control tap i.e. the smell is only noticed when the appliance is in operation.
- There may not be a natural gas leak, it may be products of combustion which are being smelled (the regulations class CO leakage from a gas fitting as a gas leak).
- The smell is from some extraneous source and mistaken for gas.
- There may be gas migration from adjoining premises.
- There may be an outside escape from a service or main which is entering the property.
- There may be naturally occurring methane (or other gases) being detected.

The gas supply will need to be turned off, the premises ventilated, no switches operated (on or off) and no naked flames or smoking permitted. Evacuation of the premises may be necessary dependant on the gas concentration.

If the cause of the smell cannot be eliminated, the Emergency Service Provider must be contacted.

6.4.5 Medium Pressure Supplies (MOP_u not exceeding 2 bar)

6.4.5.1 Where a test valve is fitted

If the MOP_u exceeds 75 mbar the previous tests are performed but any reference to the ECV is to be to the meter inlet valve (MIV). A test with LDF will then apply to all joints downstream of the ECV and upstream of the MIV at operating pressure (ensure that any regulator meter installation excess flow valve (MIEFV) is reset).

6.4.5.2 Where there is no test valve fitted

If the MOP_u exceeds 75 mbar the previous tests are performed but any reference to the ECV is to be to the meter inlet valve (MIV). A test with LDF will then apply to all joints downstream of the ECV and upstream of the MIV at operating pressure (ensure that any regulator meter installation excess flow valve (MIEFV) is reset).

1. Inspect installation, for compliance with relevant regulations and standards.
2. Ensure any open ends are sealed using the appropriate fitting.
3. Ensure all appliance isolation valves are turned ON, but all control taps and pilots are turned OFF. Raise any fold down cooker lids.
4. Turn off the ECV/ MCV.
5. Connect a pressure gauge to an appropriate test point on the installation.
6. Ensure gauge is zeroed before moving on with the test.
7. Release any pressure in the system to atmospheric pressure via a suitable point in the installation, for example a cooker burner, and reseal/ turn off.
8. Carry out a let by test on the **emergency control** as follows:

- Hold open the re-arming lever on the MIEFV (see figure 6.3) to balance the pressures between upstream and downstream of the regulator.
- With the re-arming mechanism in the open position check for any pressure rise on the gauge for 1 minute.
- If there is a perceptible movement on the gauge, the ECV may be passing.

Figure 6.3:

- If let by is suspected on the ECV, contact the National Gas Emergency service call centre, make the installation safe and suspend the test until the valve is repaired or replaced.

10. After a successful let by test, reset the release mechanism.
11. Carry out a let by test on the **regulator** as follows:

- Open the ECV slowly.
- With the ECV in the open position check for any pressure rise on the gauge for 1 minute.
- If there is any perceptible movement on the gauge, the regulator may be passing.
- If let by is suspected on the primary regulator, contact the Meter Asset Manager (MAM), make the installation safe and suspend the test until the regulator is repaired or replaced.

12. After a successful let by test, release any pressure from the system.
13. Operate any release mechanism on the regulator then SLOWLY open the meter control valve (do not snatch the valve) and raise the pressure to 19 mbar.
14. Turn off the gas supply.
15. Allow 1 minute for temperature stabilisation.
16. Carry out a tightness test for a further 2 minutes.
17. Any pressure drop must not exceed that stated in table 6.1.
18. If there is a smell of gas or the pressure drop exceeds that stated in table 6.1, the source of the leak must be traced and repaired.
19. Retest installation to confirm tightness. Where a smell of gas has been detected and subsequently repaired an installation can only be deemed tight where there is no perceptible movement of the gauge.
20. With the ECV on and the regulator re-armed, test any connections upstream of the regulator or test valve and any disturbed joints with LDF. Remember and wipe dry all joints after testing with LDF.

6.5 Purging Installations to UP 1B

Meter Type	Purge Volume depending on Pipework Size	
	≤ 28mm	> 28 mm
U6/ G4	0.01 m^3	0.01 m^3 plus 1.5 x $(IV_p + IV_f)$
E6	0.01 m^3	0.0036 m^3 plus 1.5 x $(IV_p + IV_f)$
U16	0.03 m^3 plus 1.5 x $(IV_p + IV_f)$	

Table 6.2: Purge volumes

IGEM UP 1B describes two methods of purging an installation depending on its volume:

Method 1 – Installation Volume Less than or Equal to 0.02 m^3:

This method allows the purge gases to vent freely into a well ventilated internal space. The vent gases can be released into atmosphere either through an appliance burner or by splitting a disconnecting union at the farthest point on the installation. It is permissible to hold a source of ignition at the burner head when purging through a burner. This will limit the amount of un-ignited purge gases in atmosphere.

Method 2 – Installation volume exceeds 0.02 m^3:

The purge gases must be vented through an open burner attached to a suitable point on the installation. An open burner may be a hotplate burner on a gas cooker or a temporary burner attached to the pipework. Enclosed burners must not be used for this purpose. Due to the volume of gases being vented into the internal space the atmosphere within the area may contain high concentrations of flammable gases even when adequately ventilated. To reduce this hazard it is necessary to "flare off" the vent gases by applying a constant source of ignition to the burner during the purge.

To determine which of the methods apply, the installation volume must be calculated (see section 6.4.1).

6.5.1 Calculating Purge Volume

As seen from the table where the pipework is in excess of 28 mm for U6 and E6 meters or the installation includes a U16 meter, the purge volume of the installation must be calculated. U6 & E6 meters with pipework of 28 mm or less have a fixed 0.01 m^3 purge volume.

A purge is only deemed complete when the calculated purge volume has been achieved. This can be proven by checking the volume of gas passed during the purge at the meter.

Calculating the purge volume:

Take the following example

The installation comprises of the following:

U16 meter:
6 m of 32mm steel pipe.
3 m of 22 mm copper pipe.

Calculate the volume of the installation pipework

6 m of 32 mm steel = 6 m x 0.0011 m^3 = 0.0066 m^3
3 m of 22 mm copper = 3 x 0.00032 m^3 = 0.00096 m^3

$\mathbf{IV_p}$ = 0.0066 m3 + 0.00096 m^3 = 0.00756 m^3
$\mathbf{IV_F}$ = 10% of 0.00756 m^3 = 0.000756 m^3
Calculate the purge volume of the pipework:

$\mathbf{PV_p}$ = 1.5 x (0.00756 m^3 + 0.000756 m^3)
= 1.5 x 0.008316 m^3
= 0.012474 m^3

Calculate the purge volume of the meter:

From the table it states a purge volume (PV_m) of 0.03 m^3 for a U16 meter.

Therefore the total purge volume **(PV) = $PV_m + PV_p$**

$= 0.03\ m^3 + 0.012474\ m^3$

$= \mathbf{0.042474\ m^3}$

Since U6, E6 and U 16 meters only register to 3 decimal places we can round the purge volume up to 0.043 m^3

6.5.2 Purge Procedure (IV less than 0.02 m^3)

1. Open doors and windows to ventilate area direct to outside air.
2. Extinguish all sources of ignition, do not smoke, do not operate electrical switches.
3. Inform the responsible person of your actions.
4. Ensure all appliances are OFF and slowly turn on meter control valve.
5. Note the position of the test dial or test drums on the meter depending on whether it is metric or imperial.
6. Go to a suitable purge point furthest from the meter. This could be an appliance burner or disconnection union (on the appliance or installation pipework).
7. Allow gas to pass for a short period of time. Turn off or retighten the fitting and check the volume passes through the meter. Keep passing gas until purge volume has been achieved.
8. Test any disturbed joints with LDF.
9. Once the purge volume has been passed, light the appliance to confirm a stable flame picture.

6.5.3 Purge Procedure (IV > 0.02 m^3)

1. Open doors and windows to ventilate area direct to outside air.
2. Extinguish all sources of ignition, do not smoke, do not operate electrical switches.
3. Inform the responsible person of your actions.
4. Ensure all appliances are OFF and slowly turn on meter control valve.
5. Note the position of the test dial or dm^3 drums on the meter depending on whether it is metric or imperial.
6. Go to a suitable purge point furthest from the meter. This could be an appliance or a temporary installed open burner.

7. Turn on burner control tap and allow gas to flow. Ensure a constant source of ignition is available at this time.
8. The air/gas mixture must be continually ignited until a stable flame exists at the burner head.
9. Turn off the burner and note the reading on the meter to confirm the volume of gas passed.
10. Where necessary remove temporary burner & test any disturbed joints with LDF.

6.6 IGE Documents - Summary of Scope

IGE/UP/1B

- Replaces the procedures laid down in British Standards BS 6891 [Installation of pipework in domestic premises] and BS 6400 [Installation of domestic sized meters].
- It covers work on gas installations down stream of a primary meter control valve where the supply operating pressure does not exceed **75 mbar** (low pressure installations).
- Where the supply pressure is over **75 mbar** but does not exceed **2 bar** (medium pressure) down stream of a test valve.
- The maximum operating pressure of the installation does not exceed **21 mbar**.
- The diameter of the installation pipework does not exceed **35 mm copper or 32 mm steel**.
- An installation **volume not exceeding 0.035 m^3** including any meters and allowance for fittings.
- The primary meter maximum rated capacity does not exceed **16m^3/h** [U6 (G4), U16 (G10) and E6 metered installations].
- Natural gas installations only.

If out of Scope ↓

IGE/UP/1A

- Industrial & commercial natural gas installations including larger Domestic if applicable.

- Any section of pipework downstream of the emergency control valve with a **nominal bore not exceeding 150mm (6").**
- An installation **volume not exceeding 1 m^3** including any meters and allowance for fittings.
- Low pressure supplies (up to **75 mbar**) with a design operating pressure **not exceeding 40 mbar** at the outlet of the primary meter regulator.
- Natural Gas Installations Only.

If out of Scope ↓

IGE/UP/1

- Industrial & commercial gas installations.
- Pipework containing **Natural gas, Butane, Propane, LPG/Air and coal gas**.
- For Natural gas, pipework from the primary meter emergency control valve including any plant/ appliance pipework.
- **For LPG, pipework of volume greater than 0.02 m^3** from the bulk storage vessel or cylinder valve excluding service pipework but including any plant/ appliance pipework. LPGA COP TM62 used below 0.02 m^3.
- Maximum operating pressures not exceeding **16 bar** (The scope of the document does not apply to installations where the maximum operating pressure of the installation is in excess of 75 mbar with no meter inlet valve installed between the primary regulator and meter).
- **Any size of pipework of any volume**.

7. Checking and Setting Regulators

7.1 General

Gas regulators are imperative for the safe operation of any gas system. From district supplies down to the supply of gas to an appliance, gas regulators ensure gas is delivered at the correct pressure under varying load and operating conditions.

In most accounts regulators allow some form of adjustment which will enable a competent person to alter the operational parameters to suit that of the downstream gas system and/ or appliance. It is a stipulation of the Gas Safety (Installation and Use) Regulations that when any competent person adjusts a gas regulator of any kind they must thereafter reseal it to guard against any unauthorised tampering. In the case of a primary regulator any adjustment must only be carried out by the gas transporter or any person acting on their behalf.

There is a legal requirement for any regulator supplying gas through a primary meter to have some form of automatic protection to limit the pressure of the downstream gas system in the event the regulator fails. In most accounts for installations supplied at low pressure (less than 75 mbar) this is done through the normal component design. Where the supply pressure is 75 mbar or above (medium pressure) additional safety devices must be installed such as a slam-shut, OPSO, pressure relief valve etc. This will be explained in more detail throughout this section.

7.2 Regulator Types

The types of regulator which a domestic gas engineer will encounter are:

- Low pressure, double diaphragm, compensated regulator.
- Medium to low pressure regulator either single or two stage.
- Simple type appliance regulator.
- Servo operated regulator (used as part of a multifunctional control).
- Zero rated regulator (normally used as part of an air/ gas ratio control).

7.2.1 Low Pressure Double Diaphragm Compensated Regulator

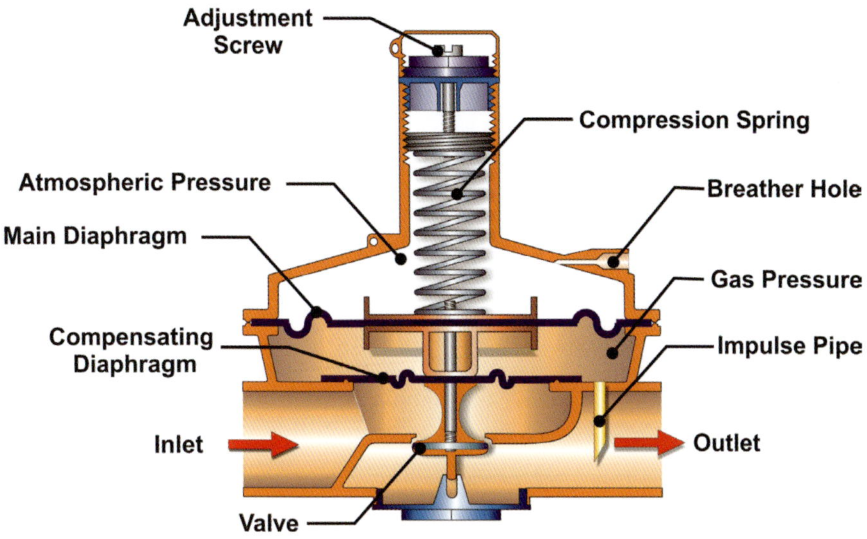

Figure 7.1 Constant pressure regulator

The construction of a typical double diaphragm, compensated regulator consists of a main diaphragm and a smaller compensating diaphragm connected to a valve. Above the main diaphragm is an air chamber which contains a compression spring. This chamber is maintained at atmospheric pressure via a small breather hole which allows the air to enter or discharge depending on the movement of the diaphragm. The internal thread in the breather hole allows a small bore pipe to be connected to the regulator when it is installed in contaminated atmospheres, such as joinery workshops etc. This will ensure the breather is kept clear of foreign matter which could damage the internal components affecting the safe operation of the regulator.

Additional care must also be given to prevent the ingress of water and moisture into the regulator through the breather. Water and moisture will cause corrosion of internal steel components, failure of other components and, in the winter time freeze, causing the regulator to malfunction.

The spring is used to exert a force on the top of the diaphragm, this force being adjustable by compressing or decompressing the spring by means of an adjustment screw on the top of the spring. This screw can only be accessed by removing a cap which must be sealed after adjustment.

With no appliances operating the pressure at the outlet is transmitted through an impulse pipe onto the underside of the main diaphragm. As the pressure increases, the force exerted on the underside of the diaphragm increases until it overcomes that of the spring. This will then pull the valve up onto its seating effectively stopping the flow of gas through the regulator. This is called "lock-up".

When we turn an appliance on the pressure in the outlet of the regulator decreases until the force of the spring overcomes that exerted by the outlet pressure. The spring will then push the diaphragm down, pushing the valve off its seating far enough to replace the gas used by the appliance. As the flow of gas increases the pressure at the outlet of the valve decreases. This reduced pressure is transmitted to the underside of the main diaphragm via the impulse pipe. As the force on the underside of the diaphragm is now reduced the diaphragm is forced down by the spring until the pressure under the diaphragm is equal to that exerted by the spring. At this point the valve will be at a position where the amount of gas passing between the valve seat and the valve is enough to maintain the desired operating pressure. If another appliance is turned on, the drop in pressure would again be transmitted on the underside to close the valve of the diaphragm with the valve moving downwards to replace the additional gas being used.

To increase the operating pressure of the installation we would screw down (clockwise) the adjustment screw which will then compress the spring. This will exert a greater force on the top of the diaphragm requiring a greater pressure on the underside. To increase this pressure we would require more gas to flow between the valve and valve seating. Alternatively, to decrease the pressure we would screw up (anticlockwise) the adjustment screw this will decompress the spring reducing the force on the top of the diaphragm in turn reducing the pressure and flow of gas required to move the diaphragm.

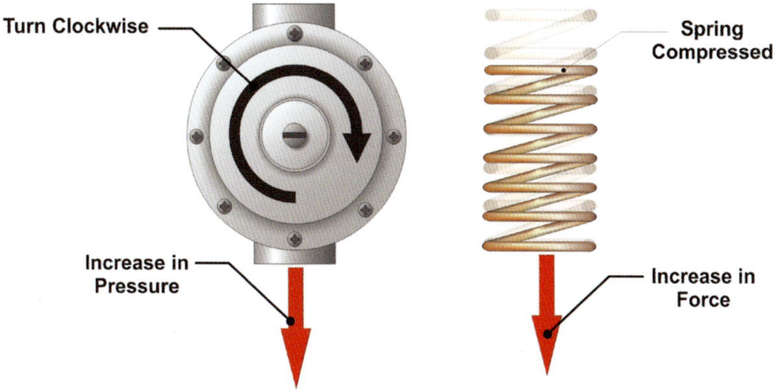

Figure 7.2 Increase Pressure Turn Clockwise

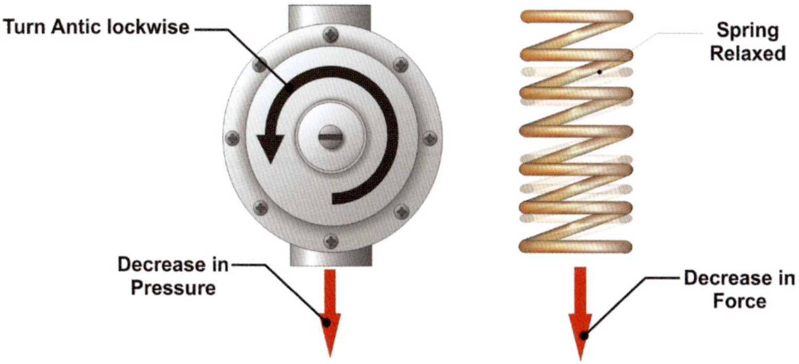

Figure 7.3 Decrease Pressure Turn Anticlockwise

The small auxiliary diaphragm is used to compensate for the effects of unequal pressures on the valve created by the higher inlet pressure on the top of the valve and lower outlet pressure on the underside. This diaphragm is also affected by both of these pressures hence cancelling any downward forces generated by the pressure differences.

The normal operating pressure of a low pressure gas installation is **21 mbar ± 2 mbar**, however we must take into account that non-domestic installations may operate at higher pressures.

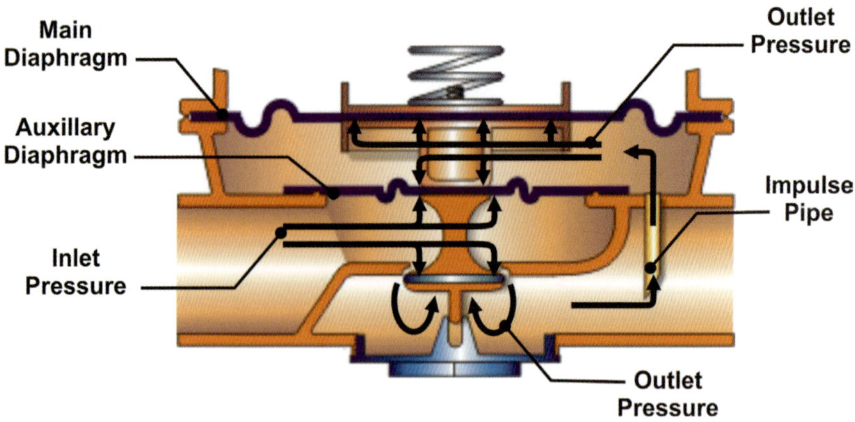

Figure 7.4 Pressures acting on auxiliary diaphragm

Primary regulators may be of the "straight through" or "angled" type. For domestic primary meter installations, other than concealed meter boxes, the regulator outlet is designed to attach directly on to the primary meter with the inlet connection to the emergency control valve (meter control valve) by means of a flexible corrugated stainless steel tube (anaconda). This type of configuration using an angled type regulator makes for a more compact installation. The anaconda and meter connection may require to be assembled onto the regulator or come pre-assembled as part of a meter kit. An example of primary meter installation with an angled regulator is shown in figure 7.5.

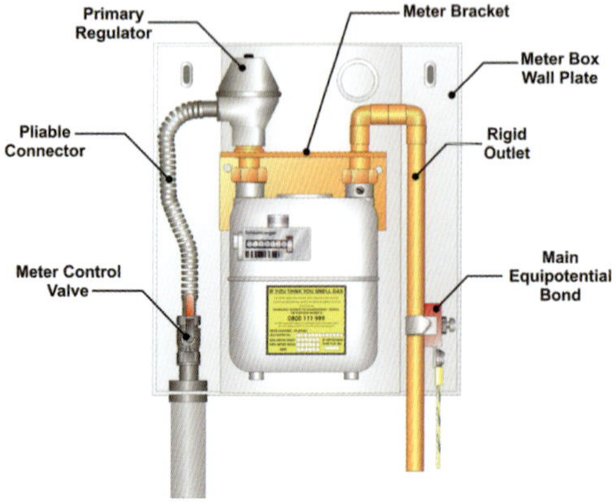

Figure 7.5 Primary meter installation

7.2.2 Medium to Low Pressure Regulator

Medium to low pressure regulators may be either direct or indirect acting depending on their application. The majority of primary regulators used for domestic applications are of the indirect acting type, using a system of levers attached to the diaphragm to ensure positive movement of the valve against the higher incoming pressures.

Medium to low pressure regulators may be single or two stage. The single stage regulator, as it's name suggests, reduces the pressure from the medium pressure supply (75 mbar up to 2 bar) through a single stage means of pressure reduction to achieve the low pressure at the outlet (21 mbar for a natural gas installation). This type of regulator has a single main diaphragm which operates the main valve through a series of levers. The most common manufacturer of this type of valve is Elster Instromet (formally Jeavons) where the J125 model was commonly used as a primary regulator. See figure 7.6.

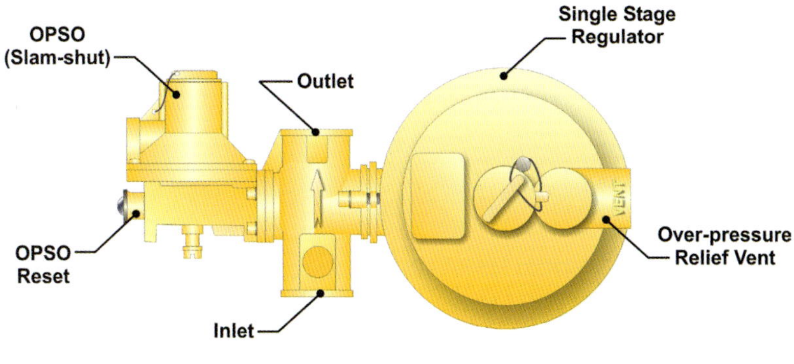

Figure 7.6 Single Stage Regulator

A two stage regulator incorporates two diaphragms, each used to reduce the incoming medium pressure supply down to low pressure in two stages. A typical two stage regulator is shown with the cut out drawing in figure 7.7. In most accounts this type of regulator is preset and cannot be adjusted. If found faulty or incorrectly set, they must be replaced.

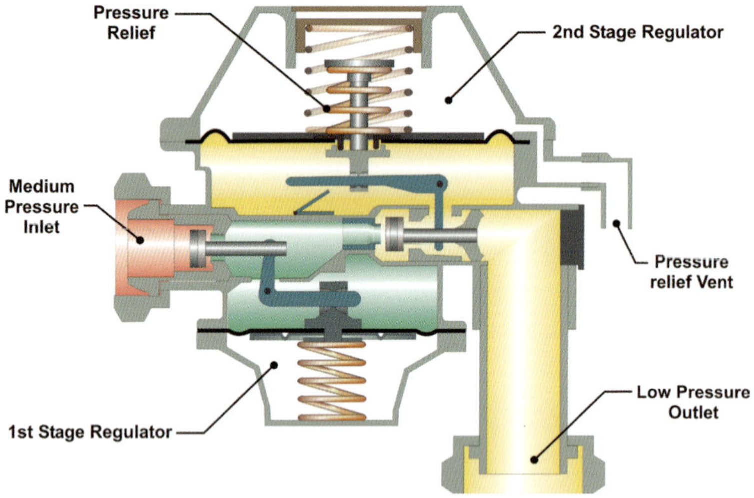

Figure 7.7 Two stage medium to low pressure regulator construction

As specified previously, additional safety devices must be installed where the supply pressure is 75 mbar and above. These safety devices may be installed as separate units or incorporated within the regulator assembly. Excess pressure well in excess of the design pressure of a low pressure system can result in damage to components and controls within the gas installation. In extreme circumstances components, controls or pipe may fail resulting in gas escaping from the installation.

The additional safety devices include a pressure relief valve (PRV) and over pressure safety shut off valve (OPSO – commonly known as a slam-shut). Some additional safety features may also be included for example under pressure shut-off valve, excess flow valve.

The medium to low pressure regulator uses the same basic operating principles as a low pressure regulator with the addition of the valve lever assembly. Incorporated within the main diaphragm is a spring loaded valve which acts as a pressure relief valve. When activated the additional pressure lifts the vent valve allowing gas to vent to atmosphere through a fixed opening. This vent opening has the facility to pipe the vent gases to outside depending on location. Some vent openings incorporate a flame trap consisting of a stainless steel mesh which must be removed when affixing an additional vent pipe.

Nominal pressure settings for a medium to low pressure regulator as per BS 6400 part 2:

Regulator Lock up pressure – maximum 27.5 mbar
Relief valve opening pressure – 35 ± 3.5 mbar
Slam-shut operating pressure – 47.5 ± 2.5 mbar

7.2.3 Simple Appliance Regulator

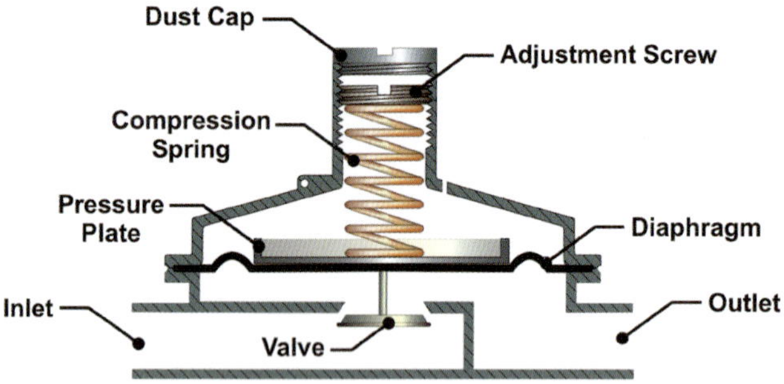

Figure 7.7 Simple Regulator Construction

An appliance regulator is used to ensure a constant pressure is maintained at the burner injector(s). This pressure is used to quantify the amount of gas injected into the burner relative to the appliance designed heat input. A test point is normally supplied by the manufacturer as near as practical to the injector to allow this pressure to be accurately measured. The manufacturer will specify at what location and under what conditions this pressure requires to be measured. This pressure is known as the burner pressure and is stated by the manufacturer, where required, on both the installation instructions and on the appliance data badge. Appliances using a zero rated regulator as part of the air/ gas ratio control may not state any burner pressure, but instead refer to the minimum inlet pressure at the appliance with the heat input and combustion performance parameters.

It is a requirement of regulation 26(9) of the GSIUR that where work is performed on an appliance that the burner pressure and/ or heat input is measured and adjusted as necessary to the manufacturers recommended setting.

In most accounts appliances such as gas fires, water heaters, cookers, tumble dryers and leisure appliances have a fixed burner pressure normally measured when the appliance is on it's highest setting. Control is normally offered through a customer operated control such as a gas valve. However, for the likes of central heating boilers and ducted air heaters there is a requirement for some flexibility in their operation to suit the heating demands of the premises. These appliances may be:

- **Fixed Rated** - The heat input for this type of appliance is fixed and cannot be adjusted out with this setting. They normally operate in a simple on/off cycle.

- **Range Rated** - This type of appliance allows the manufacturers to produce a limited number of appliances to suit a number of different applications. The burners are designed to operate safely over a range of burner pressures. These pressures are normally stated as min, mid and max. This type of arrangement allows flexibility on the installation of central heating boilers and air heaters by giving the commissioning engineer the facility to adjust the appliance to suit the heating requirements of the premises. Once set the appliance operates on the on/off cycle.

- **Modulating** - A modulating appliance is one which has a minimum and maximum heat input setting. The burner pressure adjusts continually anywhere between these two settings depending on the heating and/or hot water demand from the system normally dictated by flow and/or return temperatures.. Most modern gas central heating boilers and some types of air heater operate in this way increasing the efficiency of the appliance.

An appliance regulator must always be adjusted to the manufacturers specified settings. Too high a pressure will result in too much gas being introduced into the burner resulting in poor combustion (over-gassed). Alternatively too low a pressure may result in the appliance not achieving it's required heat input affecting the appliance performance.

7.2.4 Servo Operated Regulator (Multifunctional Control)

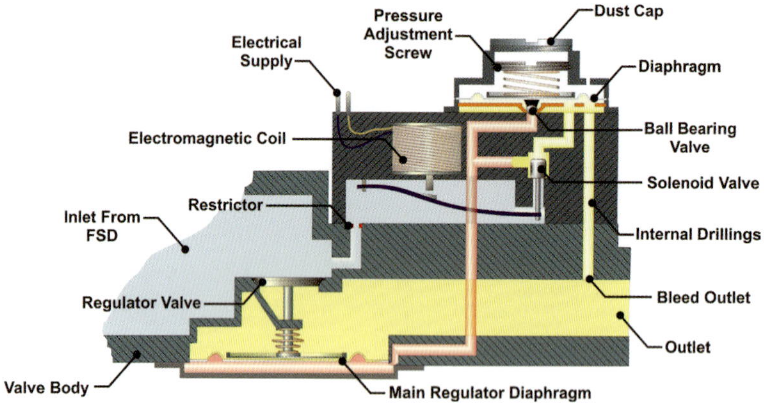

Figure 7.8 Multifunctional control with servo assisted regulator

Figure 7.8 shows a cross section through a multifunctional control incorporating a servo assisted regulator. This type of regulator is indirect acting as the pressure sensing diaphragm and pressure adjustment is not located within the gas stream. A small amount of inlet pressure is transmitted through a restricting orifice via the solenoid valve to the underside of a sensing diaphragm through drillings within the valve body. The sensing diaphragm is attached to a small valve. This valve, when open allows pressure to be transmitted to the underside of the main diaphragm which in turn will push the regulator valve in an upward direction. The amount of movement is dependant on the pressure allowed to flow to the underside of the main diaphragm. As the main valve opens gas will flow to the burner. As seen from the diagram another drilling connects the outlet pressure to the underside of the small sensing diaphragm. The movement of the sensing diaphragm is dictated by the pressure difference between the inlet and outlet gas. If the gas pressure at the outlet is lower than required the pressure difference is greater pushing the sensing diaphragm upwards allowing a higher pressure to be transmitted to the underside of the main diaphragm moving the valve upwards allowing more gas to flow. As this pressure increases the differential becomes less therefore the small valve will be pushed nearer its seating by the action of the spring reducing the pressure transmitted to the underside of the main diaphragm until the desired outlet pressure is achieved. The outlet pressure also acts on the top of the main diaphragm where movement of the main valve is mainly determined by the difference in pressure between the underside and top of this diaphragm The valve will continually adjust depending on inlet and outlet pressures to maintain a constant outlet pressure. Adjustment of the regulator acts similar to that of a normal regulator by adjusting the loading on the small diaphragm by means of a spring. This adjustment is made at a point specified by the valve manufacturer.

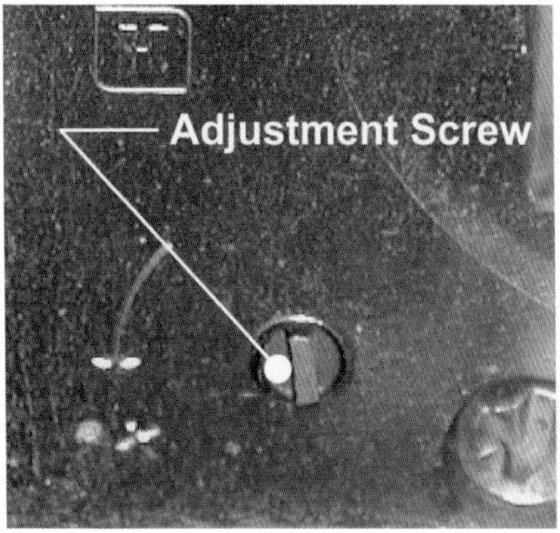

Figure 7.9 Regulator adjustment screw on a twin solenoid Multifunctional control

7.2.5 Zero Rated Regulator.

The zero rated regulator is not a new control. It has been used for many years within the industrial and commercial sector. What is new is its recent inclusion as a control on domestic appliances. In the industrial application it is found as a separate control component, in the domestic application it is incorporated into the multi-functional control.

The construction of a zero rated regulator is similar to that of a normal regulator, however instead of the diaphragm reacting to a positive pressure at the outlet of the control it responds to a negative pressure (suction) generated by an air source, normally a fan.

Although this control is called a zero rated regulator it does not mean that the gas is supplied at zero pressure. The pressure supplied through the regulator is equal and opposite to the negative pressure generated by the air source either directly or indirectly by means of the venturi or measured orifice. For example if a fan generates a negative pressure of minus 4 mbar the regulator would have to supply a positive pressure of 4 mbar for the gauge to read zero (+4mbar – 4 mbar = 0 mbar). As the fan pressure changes the regulator will adjust to suit, however this adjustment will not be recognised on the gauge as this will always register zero. Fundamentally in all accounts any adjustment should be backed up by taking a gas rate and flue gas analysis to the parameters set by the appliance manufacturer. Small adjustments can create significant problems with the safe operation of the appliance.

These controls are commonly used within the control train of air/gas ratio valves (see section 7.2.6).

7.2.6 Air/ Gas Ratio Control

Air/gas ratio control valves are used extensively on modern appliances due to their exceptional capability to modulate over a wide range. This becomes important when achieving higher efficiency on the appliance operation. The majority of these controls operate on the same principles with variation on design determined by the appliance manufacturer.

As mentioned previously this type of control incorporates a zero rated regulator and in most accounts operate at a 1:1 ratio between the gas and air, for example if the fan produces a negative pressure of say 3 mbar the valve will deliver gas at a positive pressure of 3 mbar.

The gas is induced into the air stream normally through some form of measured orifice. This can be the likes of a small bore open ended pipe, injector, restrictor plate or threaded bush fitting.

The air flow to the burner is controlled by means of a multi-speed fan unit. The speed of the fan unit is dictated by some form of electronic control either on the fan itself or by way of a PCB or in some accounts both. The configuration of the air/gas ratio control is dictated by the location of the point at where the gas is induced into the air stream relative to the fan. This point may be either on the positive or negative side of the fan unit.

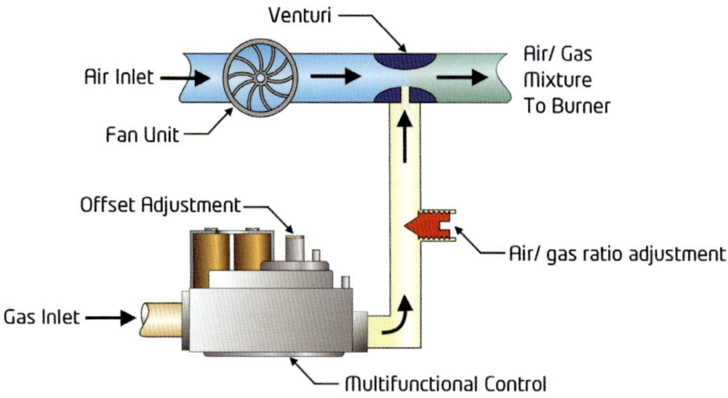

Figure 7.10 Air/ Gas Ratio Valve with gas connected to positive side of fan.

Figure 7.10 illustrates the connection of the gas supply to the positive side of the fan unit. As air is pushed through the venturi it generates a negative pressure at the throat enough to suck gas into the air stream. The amount of negative pressure generated is relative to the speed of the fan. If the fan speeds up or slows down, the amount of gas induced will increase or decrease accordingly, maintaining the correct air/ gas ratio for complete combustion. The gas is mixed with the air stream as it flows to the burner.

The configuration for the gas connected to the negative side of the fan is represented in figures 7.11 and 7.12. In this type of system all connections and tapping are maintained at a negative pressure reducing the risk of leakage. The gas may be induced into the air stream either by a fixed orifice opening within the air stream, with or without a venturi, or connected directly to the inlet of the fan unit. With this system an additional impulse tube may be connected to the top of the sensing diaphragm. The tube may be connected into the incoming air stream or a pressurised chamber within the appliance (figure 7.12). The pressurised chamber normally houses the burner, combustion chamber, heat exchanger, fan unit and associated controls and pipework. A sealed cover encloses the chamber to allow access for maintenance and repair. The impulse tube, where fitted, must be connected to it's associated point(s) on the appliance as the pressure from this point is used to "load" the top of the sensing diaphragm. Failure to connect this tube will result in the incorrect operation of the air/ gas ratio control which may result in high CO levels within the flue gases.

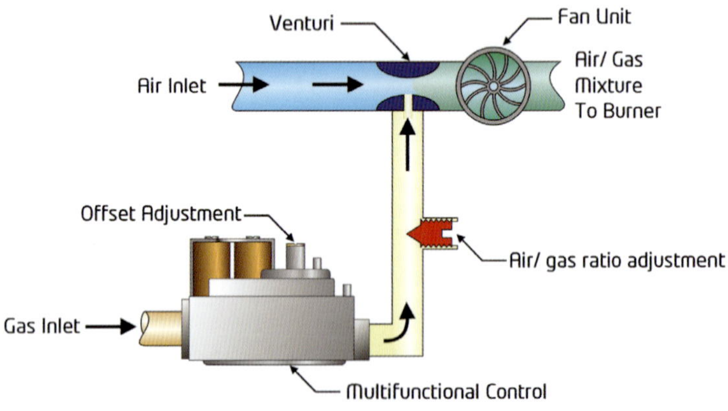

Figure 7.11 Air/ Gas Ratio Valve with gas connected to negative side of fan

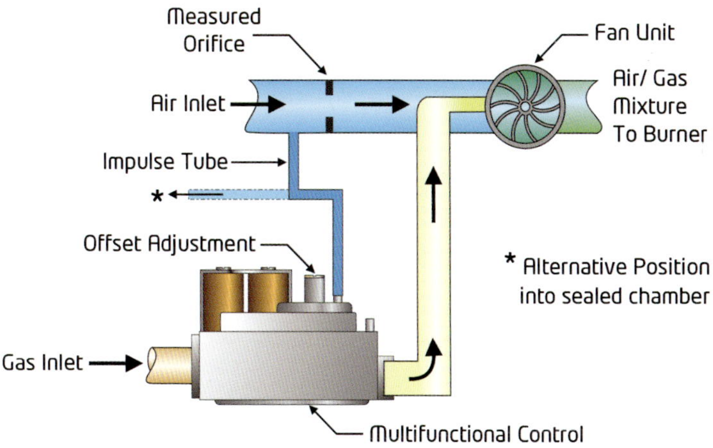

Figure 7.12 Air/ Gas Ratio Valve with gas connected to negative side of fan with impulse tube

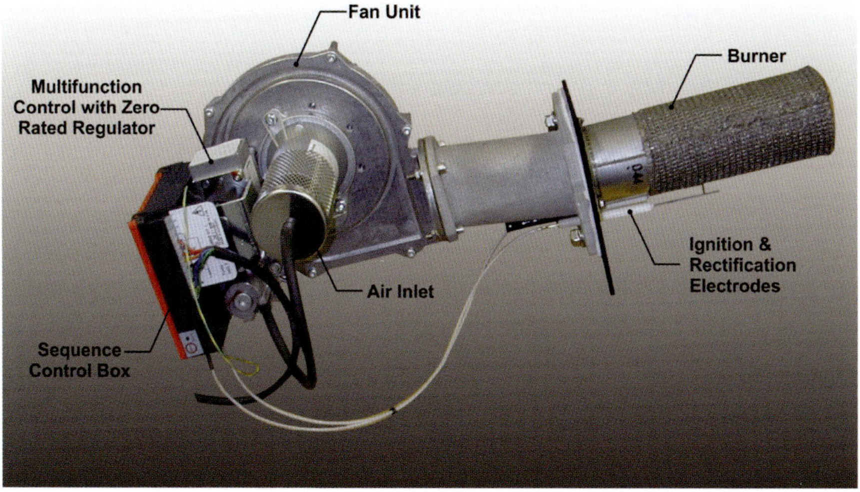

Figure 7.13 Air/ Gas Ratio Valve, fan and burner assembly

7.2.6.1 Adjusting Air/ Gas Ratio Valves

Any adjustment of an air/gas ratio valve MUST be carried out with strict adherence to the appliance manufacturers specific instruction. Some manufacturers do not allow adjustment of this valve. In this case under no circumstances should any adjustment be made. When tested and it is found the valve does not operate within specified parameters then a replacement must be installed. Unauthorised adjustment can result in poor combustion performance which can cause flame distortion resulting in damage to boiler components and high levels of carbon monoxide being created.

Where adjustment is authorised there is normally only two settings which can be altered, namely air/ gas ratio and offset. The fan speed control is normally factory preset with any adjustment reserved for the manufacturer or an agent acting on their behalf. Specialised manufacturers training is required.

Prior to adjusting any setting it is important that the inlet pressure to the appliance is measured and confirmed as satisfactory. In addition, flue gas analysis and/or a gas rate are normally required. Any person using a flue gas analyser must be proved competent to use the equipment and interpret any results obtained.

Air/gas ratio adjustment

Adjustment of the air/ gas ratio control may be either on the main valve, part of the venturi assembly or as a separate assembly within the gas stream. The adjuster facility may be also known as a throttle, ratio adjuster or obturator. The manufacturers instructions will indicate the relevant point of adjustment.

As mentioned previously, the air gas ratio valve requires the fan to suck in a measured quantity of gas relative to the air flow. Adjustment of the air/ gas ratio ensures that the optimum amount of gas is induced relative to the volume of air to achieve the best possible combustion results. An analysis of the flue gases is required to ensure that CO_2 and/or CO levels meet that as stated by the manufacturer. When taking any flue gas readings allow the results to stabilise after any adjustment before carrying out any further alteration.

This adjustment is normally performed at the appliances maximum gas rate.

Offset adjustment

When the gas pressure is equal and opposite to that generated by the air stream the offset is regarded as zero. When an appliance starts to modulate the pressures within the appliance and flue system changes. The levels of change are dictated by different factors such as flue orientation and length. Given this as the appliance modulates to it's minimum setting these factors can cause the air/gas ratio setting to alter slightly which can affect the combustion. To combat this we can slightly offset the gas against the air at the minimum setting to ensure satisfactory combustion through out the appliance modulating range. The location of the offset adjuster and comparable flue gas readings will be dictated by the appliance manufacturer. The gas is normally set slightly lower than the air pressure to achieve the best combustion results. This is referred to as a negative offset.

Due to the small pressure range involved in adjusting the offset a manometer which reads down to 2 decimal places may be required.

Final Performance Test

After any adjustment of an air/gas ratio valve it is advisable to recheck the inlet pressure and gas rate of the appliance to ensure that they are within the parameters set by the manufacturer.

7.3 Setting Primary Regulators

Pressure Profile

The pressure profile of a regulator is usually provided in the form of a graph and it details the performance of the device. A typical profile may appear as shown in figure 7.14. This shows that the device will provide an operating pressure within the tolerances of 21+/- 2 mbar provided the flow rate is not outside the minimum/maximum flow rates, the maximum flow rate being 6 m^3/h in this case. Therefore, when gas is flowing at 50% of capacity the pressure may be operating perfectly at 21 mbar. If the flow is reduced the operating pressure (OP) will increase and if the flow is increased the O.P. will decrease.

Engineers are unable to measure the O.P. of the regulator immediately at its outlet; the first downstream test point will be at the gas meter outlet connection. Although this will not be the true O.P. of the regulator as there will be pressure absorption through the meter (maximum of 4 mbar under full flow conditions) nonetheless it is the point where a measurement is taken.

When an operative is checking the operating pressure of an installation which has no appliances connected, the industry meter regulator test device must be used. This device should ideally provide a flow rate of 3 m^3/h but must not be less than 0.5 m^3/h.

To ensure we adjust the primary regulator to the correct operating pressure we require to have an adequate flow of gas in a similar range to that of the industry meter regulator test device. Industry states that we should have either the largest appliance in operation or, where that appliance is a gas cooker or hob, three of the hotplate burners. As seen from the pressure profile if we were to adjust the regulator with only a pilot or a small burner on, the valve would be very close to its seating since very little gas is required to maintain the outlet pressure. When an appliance is then turned on we would find the operating pressure is lower than that required. Alternatively if we set the regulator with all appliances on the valve would be fully open, hence when only one appliance is operated we would find the operating pressure above the desired value.

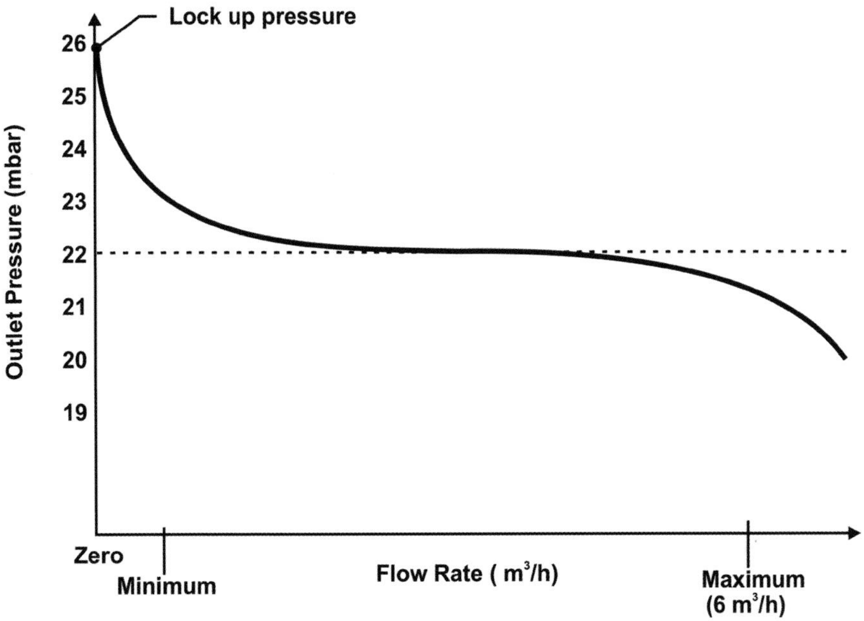

Figure 7.14 Regulator pressure profile

7.3.1 Standing Pressure

Standing Pressure is normally measured at the Meter Test Point and registers the pressure of gas in the installation when there is no gas being used. The main purpose of this measurement is to determine whether or not the meter regulator is closing properly. It is important to run an appliance for a short period of time as the gauge may be registering the initial "surge" pressure when the ECV is first opened.

Other Names:	**Lock up pressure**
	Static pressure
Typical Pressure:	**23 – 26 mbar**
Maximum Pressure:	**Not to exceed 30 mbar for**
	Low Pressure Installations
	Not to exceed 27.5 mbar for
	Med Pressure Fed Installations
Method:	**Gas "ON"**
	Operate appliance
	Appliance "OFF" (including pilots)
	Read Pressure

7.3.2 Operating Pressure (Low pressure systems)

Working pressure is also measured at the meter test point and is the pressure which the meter regulator provides at the meter outlet.

Other Names:	**Working pressure**
Expected Pressure:	**21 mbar ± 2 mbar**
Method:	**Gas "ON"**
	Operate the largest rated appliance at its maximum rate. If a cooker is used, with three hotplate burners on.

7.3.3 The logical sequence to combine these two procedures

- Turn the ECV off and connect a U-gauge to the meter test point.
- Turn the ECV on slowly (to prevent the water being blown from the gauge).
- Operate the appropriate number of appliances.
- Read the U-gauge for the OPERATING PRESSURE.
- Turn off the appliance(s) including pilot flame if applicable.
- Return to the U-gauge and read the STANDING PRESSURE.

7.3.4 Regulator Creep

This is a condition in which the valve has not formed an effective seal against its seat and although the valve has locked-up a small leakage (let-by) is occurring. If left e.g. overnight, the pressure in the outlet will rise to whatever the pressure is in the regulator's inlet. This could be anything up to 75 mbar in the case of a low pressure installation. This is a fault condition and should be rectified by the person responsible for the regulator.

7.4 Procedure For Checking Burner Pressure

This procedure must not be used as a substitute for the manufacturers specific instruction.

- Check and zero pressure gauge.
- Turn OFF the appliance to be tested.
- Locate the correct test point from which a reading will be taken (refer to manufacturers instructions).
- Remove or loosen the test point screw as required and connect a suitable pressure gauge. Ensure any tubing used is suitable and not damaged. Any escape of gas will affect the pressure recorded but more importantly may ignite off the naked flame of the burner.
- Turn the appliance on and allow the appliance to heat up until it's operating temperature has been achieved. The time take will be specified by the manufacturer but normally 10 minutes should suffice.
- Record the pressure reading and compare against the manufacturers recommended setting (see instructions or data badge).
- Adjust the pressure, where necessary, at the appliance regulator until a satisfactory reading has been recorded.
- Turn OFF the appliance and remove the pressure gauge.
- Tighten or reseal the burner test point.
- Turn on the appliance and check the test point for gas tightness using a suitable leak detection fluid.

8. Gas Industry Unsafe Situations Procedures

8.1 Dealing with Unsafe Situations in Customer's Premises

The Gas Industry Unsafe Situations Procedures (GIUSP) were born out of the fact that gas operatives required guidance to help identify, correctly classify and make safe any unsafe situation which they may encounter during their daily course of work. It must be noted that in all accounts any gas operative working on gas systems has a legal duty of care to the customer such that they must ensure that any gas installation in which they are involved with, whether directly or indirectly, does not pose a danger to life or property. To highlight any defect which may cause concern, the Gas Safety (Installation & Use) Regulations specifies the minimum checks which must be carried out to ensure an installation can be used safely. In the first instance, for existing appliances, reference should be made to the manufacturer's instruction as to any special requirements. Where an operative feels there is an unacceptable level of risk, these procedures outline how they should deal with the situation dependant on that level of risk.

The scope of the GIUSP covers all EXISTING installations and appliances using 1st, 2nd or 3rd family gases installed within both domestic and non-domestic premises (excluding industrial process).

All new appliance/installations must be installed and fully commissioned as per Manufacturers Instructions and any other relevant industry regulations and standards. Any new appliance/installation which is not commissioned must be disconnected from the gas supply and sealed using an appropriate fitting.
A "do not use" label must be attached until such commissioning has been done.

It must be recognised that when working in a customers' premises we cannot instinctively disconnect or turn off an installation and/or appliance without due regard to the customer. Under the Gas Safety (Rights of Entry) Regulations only officials of The Public Gas Transporters have the right to enter premises where there is a threat to life and/or property to make the installation safe. We have been invited into the customer's premises to do work, for this reason we must seek permission from the customer before we can take any further action.

The GIUSP provides the gas operative with a recommended procedure which is designed to assist them in meeting their legal obligations. It is their duty to warn the customer of any hazards which may exist and providing them with a recommended course of action. Specific labels and notices are used to document and highlight any defective installations and/or appliances. In all accounts our first communication with the customer will be verballty where the situation is explained and recommended actions given. This information is enforced by the application of labels to the defective installation/ appliances warning others of these dangers.

In addition written notification must then be given to the customer by way of a Warning Notice. The customer must sign this notice as proof that they clearly understand the situation and are fully aware of any hazards or potential hazards which may exist.. A copy is left with the customer and a further copy retained by yourself and your company. This is a legal document which could be used in a court of law.

8.1.1 Visual Risk Assessment of Gas Appliances

When working in a customers premise gas operatives may encounter other additional appliances not associated with the gas work they are doing, for example repairing a cooker with an open flue boiler located in the same room. In addition appliances may require to be relit after a temporary interruption to the gas supply either through isolation to allow work to be performed or cessation of supply due to failure of the network.

Even though no "work", as defined in the gas safety (installation and use) regulations, has been performed the gas operative is required to carry out a visual risk assessment of these appliances. The extent of which is dependant on whether or not an interruption of the gas supply has occurred.

Visual Risk Assessment With No Interruption to Supply:

The following five "trigger" points will require to be performed on existing appliances where no gas work has been undertaken. It should be noted that if the gas operative does perform any associated work with these appliances the safety checks as defined in regulation 26(9) must be carried out.

1. **Location** – Check whether the room and/or area is suitable for the appliance(s) installed and if it meets the requirements of the manufacturer, current industry legislation, standards and procedures.
2. **Stability and Security** – examine the appliance to ensure it is both stable and securely affixed such that it can operate safely under normal operating conditions.
3. **Ventilation** – Where appropriate, check if there is an adequate supply of ventilation for the appliance to operate safely.
4. **Flueing** – Examine any open-flued or room sealed appliance to ensure the flue system (including any casing seals) is intact and satisfactory for the removal of products to the outside atmosphere (note: this does not include a flue flow or spillage test only a visual inspection).
5. **Signs of Distress** – Check appliance and surrounding area for signs of discolouration, heat damage or spillage.

Visual Risk Assessment With a Temporary Interruption to Supply:
Where the gas supply has been interrupted for any reason and subsequently re-established, the appliances affected will require to be relit. In this occasion in addition to the five "trigger" points as mentioned, the gas operative is required to carry out an additional visual inspection of the flame picture.

There is no requirement by industry to record the results of any visual risk assessment, however it is recommended that the gas operative records that a visual risk assessment has been performed. Where an unsafe situation has been identified or is suspected, the GIUSP must be applied with appropriate action taken.

8.1.2 Non Domestic Installations

Due to the size and diversity of non-domestic installations all or part of the installation may not be within the scope of the Gas Safety (Installation and

Use) Regulations. To ensure we meet our legal obligations the same safety principles contained within the industry unsafe situations can be applied to determine the level of risk.

The responsible person must be consulted in all accounts before taking any action with regard to unsafe situations. Provision of accurate records and test results will assist the responsible person in ascertaining the level of risk and action required. Only in extreme circumstances where any delay in contact with the responsible person would result in an immediate danger to life and/ or property should any non-domestic installation be shut down without prior consultation with the responsible person.

In some instances isolation of the gas supply may create a substantially higher level of risk depending on the nature of the installation. Some industrial processes require specific shut down procedures to prevent not only extensive damage to plant and equipment but also to reduce any immediate health and safety issues such as the release of toxic gases or explosion. These shut down procedures may take from a few hour to days. Re-establishment due to uncontrolled shut down may also introduce additional lengthy complex procedures.

Other premises which may require due regard with the effects of immediate isolation of the gas supply are for example hospitals, care homes, research facilities, animal housings such as reptile enclosures etc. Substantial evacuation procedures may be required.

8.1.3 Hierarchy of Documentation

Legislation, standards and procedures used within the gas industry evolve and change continuously. For the gas operative to apply good engineering judgment, experience and a fundamental knowledge of current legislation, standards and procedures is important. The hierarchy of documentation is designed to assist the gas operative to understand the level of requirement associated with each document from legal to advisory status. However, it does not detach from the importance of each document, no matter on it's position within this hierarchy, in achieving safe working practices. The list provided should not be regarded as definitive.

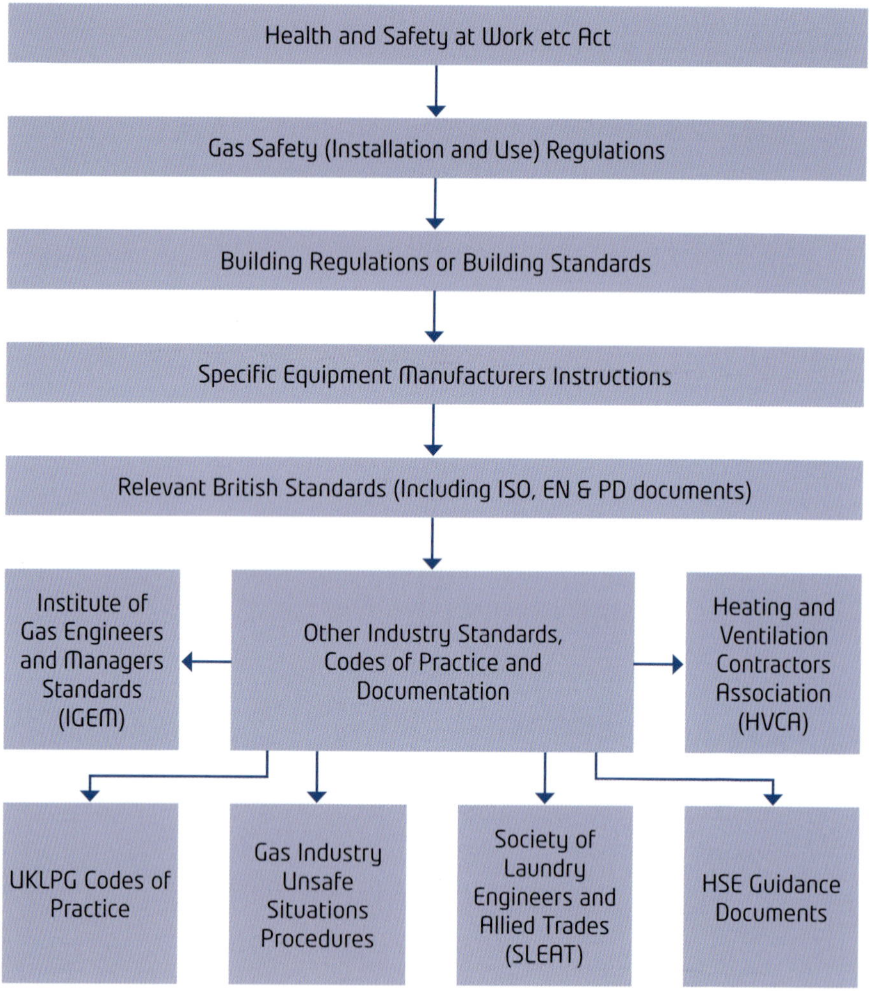

Hierarchy of Gas Legislation, Standards and Procedures

8.2 Reporting of Injuries, Diseases and Dangerous Occurrences Regulations (RIDDOR)

It is a statutory requirement of all members of a class of persons approved by the Health and Safety Executive (HSE) to report any unsafe situation which they have reason to believe has caused or may cause a danger to any persons from:

- An accidental leakage of gas, or
- Inadequate combustion, or
- Inadequate removal of combustion products.

Normally an installation only becomes reportable when the fault has been incurred through:

- Design
- Construction
- Installation methods
- Modification
- Servicing
- Some active operation on the installation

Where the faults are due to wear and tear, lack of maintenance or customer neglect there is no need to report the situation. However, where the fault has resulted in an incident or has been so serious that the installation has been disconnected on safety grounds, it should be reported. In all accounts the Gas Safe registered installer must exercise the unsafe situations procedure to make the installation safe.

RIDDOR Regulation 6(1) applies where there has been an incident which has resulted in death or major injury. This normally applies to carbon monoxide poisoning, fire or explosion. To report such an incident the form F250G1 is used. As soon as basic information has been gathered the HSE must be contacted within 2 hours of attending the incident (normally by a phone call) with a full report within 14 working days.

RIDDOR Regulation 6(2) applies to any other reportable situations. The form F250G2 is used. These types of situations must be reported to the HSE within 14 working days of discovery.

Any reports must be made directly to the HSE by telephone, fax, internet, email or post.

The following is a list of situations which may be reportable under RIDDOR:

1. Installations where there is a gas leak outside the tolerances of a tightness test as a result of poor workmanship or unsatisfactory fittings
2. Uncapped or open-ended pipework connected to the gas supply
3. Gas appliances which are spilling products of combustion, or show past signs of spillage with no evidence that the fault has been rectified
4. Defective flues or chimneys where they are not clearing the products of combustion
5. Any gas appliances which must be flued but are not (remember some radiant tube heaters can be flued or un-flued)
6. Appliances which are not suitable for the gas being supplied (for example natural gas appliances used with LPG)
7. Where any safety device has been rendered inoperative, for example a flame supervision device
8. Where an appliance is connected to the gas supply through a fitting made of inappropriate materials for example garden hose
9. Any appliances which are dangerous through faulty servicing

8.3 Unsafe Situations Categories

There are three different categories of unsafe situations depending on the level of hazard which exists, however a fourth has been introduced specifically for the Emergency Service Operative and is not used by any other gas operative. These are:

- Immediately Dangerous
- At Risk
- Not To Current Standards
- Concern for Safety (only used by ESP)

8.3.1 Immediately Dangerous (ID)

This is where an appliance/installation which, if operated or left connected to the gas supply, **WILL POSE AN IMMEDIATE DANGER TO LIFE AND/OR PROPERTY**. In general terms there are three main situations which would warrant the application of an ID classification, namely **gas escapes, spillage from a flued appliance and incomplete combustion from a flueless appliance**. If any fault within the installation has created any one of these situations then the installation may be classified as ID.

The following procedure should be employed.

- Explain situation to user/responsible person
- With their permission, try to repair any defect to make the installation safe to use
- Where the defect cannot be repaired there and then, affix a **DO NOT USE** label to the appliance/installation
- Complete a **WARNING NOTICE**, ask the responsible person to sign, leave a copy on site
- With their permission **DISCONNECT & SEAL** the gas supply
- If the customer refuses to sign the warning notice, record this on the notice and job card and still leave a copy on site
- If the customer refuses to allow disconnection of the gas supply, **endeavour to turn off appliance** and immediately contact Gas Emergency Service Call Centre

8.3.2 At Risk (AR)

This is where an appliance/installation, which if operated or left connected to the gas supply **MAY IN THE FUTURE CREATE A DANGER** to Life or Property. Again we can look at the three main general terms as specified in 8.3.1. If there is a potential to create these situations then the installation can be classed as AR.

The following procedure should be employed.

- Explain situation to user/responsible person
- With their permission, try and repair any defect to make the installation safe to use
- Where the defect cannot be repaired there and then, affix a **DO NOT USE** label to the appliance/ installation
- Complete a **WARNING NOTICE** and get the responsible person to sign, and leave a copy on site
- With their permission **TURN OFF** the appliance/installation, **DO NOT** disconnect
- If the customer refuses to sign the warning notice, record this on the notice and job card and still leave a copy on site
- If the customer refuses to turn off the appliance, indicate that it is an offence under the GSIUR to operate appliance/installation and record this on the notice and job sheet.

8.3.3 Not To Current Standards (NCS)

This is where an existing appliance/ installation does not meet the criteria laid down in current Standards, Procedures and Codes of Practice. The appliance/installation must be operating safely and **NOT POSE A RISK OR DANGER TO LIFE OR PROPERTY.**

Any NCS situation which falls within the categories 1 or 2 as stated MUST be notified to the gas user/responsible person, if the situation relates to <u>an appliance</u>. It is left to the operative's discretion to notify any other faults which may come within these categories. It is recommended that any notified NCS is done in writing using an appropriate advice notice which is signed with a copy left with the gas user/responsible person.

Please note: Customers are under no obligation to repair these defects, if the defects do not constitute a matter of safety. **However, where a natural draught open-flued or flueless appliance has been identified as having two or more NCS faults on the flue and/or ventilation, it may be treated as an At Risk situation.**

8.3.4 Concern for Safety.

The duties and responsibilities of the gas emergency service is primarily to respond to any reported escape of gas. As indicated in the Gas safety (Installation and Use) Regulations an escape of gas can include fumes from an appliance. Emergency service operatives normally have a limited scope of competence and as such when called to a property where there has been a reported smell of fumes they are only required to carry out a visual risk assessment of the installation. Where the installation has been found gas tight and there are no visual signs of an ID or AR situation, the appliance will be turned off with a concern for safety label attached. This label is used to make the customer aware that the appliance(s) has not been tested and confirmed safe to use. The safe operation of the appliance(s) can only be confirmed by an appropriately competent member of a class of persons approved by the Health and Safety Executive (HSE).

Table 8.1 Examples of Unsafe Situation Classification

1 Situation	2 Category	3 RIDDOR	4 Additional Information	5 Regulations
UNBURNT GAS ESCAPES				
From Primary Meter Installation with capped outlet.	ID	R*	* Where due to the use of unsatisfactory fittings or workmanship.	GS(I&U)R, 37
Downstream of ECV (including Primary Meter Installation). (1) Outside tolerance of tightness test. (2) Within tolerance of tightness test with a detectable smell of gas.	 ID ID	 R* R*	* Where due to the use of unsatisfactory fittings or workmanship.	GS(I&U)R, 37
Fire/Explosions.	ID	R#	Make gas installation safe (i.e. turn off). Wherever possible, do not disturb the installation pending investigation. # Report to NGT if cause of death or major injury	GS(I&U)R, 37 GS(M)R
METERS/PRESSURE REGULATION				
Meter/ regulator showing clear signs of damage from, for example: • corrosive atmosphere, • mechanical damage • contact with electrical equipment.	AR		• Primary meters inform the Gas Emergency Service on 0800 111 999 • Secondary meters Inform the "responsible person".	GS(I&U)R, 7

Table 8.1 Examples of Unsafe Situation Classification (continued)

No pressure regulation at primary meter.	ID	R	Inform the Gas Emergency Service Call Centre (0800 111 999) Note: Where LPG/Air is in use, there may be no requirement for a meter regulator (check with the Gas Supplier).	GS(I&U)R, 14
Let-by of any ECV, which forms part of a tightness test	AR		• Primary ECV inform the Gas Emergency Service on 0800 111 999 • Additional ECV's Inform "responsible person". Note: if smell of gas, must be treated as ID	GS(I&U)R
No main equipotential bonding at meter or in wrong position	NCS		Inform the responsible person.	GS(I&U)R, 18 (2)
Where required, no gas supply line diagram fixed at primary meter.	NCS		Inform the responsible person.	GS(I&U)R, 17 & 24
Medium pressure installation with no MIV	NCS		Inform the Gas Transporter.	GS(I&U)R
Incorrect gas pressure to the inlet of a gas appliance caused by either: • Installation pipework. • Meter Regulator or Network capacity (inform ESP).	(see note)		Note: • If Manufacturers minimum specified burner pressure is achieved when all appliances operational – NCS. • If incorrect pressure affects the safe operation of the appliance – ID/AR as appropriate.	GS(I&U)R -26 & 33 GS(M)R

Table 8.1 Examples of Unsafe Situation Classification (continued)

Meter Box/Compartment				
Point of gas to enter building from a meter box for example, damaged box or pipe entering building from meter box which is not sleeved.	AR		Inform the gas user to either replace or repair meter box and/or sleeve and seal gas pipework.	GS(I&U)R, 13
Medium pressure pipework entering a building from within a meter box.	AR			GS(I&U)R 13
Medium pressure fed meter installation where the low pressure gas pipe and/or MEB cable enters the property from within the meter box via the rear exit spigot.	AR		Further risk assessment work will be undertaken to determine the actions that should be taken to manage the risk posed, see Gas Safe TB 004	GSIUR
Reports Of "Fumes"				
Carbon Monoxide Detector alarm sounds or fumes reported: (1) Flued appliances: Spillage/leakage of POC's occurring, or signs of occurrence (with no evidence that the problem has been corrected). (2) Flueless appliances: Evidence of poor combustion occurring.	ID ID	R* R*	• Observe adjacent appliance(s) for satisfactory flame picture. • Examine and test for spillage as appropriate. • Visually check all other appliances in the property for safety. • Consider CO migration from another property. • Once satisfied that the appliance(s) is safe, it may be put back into operation. * If due to the use of unsatisfactory fittings or workmanship.	GS(I&U)R 37

Table 8.1 Examples of Unsafe Situation Classification (continued)

Installation Pipework				
Pipework, with an open end connected to a gas supply.	ID	R	Seal the pipework with an appropriate fitting.	GS(I&U)R, 6(2)(3)
Pipework suitable for the gas being used but in an inappropriate location/situation.	AR	R	For example PE within a building or exposed above ground PE without suitable protection.	GS(I&U)R, 7(1)
Where an emergency exists i.e gas escape with no access to the ECV or no handle on the ECV.	ID		Advise user/responsible person access is required at all times, and report to the ESP immediately.	GS(I&U)R, 9
No access to the ECV or no handle on the ECV where no emergency exists.	AR		Advise user/responsible person access is available at all times, and report to the ESP.	GS(I&U)R, 9
Restricted access to any ECV.	AR		Advise user/responsible person access is available at all times, and report to the ESP.	GS(I&U)R, 9
No additional ECV at point of entry to a building where there is no adequate access to the primary ECV.	AR		Advise user/responsible person.	GS(I&U)R, 9, 24
Pipework showing signs of damage liable to affect safety.	AR		Pipework not suitable protected against corrosion and positioned where it may suffer damage, but showing no visible signs of corrosion or damage may be treated as NCS.	GS(I&U)R, 7(1)
Pipework in unventilated duct/void or located within a cavity (not passing through by the shortest route).	AR		If the pipework is just unsleeved but passes through the cavity by the shortest route it is categorised as NCS.	GS(I&U)R, 19 (2)

Table 8.1 Examples of Unsafe Situation Classification (continued)

Pipework which passes through a wall sleeved but not sealed.	NCS		Seal sleeve if appropriate.	GS(I&U)R, 19(4)
Inadequately supported pipework.	NCS			GS(I&U)R, 7(1)
Pipework significantly undersized such that it is preventing the appliance to operate at the Manufacturers intended minimum heat input rating or affecting the safe operation of the appliance.	AR		If the undersized pipewcrk does not affect the safe operation of the appliance or affect the minimum heat input the installation may be treated as NCS.	GS(I&U)R 26,33
Air Supply (Ventilation)				
Open-flued or flueless appliances requiring purpose provided permanent ventilation where none is provided.	AR		For factory units, other forms of ventilation may be considered.	GS(I&U)R 26,33
Open-flued appliances installed in a compartment requiring purpose provided high and low level ventilation where the ventilation provision is less than 90% of the calculated ventilation requirement for each ventilator.	AR		For non-domestic plant / boiler rooms refer to manufacturer's instructions or where appropriate the relevant industry standards.	GS(I&U)R 26,33

Table 8.1 Examples of Unsafe Situation Classification (continued)

Open-flued or flueless appliance in rooms and internal spaces requiring a purpose provided permanent combustion air supply with 0% to 89% of requirement.	AR		90% to 100% is acceptable, however for non-domestic installations reference must be made to Manufacturers Instruction and Industry standards.	GS(I&U)R 26 (9)
Air supply vents which incorporate gauze/fly screen or closeable.	AR		Gauzes and fly screens do not apply to Commercial Catering establishments or Leisure activity vehicles where pest control is required. As long the mesh is clean and the vent is installed to the relevant standards.	GS(I&U)R 26 (9)
Flueless appliances installed within a room of inadequate size irrespective of ventilation provision.	AR		For minimum room volume requirements, reference must be made to the Manufacturers instructions.	GS(I&U)R 26 (9)
Open Flued Appliances.				
Incomplete or damaged flue or inadequate fixing/sealing.	AR		Examples include missing down draught diverter, flue terminal and inadequate support.	GS(I&U)R 27
Appliance connected to an unlined brick chimney, which requires to be lined due to poor condition where the POC are not leaking into the building.	AR			GS(I&U)R 27
POC's leaking into building including flues terminating in loft space.	ID	R*	* if due to the use of unsatisfactory fittings or workmanship.	GS(I&U)R 27

Table 8.1 Examples of Unsafe Situation Classification (continued)

Open Flued Appliances continued				
Automatic flue damper not interlocked to appliance gas supply.	AR			GS(I&U)R, (32)
• Flue operating satisfactory but less than 600mm rise before first bend (unless otherwise permitted by Manufacturer). • 90o bends or horizontal runs. • Unsatisfactory termination positions. • Incorrect use of flue material. Undersized flue with no evidence of adverse operation. Unsuitable flue terminals.	NCS		Where more than one flueing and /or ventilation NCS is identified, the installation must be assessed with due regard to safety. If the deficiencies are serious enough the installation may be treated as AR.	GS(I&U)R, 27
Any mechanically assisted flueing or ventilation system which is not interlocked to the gas supply.	AR		For commercial catering installations we must refer to catering sheet 23 where a risk assessment will ascertain the level of unsafe category.	GS(I&U)R, 27
Forced convection air heater with fan assisted air circulation installed in a plant room with inadequate provision for a return air path.(see note)	AR		Where the level of ventilation is adequate within the non domestic environment such that we do not depressurize the room affecting flue performance the installation may be regarded as NCS.	GS(I&U)R, 27

Table 8.1 Examples of Unsafe Situation Classification (continued)

Room Sealed Appliances				
Flue terminations located in positions where the products of combustion could enter the premises e.g next to air vents, windows, doors etc. After an indoor air quality assessment it has been found that products are entering the premises with levels in excess of acceptable limits as specified in BS 7967 e.g CO greater than 10ppm and rising.	ID	R*	Indoor concentration is measured using an electronic combustion gas analyser (ECGA) in accordance with the procedures contained in BS 7967 part 2. It should be recognised that this test is subject to prevailing ambient conditions, Where levels have not been confirmed the customer should be advised if the problem persists to contact the ESP, turn off appliance & ventilate.	GSIUR, 27
Fan assisted positive pressure type appliance with ineffectively sealed casing.	ID	R*	Further guidance can be found in Technical bulletin TB 006	GSIUR, 27
Flues in Voids				
A flue system in an enclosure/ceiling which is showing signs of distress or where there is a break in the flue with no access to carry out further investigation.	ID	R	Where appropriate a risk assessment and flue gas analysis should be carried out. If the premise is part of a number of similar properties in a block or complex, include an approximate number of properties in report summary. Further guidance can be found in Technical bulletin TB 008	GSIUR, 27 & 28

Table 8.1 Examples of Unsafe Situation Classification (continued)

No access or inadequate access to allow a satisfactory visual inspection of the chimney system and route. This may be an individual dwelling or include a number of properties in which the chimney passes through.	see note		Where a risk assessment has been carried out and no further deficiencies are evident with the chimney system and a suitable CO detector is fitted, the system may be left operational until 31st Dec 2012. Operatives may work on these appliances up to this date. The customer must be advised that after this date, if inspection hatches have not been provided, the installation will be classed as AT Risk and must not be used until access has been provided. Refer to Technical bulletin TB 008 Ed 2 for more specific information	GSIUR, 27 & 28
Chimneys - General				
Signs of distress on chimney system e.g damage such as cracking or condensate leakage from joint.	AR	R	A risk assessment should be carried out. If the premise is part of a number of similar properties in a block or complex, include an approximate number of properties in report summary.	GSIUR, 27 & 28
After carrying out a visual inspection of the chimney system it has been found that it is insecure or inadequately supported.	AR		Check for evidence such as insufficient clipping (check manufacturers instruction where applicable) and sagging.	

Table 8.1 Examples of Unsafe Situation Classification (continued)

Unsatisfactory combustion reading when using an electronic flue gas analyser on an appliance which incorporates an air/gas ratio valve. CO/CO2 reading above 0.008 CO/CO2 reading between 0.004 and 0.008	ID AR	R	Refer to specific appliance Manufacturers instruction, TB 126 or appropriate tables within BS 7967	
Incorrect grade of plastic chimney system material showing signs of distress, for example warping, discolouration, or where the entire chimney system cannot be fully visually inspected.	AR		Where the chimney system is not showing signs of distress and where there is adequate access for inspection along its full length including all joints and is adequately supported then the installation may be classified as NCS.	
Incorrect jointing methods used for chimney system eg. Screws missing from mechanical joints or non appropriate lubricant used on push-fit fittings	AR			
Appliances - General				
Appliances which must be flued but are not.	ID	R		GS(I&U)R, 27
Appliances which are unsafe due to lack of maintenance.	ID			GS(I&U)R, 26

Table 8.1 Examples of Unsafe Situation Classification (continued)

Appliances not suitable for the gas supplied.	ID	R	This is more prevalent where a NG appliance is used on LPG.	GS(I&U)R, 26
Gas controls and safety devices that affect the safe operation of the gas appliance, which are inoperable, failing to danger or are disabled.	ID	R*	* if due to the use of unsatisfactory fittings or workmanship.	GS(I&U)R 26
Evidence of distress to adjacent combustible materials.	AR			GS(I&U)R
Appliances which are found to be insecure or unstable so that they are potentially unsafe.	AR			GS(I&U)R
Situation where an appliance may be a potential source of ignition within a hazardous area.	AR		Refer to IM 28 and other industry standards on the location and use of appliances within these areas. Example of a hazardous area is a commercial garage.	GS(I&U)R
Boosted Gas Supplies				
Low pressure protection not fitted, bypassed or inoperable.	AR			
Non-return valve not fitted, or if fitted not functioning.	AR			GS(I&U)R, 38
Pressure raising equipment in an inappropriate or inadequately ventilated location or incorrectly installed	AR			GS(I&U)R

Table 8.1 Examples of Unsafe Situation Classification (continued)

Commercial Catering				
Appliances with enclosed burners with no flame supervision device.	AR		Where existing appliances are operated only by trained personnel the installation can be regarded as NCS. Refer to catering sheets 3 and 23	GS(I&U)R
Deep fat fryers and other appliances where the high limit stat is required, but is failing to operate or is not fitted.	AR			GS(I&U)R
Power extract system with no provision for air entry (make up air).	AR			GS(I&U)R
Non-Domestic Meter Installations.				
Non-domestic meter installation ventilated internally into boiler house or plant room.	AR		Any ventilation must communicate directly with outside air.	GS(I&U)R 13(1)
No line diagram affixed to primary meter installation where required.	NCS			GS(I&U)R, 24
Insufficient ventilation into meter compartment.	NCS			GS(I&U)R 13(1)

9. Gas Rate & Heat Input

To meet the requirements of the Gas Safety (Installation and Use) Regulations, when we perform work on a gas appliance we are required to take either a burner pressure or heat input or where necessary both (Regulation 26/9). In most occasions, normally with atmospheric burners, taking the burner pressure is sufficient to determine whether or not an appliance has been set to burn the correct amount of gas as specified by the Manufacturer. However, in some circumstances the burner pressure may not be enough to determine the correct operation of the appliance. This becomes more evident with high efficiency appliances which use air/gas ratio valves incorporating zero rated regulators. These appliances normally require a heat input calculation in addition to a combustion analysis as part of their commissioning procedure.

9.1 Gas Rate

Before we can determine the heat input of any appliance we must initially calculate the gas rate. This being the quantity of gas used by an appliance in a specific period of time, normally one hour.

The gas rate is measured in either:

- Imperial – ft^3/hr
- Metric – m^3/hr

9.1.1 Imperial Calculation

Imperial meters have a small circular dial which we call the test dial. One full revolution of this dial indicates a specific quantity of gas used in ft^3. This could be 1, 2, 5 or 10 ft^3 depending on the size of the meter. To calculate the gas rate we time one complete revolution of this test dial, measured in seconds.

Figure 9.1: Imperial Test Dial

Insert the time for one complete revolution into the following formula.

$$\text{Gas Rate (ft}^3\text{/hr)} = \frac{3600 \times \text{Number of ft}^3 \text{ per rev. of test dial}}{\text{Time taken for one complete revolution (sec)}}$$

3600 represents the number of seconds in one hour

Note: The appliance should be operated for a sufficient period of time, normally 10 minutes, to allow it to heat up. Make sure all appliance and external controls such as room and boiler stats are set at a level which is high enough to ensure the appliance will stay on during the test duration. Modern appliances normally have a commissioning setting which will lock the appliance at a desired setting and stop modulation (remember and reset the control to "run" mode after a satisfactory calculation has been obtained).

Example:

When checking the gas rate of a gas fire from an imperial gas meter with a 1 ft^3 test dial. The dial took 2 minutes and 45 seconds (165 seconds) for one complete revolution.

$$\text{Gas rate (ft}^3\text{/hr)} = \frac{3600 \times 1 \text{ ft}^3}{165 \text{ seconds}}$$

$$= 21.82 \text{ ft}^3\text{/hr}$$ (answer rounded up to 2 decimal places)

9.1.2 Metric Calculation

Since a metric meter does not have a test dial, the gas rate is calculated using a different method. As we can see from figure 9.2, the index of the meter is split into two distinct sections. The five drums within the black surround represent m^3, the further three drums in the red surround are dm^3. To calculate the gas rate we log the first reading on the meter. After a minimum of 2 minutes we will then log a second reading. Please note the time duration and index reading are logged when the unit dm^3 drum or digital readout turns to the nearest whole number. To calculate the gas rate we use the following formula:

$$\text{Gas Rate (m}^3\text{/h)} = \frac{\text{(2nd reading - 1st reading)} \times 3600}{\text{Time taken (sec)}}$$

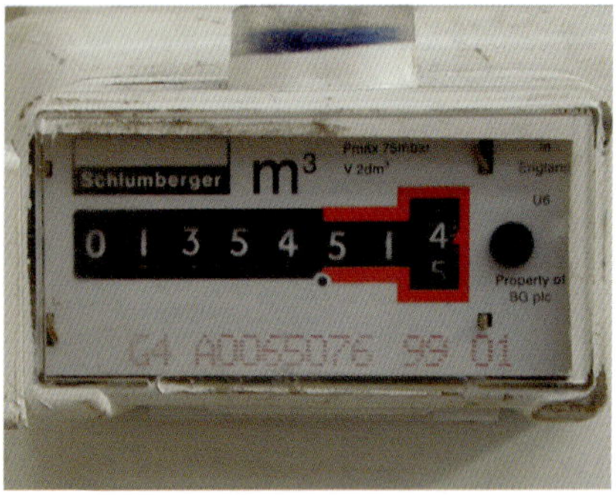

Figure 9.2: Metric Meter

Example:

The test dial on a metric G4 meter at the start and end of the test period is given below. The time taken was 2 minutes and 3 seconds (123 seconds). The extra time was due to the unit dial reaching the nearest whole number.

1st Reading at start of test

2nd Reading at end of test

$$\textbf{Gas Rate (m3/h)} = \frac{(2.436 - 2.415) \times 3600}{123 \text{ seconds}}$$

$$= \frac{0.021 \times 3600}{123 \text{ seconds}}$$

$$= 0.615 m^3/h$$ (answer rounded up to 3 decimal places)

9.2 Heat Input

The heat input is the amount of heat produced by an appliance in a given time. When we have measured the quantity of gas used by an appliance by calculating the gas rate, we use the Calorific value of the gas to determine the amount of heat energy generated by that quantity of gas. To ensure accurate calculation an up to date calorific value may be obtained from either the customers energy bill or from their supplier.

The heat input can be measured in either:

- Imperial measurement – btu/hr
- Metric measurement – kW

Today most Manufacturers give the appliance rated heat input as a metric NET value.

The calculation to convert gross to net heat input is:

Net heat input = gross heat input ÷ 1.11

The heat input can be calculated by either imperial or metric methods. Again this will depend on what type of meter was used to calculate the gas rate. We must remember that when we physically calculate the heat input, the result will be gross and **NOT** net. We can only measure all the gases passing through the meter.

9.2.1 Imperial Calculation

Heat Input (btu/hr) = Gas Rate (ft^3/hr) x Calorific Value (btu/ft^3)

An average imperial calorific value would be 1040 btu/ft^3. **To convert btu/hr to kW we divide by 3412.**

Example:

If we take the example from section 9.1.1 we calculated the gas rate as 21.82 ft^3/hr. If we use this figure and place it into the equation above we can calculate the heat input of the gas fire.

Heat Input (btu/hr) $= 21.82\ ft^3/hr \times 1040\ btu/ft^3$

$= 22{,}693\ btu/hr$

Convert to kW $= 22{,}693\ btu/hr \div 3412$

$= 6.65$ **kW Gross (5.99 kW net)**

9.2.2 Metric Calculation

$$\text{Heat Input (kW)} = \frac{\text{Gas Rate } (m^3/hr) \times \text{Calorific Value } (MJ/m^3)}{3.6}$$

An average metric calorific value would be 38.76 MJ/m^3. 3.6 is a constant which converts MJ/hr into kW.

Example:

If we take the example from section 9.1.2 we calculated the gas rate as 0.615 m^3/h. If we use this figure and place it into the equation above we can calculate the heat input using the calorific value 38.76 MJ/m^3.

$$\text{Heat Input (kW)} = \frac{\text{Gas Rate } (m^3/hr) \times \text{Calorific Value } (MJ/m^3)}{3.6}$$

$$= \frac{0.615\ m^3/h \times 38.76\ MJ/m^3}{3.6}$$

$= 6.6215$ **kW Gross (5.97 kW net)**

9.2.3 Heat Input Tables (Net)

The following tables are provided as a quick references when calculating the NET heat input of an appliance. The net value is given as most manufacturers state the heat input as a net value. An average calorific value is used for ease of calculation.

Imperial Meter - Natural Gas (average calorific value 1040 btu/ft³)										
sec	kW Heat input (Net)									
	0	1	2	3	4	5	6	7	8	9
0		989.51	494.76	329.84	247.38	197.90	164.92	141.36	123.69	109.95
10	98.95	89.96	82.46	76.12	70.68	65.97	61.84	58.21	54.97	52.08
20	49.48	47.12	44.98	43.02	41.23	39.58	38.06	36.65	35.34	34.12
30	32.98	31.92	30.92	29.99	29.10	28.27	27.49	26.74	26.04	25.37
40	24.74	24.13	23.56	23.01	22.49	21.99	21.51	21.05	20.61	20.19
50	19.79	19.40	19.03	18.67	18.32	17.99	17.67	17.36	17.06	16.77
60	16.49	16.22	15.96	15.71	15.46	15.22	14.99	14.77	14.55	14.34
70	14.14	13.94	13.74	13.55	13.37	13.19	13.02	12.85	12.69	12.53
80	12.37	12.22	12.07	11.92	11.78	11.64	11.51	11.37	11.24	11.12
90	10.99	10.87	10.76	10.64	10.53	10.42	10.31	10.20	10.10	10.00
100	9.90	9.80	9.70	9.61	9.51	9.42	9.34	9.25	9.16	9.08
110	9.00	8.91	8.83	8.76	8.68	8.60	8.53	8.46	8.39	8.32
120	8.25	8.18	8.11	8.04	7.98	7.92	7.85	7.79	7.73	7.67
130	7.61	7.55	7.50	7.44	7.38	7.33	7.28	7.22	7.17	7.12
140	7.07	7.02	6.97	6.92	6.87	6.82	6.78	6.73	6.69	6.64
150	6.60	6.55	6.51	6.47	6.43	6.38	6.34	6.30	6.26	6.22
160	6.18	6.15	6.11	6.07	6.03	6.00	5.96	5.93	5.89	5.86
170	5.82	5.79	5.75	5.72	5.69	5.65	5.62	5.59	5.56	5.53
180	5.50	5.47	5.44	5.41	5.38	5.35	5.32	5.29	5.26	5.24

Table 1 - Imperial Meter Heat Input

Table 1 is based on a U6 meter with a 1ft³ test dial. It is divided into tens (left hand side column) and units (3rd top row) seconds. Take for example the test dial took 67 seconds for one complete revolution. Go down the LHS column to 60 then along the row until you reach the 7 unit column this will give you a net heat input of 14.77 kW. Where the test dial is more than 1 ft³ per rev, multiply the figure given in the table by the number of ft³ on the test dial to calculate the required heat input. For example if you had a 5 ft³ test dial and it took 67 seconds for one complete rev, this would give a heat input of 14.77 kW multiply this by 5 and it will give you the actual heat input for that meter, in this case 73.85 kW.

Tables 3 and 4 are for metric meters based on a test time of 120 sec.

Metric Meter - Natural gas (average calorific value 38.76 MJ/ m³)										
dm³	kW net Heat input (Net)									
	0	1	2	3	4	5	6	7	8	9
0		0.29	0.58	0.87	1.16	1.45	1.75	2.04	2.33	2.62
10	2.91	3.20	3.49	3.78	4.07	4.36	4.66	4.95	5.24	5.53
20	5.82	6.11	6.40	6.69	6.98	7.27	7.57	7.86	8.15	8.44
30	8.73	9.02	9.31	9.60	9.89	10.18	10.48	10.77	11.06	11.35
40	11.64	11.93	12.22	12.51	12.80	13.09	13.39	13.68	13.97	14.26
50	14.55	14.84	15.13	15.42	15.71	16.00	16.30	16.59	16.88	17.17
60	17.46	17.75	18.04	18.33	18.62	18.91	19.21	19.50	19.79	20.08
70	20.37	20.66	20.95	21.24	21.53	21.82	22.12	22.41	22.70	22.99
80	23.28	23.57	23.86	24.15	24.44	24.73	25.03	25.32	25.61	25.90
90	26.19	26.48	26.77	27.06	27.35	27.64	27.94	28.23	28.52	28.81
100	29.10	29.39	29.68	29.97	30.26	30.55	30.85	31.14	31.43	31.72
110	32.01	32.30	32.59	32.88	33.17	33.46	33.75	34.05	34.34	34.63
120	34.92	35.21	35.50	35.79	36.08	36.37	36.66	36.96	37.25	37.54

Table 2 - Metric Meter Net Heat Input - 0 < 130 dm³

dm^3	Metric Meter - Natural gas (average calorific value 38.76 MJ/ m^3)									
	kW net Heat input (Net)									
	0	1	2	3	4	5	6	7	8	9
130	37.83	38.12	38.41	38.70	38.99	39.28	39.57	39.87	40.16	40.45
140	40.74	41.03	41.32	41.61	41.90	42.19	42.48	42.78	43.07	43.36
150	43.65	43.94	44.23	44.52	44.81	45.10	45.39	45.69	45.98	46.27
160	46.56	46.85	47.14	47.43	47.72	48.01	48.30	48.60	48.89	49.18
170	49.47	49.76	50.05	50.34	50.63	50.92	51.21	51.51	51.80	52.09
180	52.38	52.67	52.96	53.25	53.54	53.83	54.12	54.42	54.71	55.00
190	55.29	55.58	55.87	56.16	56.45	56.74	57.03	57.33	57.62	57.91
200	58.20	58.49	58.78	59.07	59.36	59.65	59.94	60.24	60.53	60.82
210	61.11	61.40	61.69	61.98	62.27	62.56	62.85	63.15	63.44	63.73
220	64.02	64.31	64.60	64.89	65.18	65.47	65.76	66.05	66.35	66.64
230	66.93	67.22	67.51	67.80	68.09	68.38	68.67	68.96	69.26	69.55
240	69.84	70.13	70.42	70.71	71.00	71.29	71.58	71.87	72.17	72.46

Table 3 - Metric Meter Net Heat Input - 130 < 250 dm^3

10. Safety Devices & Controls

Any person working in the domestic gas sector must be familiar with the purpose and operation of an extensive range of gas controls. From simple gas taps through to a sophisticated burner control systems, the gas operative must have the ability to ensure safe and reliable operation of every control within their working environment. It is important when installing or replacing any control that it is suitable for the gas being used. Where these controls form part of an appliance only replacement controls specified by the manufacturer must be used. Relevant information which will assist in the correct identification of specific controls are: control type, make and model number. appliance type, make and model, serial number, gas council numbers of both the appliance and component etc. For older appliances alternative controls recommended by the manufacturer may be required.

We can split the main purpose of controls into the following categories:

- Gas pressure regulation (see section 7)
- Flow control (within all or part of an installation)
- Temperature
- Flame supervision
- Multifunctional
- Temperature
- System monitoring/ safety

10.1 Flow Controls

Many different types of gas flow controls will be encountered within domestic gas installations and appliances.

10.1.1 Taper Plug Valves

Construction and Operation

This valve consists of a tapered brass or aluminium plug (sometimes referred to as the barrel) through which a slot is cut. The plug is inserted into the body of the valve which has an identical tapered recess and is held into the valve body by means of a spring or nut. The movement of the plug is usually restricted to 90° or 180° by means of a niting plate or niting washer.

The plug is lubricated by graphite grease (a high temperature lubricant) which ensures that the valve can be operated with ease and most importantly that it remains gas tight. The valve is operated manually by means of the handle or knob which can be fixed or loose, metal or plastic.

These valves are commonly used for the purpose of isolating appliances or installations.

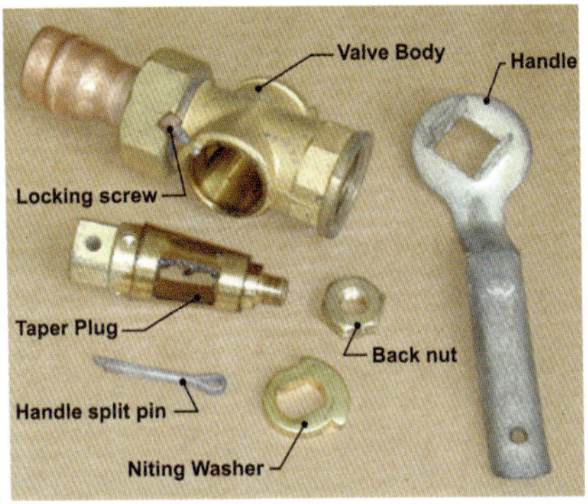

Figure 10.1 Taper plug valves

10.1.2 Ball Valves

Construction and Operation

These valves consist of a chromium plated brass sphere with a circular hole cut through along the line of the axis. The sphere (or ball) is located in a nylon seat which effects a gas tight seal when the valve is turned OFF. The valve is operated by turning a spindle which has either a screwdriver slot or a handle attached.

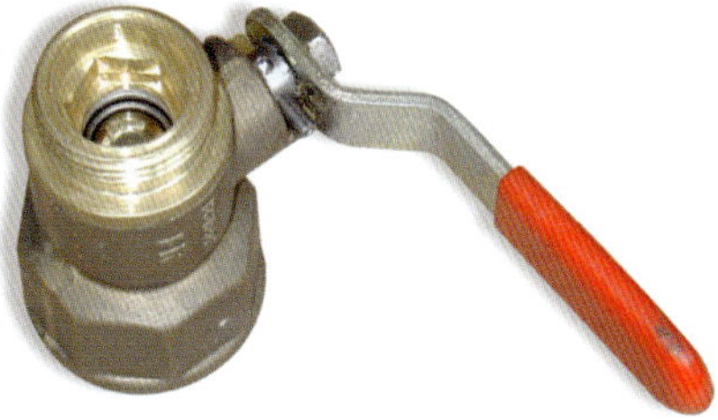

Figure 10.2 Ball Valve

These valves are commonly used for the purpose of isolating appliances and more recently they are being used as emergency/meter control valves. The valves are maintenance free and cannot be repaired if they are found to be leaking externally or internally (let by) or if they are difficult to operate.

10.1.3 Manual Disc on Seat Valves

Construction and Operation

These valves consist of a washer or "O" ring (usually neoprene) attached to a disc which is then driven onto a seat by means of screw thread or spring.

Figure 10.3 Fire pedestal elbow

Applications

These valves quite often have specific applications. One manufacturer uses this type of valve as the means of gas isolation for a single point water heater. It is also used exclusively as the means of isolation when connecting gas fires and wall heaters by 8 mm chrome/brass pipe.

10.1.4 Self Sealing Disc on Seat Valve

Self sealing valves (bayonet plug in sockets) are also used in conjunction with flexible gas pipes for cookers and tumble dryers. The "micropoint" gas pipework system also uses this type of valve at each wall socket.

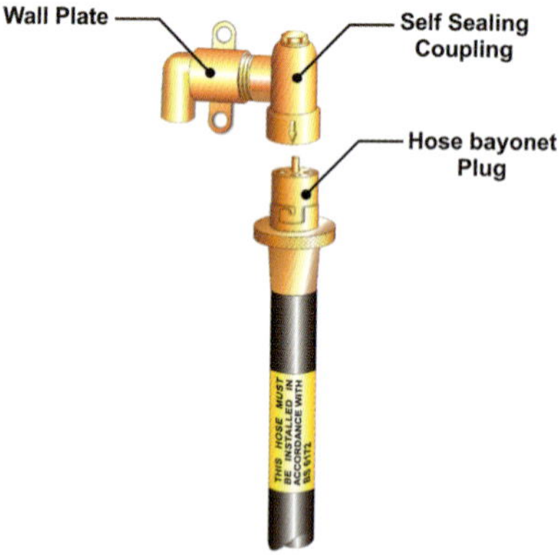

Figure 10.4 Cooker bayonet

10.1.5 Gas Taps

These are found on appliances of which the user controls the throughput such as gas fires and cookers. They consist of a taper plug which is held in position by a compression spring. They often have a large orifice through which gas flows when the valve is turned to the high position and a much smaller orifice through which gas flows when the valve is turned to the low position. Excessive application of lubricating grease can result in the flame extinguishing at low settings.

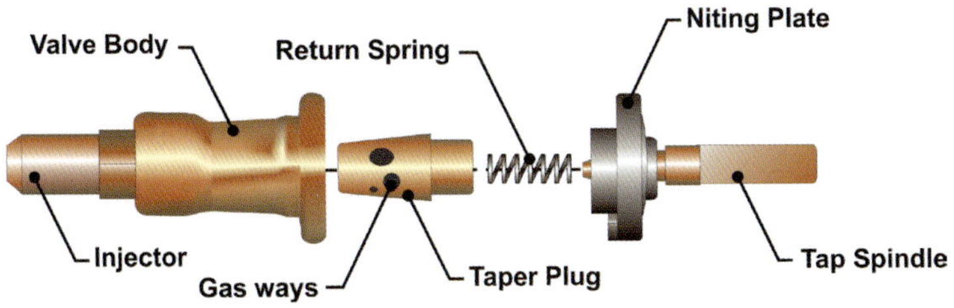

Figure 10.5 Gas tap

10.1.6 Cooker Lid Safety Cut Off Valve

This mechanism is unique to gas cookers with drop down lids. There are many different valve designs but the common feature is that if the lid is dropped without the hotplate burners being turned off this valve will extinguish the burners. Some valves require to be manually reset.

Figure 10.6 Cooker lid valve

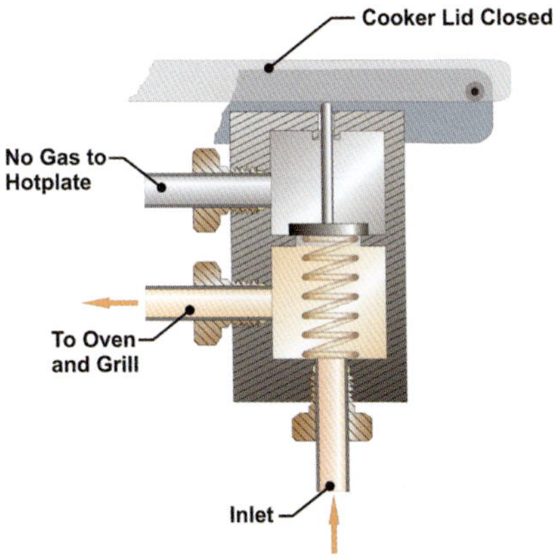

Figure 10.7 Lid valve in closed position

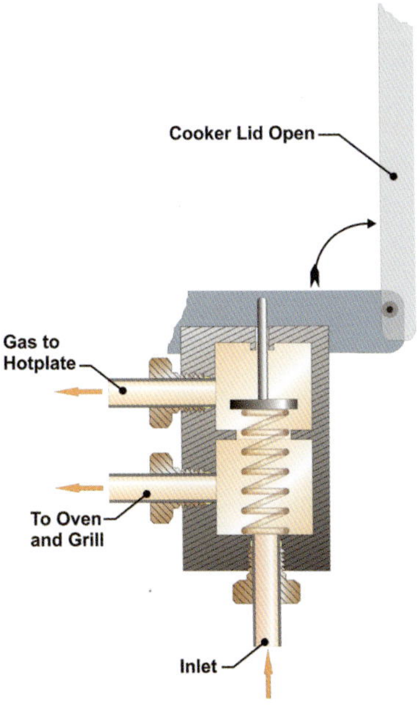

Figure 10.8 Lid valve in open position

10.1.7 Solenoid Valves

Electrically operated gas valves are known as "solenoids" when direct acting and "operators" when indirect. Their purpose is to turn ON or OFF a gas supply by electrical means and are either fitted on the supply pipe to the appliance/s or are an integral part of the appliance. When indirect they are usually part of a multifunctional unit.

Construction and Operation

A solenoid is an electrically controlled gas valve which is usually constructed so as to be normally closed, that is to say that when no power is present (can be D.C. but usually A.C.) the gas valve is closed and when power is applied (can be 24 or 240V), the valve opens. The coil or windings are arranged in a cylindrical fashion around the soft iron core which is free to move up or down within the coil. The gas valve is attached to the core and is pushed onto its seat by the return spring when no power is present so preventing the gas flow through the solenoid, the gas pressure helps to push the valve onto its seat. When power is switched on a current flows through the coil generating an electromagnetic field which is powerful enough to overcome the force of the return spring and lift the core upwards and the valve away from its seat so allowing gas to flow through the solenoid valve.

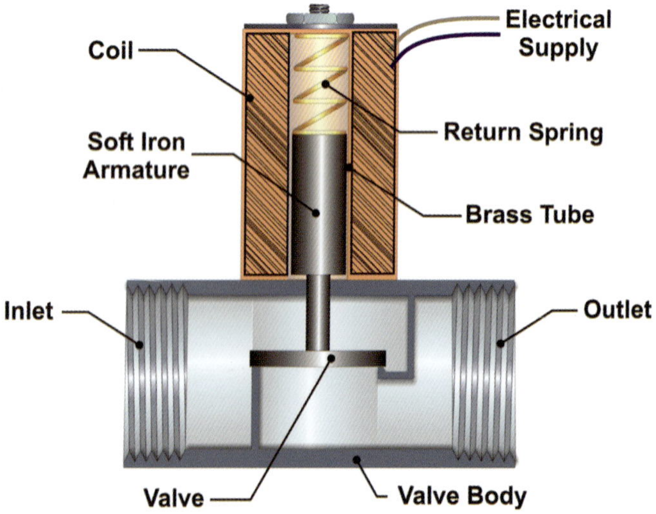

Figure 10.9 Construction of Solenoid Valve.

10.2 Temperature Control

10.2.1 Thermostatic Valves & Switches

The purpose of a thermostatic control device is to automatically maintain or limit the temperature of a given situation e.g. air temperature, water temperature or the maximum temperature of a boiler heat exchanger. There are many different types of thermostat ('stat) available, but they will fall into one of two categories, either direct acting or indirect acting.

Direct Acting 'stats

This category of 'stat will directly control the flow of gas to the main burner of the appliance. It will either turn it ON and OFF or, UP and DOWN. An example of a direct acting 'stat is the thermostat on a cooker oven, all the gas flowing to the main burner will flow through the 'stat first.

Indirect Acting 'stats

With an indirect acting thermostat, the 'stat controls the flow of gas to the main burner by utilizing another device to control the flow of gas to the burner, e.g. an electrical thermostat (room 'stat) working in conjunction with a solenoid valve to control the flow of gas to a boiler.

10.2.2 Liquid Expansion Thermostatic Valve

Construction and Operation

The principle of operation of this 'stat is that liquid, when heated, expands. The liquid is contained in a copper phial and is connected to a flexible, metal bellows by means of a capillary tube. The phial is located at the point where the temperature is to be sensed. The gas valve is attached to the bellows by a valve stem which in turn is attached to the bellows by a coarse thread. When the temperature increases, the bellows expand moving the valve onto its seat, stopping the gas flow to the burner via that route. A by-pass screw allows a small flow rate to the burner so that when the temperature is reached, the burner is not extinguished but remains on at a by-pass rate. This by-pass is nonadjustable and is designed to maintain the desired temperature. The disc on seat valve is assisted onto its seat by means of a spring. If the temperature falls, the liquid contacts as do the bellows which pull the valve away from its seat, so restoring the main gas rate to the burner. Set temperature adjustment is achieved by the temperature adjustment bar which when turned, will move the valve closer to or further from its seat so resulting in a lower or higher temperature before by-pass rate is achieved. Although calibration of the 'stat can be performed on site it is normal practice to exchange the 'stat due to the time this may take.

Applications

This valve is most commonly found (as part of the thermo-tap assembly) on gas cooker ovens. The current manufacturers are Concentric, Diamond H and Coprecci. It can also be found on back circulator units such as the Main Carina E and Eastam Maxol EM10D, but these appliances are not as popular as they once were.

Figure 10.10 Cooker thermostat

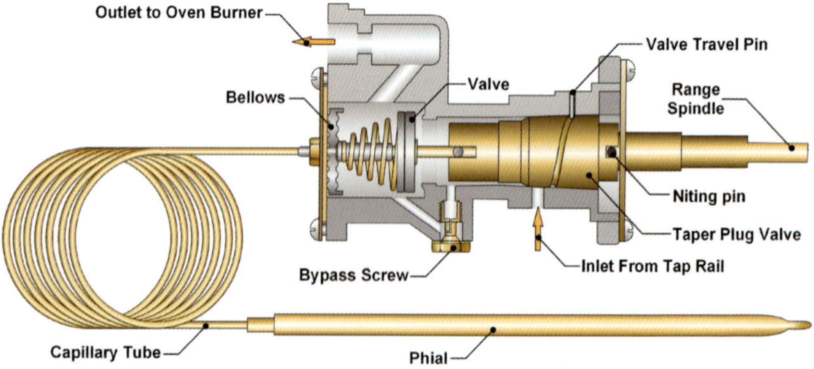

Figure 10.11 Compensated governor

10.2.3 Liquid Expansion Thermostatic Switch, Remote Sensor

Construction and Operation

The phial is positioned wherever the temperature is to be sensed (e.g. in the top of a boiler heat exchanger). The phial, capillary tube and bellows contain a liquid which will expand when heated and when this occurs the bellows will open to accommodate the expansion. The bellows act on the armature which can pivot about the left hand end, at the other end of the armature is an electrical switch contact which normally rests against another electrical switch contact which is fixed. An electrical circuit is connected to the electrical connections of the thermostatic switch and when the contacts are "made" a current can flow. When the contacts separate (due to the liquid expansion) the current flow ceases. The temperature at which the contacts open can be altered by the operator adjusting the setting of the control knob, this action causes the spindle to move in or out on its thread, this in turn causes more or less compression of the spring causing more or less force to act on the armature. The more force which acts on the armature due to the spring, the more expansion is required by the bellows to separate the contacts and therefore a higher operating temperature is obtained and vice versa. This thermostatic switch normally controls the gas flow by switching a solenoid gas valve on and off.

Applications

This type of thermostatic switch is commonly found on cental heating boilers (Baxi, Glowworm, Caradon, etc.) and combi boilers (Vokera, Ravenheat, etc.). The phial is located within the top of the heat exchanger.

Figure 10.12 Liquid expansion thermostatic switch

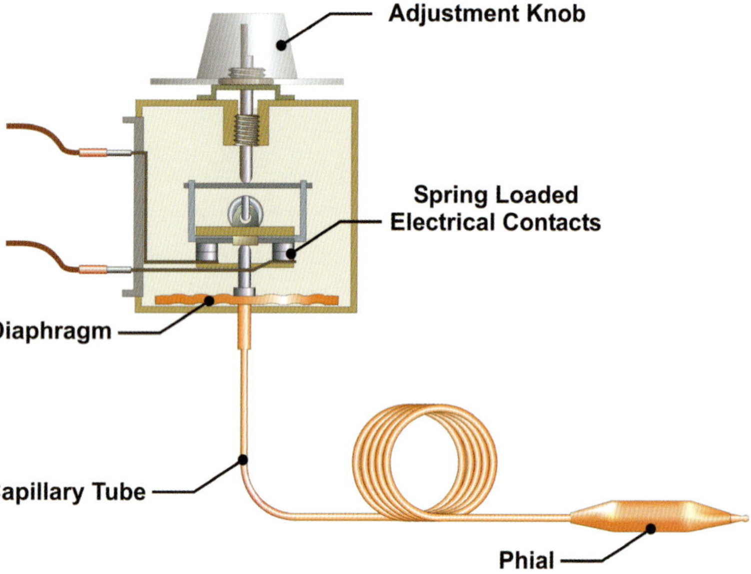

Figure 10.13 Liquid expansion thermostatic switch

10.2.4 Thermo-disc

These 'stats are known as thermo-discs due to their construction. They consist of an electrical switch contained in a plastic housing, which is activated by a bi-metallic disc. The disc will flex at a predetermined temperature. The 'stat is attached in position by screws which pass through the fixing clip. The switch is connected in circuit to a solenoid valve by wires attached to the electrical connections. The switch usually breaks on temperature increase but can be made so that it makes on temperature increase. They are usually automatic reset but can be manual (look for the reset button). The plastic housing is approximately 15 mm in diameter and 15 mm high.

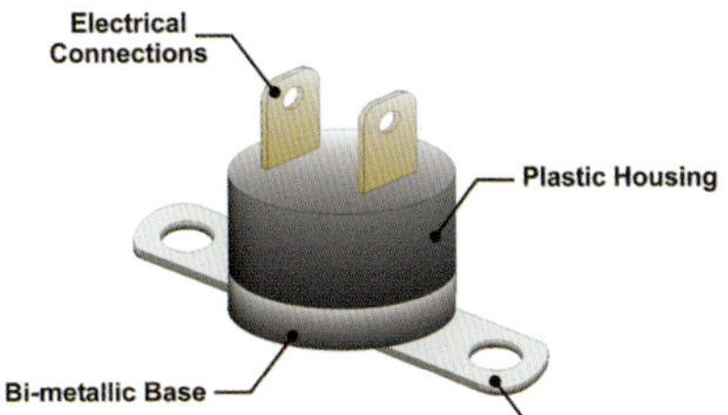

Figure 10.14 Disc stat

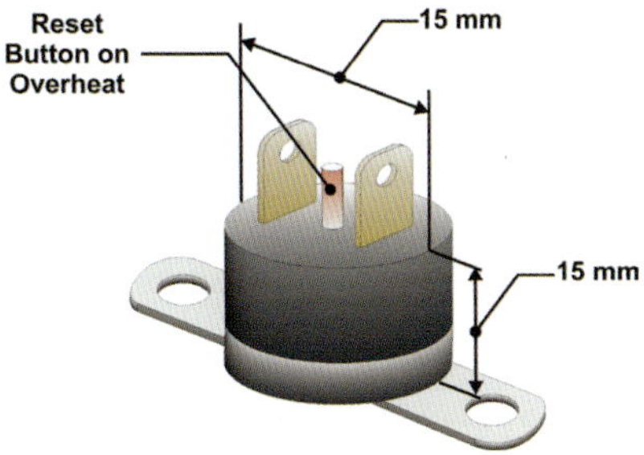

Figure 10.15 Disc overheat stat

Applications

This 'stat is extensively used on CH boilers (wall mounted, free standing, combi, system), tumble dryers and warm air units. The 'stat is clamped onto the part of the appliance where the temperature is to be sensed, sometimes a heat conducting paste is used to improve thermal conductivity. They can be used in applications other than temperature control (spillage sensing) although this is their primary function. When incorporated into a thermocouple circuit (thermoelectric FSD) they can provide overheat protection.

10.2.5 Thermistor

Thermistors are solid state electrical devices, i.e. do not contain any moving parts. They contain materials, which, when heated, either decrease or increase in electrical resistance. This variation in resistance can be monitored by a printed circuit board to activate an electrical solenoid to control the flow of gas to a burner.

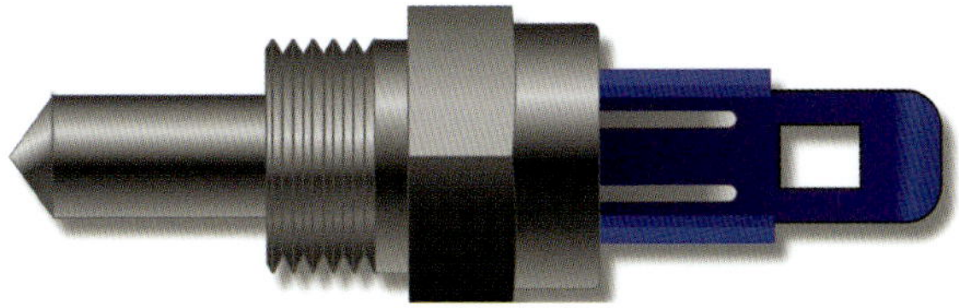

Figure 10.16 Thermistor

10.3 Flame Supervision Devices

10.3.1 Flame Rectification (Ionisation)

This is an electronic method of flame safety device and is very quick acting in response to flame failure, usually less than one second.

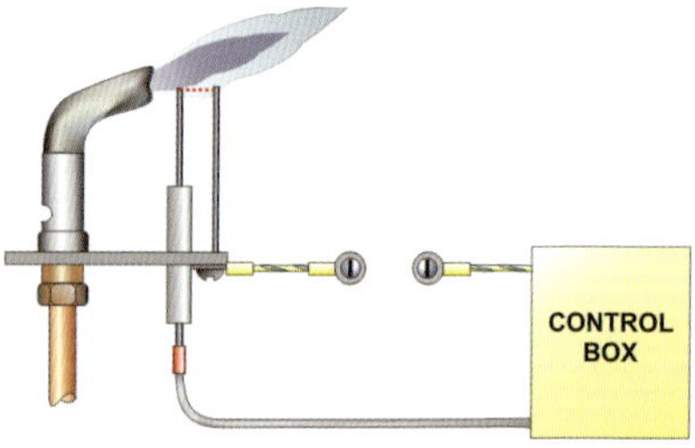

Figure 10.17 Flame rectification

Construction and Operation

The flame sensor is in the form of an electrode (similar to an ignition electrode) which is positioned approximately 10 mm or more from the burner head. A wire (not unlike the H.T. lead of an ignition electrode) connects the electrode to the printed circuit board (PCB).

The principle of operation of this system is based on the fact that due to the high temperature within a flame there are positively charged particles known as ions. These particles can be used to conduct an electrical current between the sensing electrode and the burner - but this can only happen when a flame is present. How the system works is as follows. A solenoid valve is opened to allow gas to flow to the burner (pilot or 1st stage depending on the manufacturer) and at the same time the ignition transformer creates a spark at the ignition electrode. Assuming that the gas ignites, the current which is flowing from the PCB to the sensing electrode will be conducted through the flame to the earthed burner and from there the circuit is completed to the PCB. As soon as the PCB senses that a current is flowing in this circuit the ignition spark stops and the main gas is energised. If at any time the flame is extinguished then the current flow will cease and the PCB will stop the main gas flow. If after a period of trying to re-ignite a flame is not re-established, the burner control system will "lockout" although not all appliances have this particular feature.

The system is called flame rectification (as opposed to flame conduction) due to the ability of the system to discriminate against short circuit conditions (loose lead touching the appliance case or a piece of soot bridging the gap) producing an erroneous flame signal. This is due to the design of the system which is based on an alternating current (A.C.) and not a direct current (D.C.). The current itself is very small and is in the region of 5 to 30 micro amps (μA). The PCB amplifies the current and a flame relay controls the power to the gas solenoids.

N.B. Some manufacturers have combined both electrodes into one (ignition and sensing). Once the spark has ignited the gas the purpose of the electrode changes to that of flame sensing (the Baxi Solo 2 PF for example).

Testing (CH boilers, water heaters and ducted air heaters)

With the main burner operating, isolate the gas supply at the appliance isolation valve and check by either of the method detailed below.

- The appliance goes directly to lockout (within a maximum time of 60 seconds) and does not attempt to relight when the gas supply is restored (see notes 1 and 2).
- The appliance goes to lockout after a number of re-ignition attempts (within a maximum time of 2 minutes) and does not attempt to relight when the gas supply is restored (see notes 1 and 2).
- The appliance ignition system continues to spark during the period the gas supply is isolated and normal ignition sequence is achieved when the gas supply is restored (see note 1).

Note 1: Before the gas supply is restored it is recommended that a delay of 2 minutes is allowed to ensure dispersal of any residual gas/air mixture.

Note 2: Following any of the above tests, the appliance should be checked for normal ignition sequence after resetting as necessary.

10.3.2 Thermo-electric FSD Construction and Operation

A thermoelectric flame supervision device is used to detect the presence of a flame through the heat generated by the flame. It works on the principle that when two dissimilar metals are joined together at one end and heated a small electrical current is generated. This principle is the basis in which a thermocouple works. When the tip of the thermocouple is heated by a flame, normally a pilot burner, it generates a small electrical current which we can then be transmitted to the control.

The construction of the thermo-electric FSD is shown in figure 10.18. It consists of a small electromagnet, spring loaded main valve, interrupter valve and thermocouple. In the rest position, the gas is prevented from flowing through the valve to the pilot and main burner by the main spring loaded valve. The underside of the valve is constructed of a soft iron material which is attracted by a magnetic field. To establish the pilot flame we are required to push down the reset button. This pushes both the interrupter valve onto its seating (stopping gas flowing to the main burner) and the main valve off its seating onto the small electromagnetic coil. This action allows gas to flow to the pilot where it can then be ignited. The when ignited the pilot flame heats the thermocouple. As the thermocouple heats up it starts to generate a small current enough to energize the electromagnet. As the current becomes stronger the generated magnetic field becomes enough to hold open the main valve. As the reset button is released gas is now allowed to flow through both valves towards the burner. The main valve will remain open as long as a current is generated by the thermocouple.

If the gas supply is interrupted, by either failure of the gas supply or turning off the pilot, the thermocouple will then cool. The electromagnet will then de-energise allowing the main valve to close. This will normally happen within 30 seconds, however the manufacturer will specify the maximum time allowed for shut off.

Testing

The following applies to Central Heating Boilers, Water Heaters and Ducted Air Heaters.

"Click Test"

With the main burner operating, isolate the gas supply at the appliance isolation valve and check the time taken for the thermoelectric, magnetic valve to close. The maximum operating times are given in the table below. Following closure of the valve, restore the gas supply at the appliance isolation valve and check that there is no gas at the main burner before relighting the appliance.

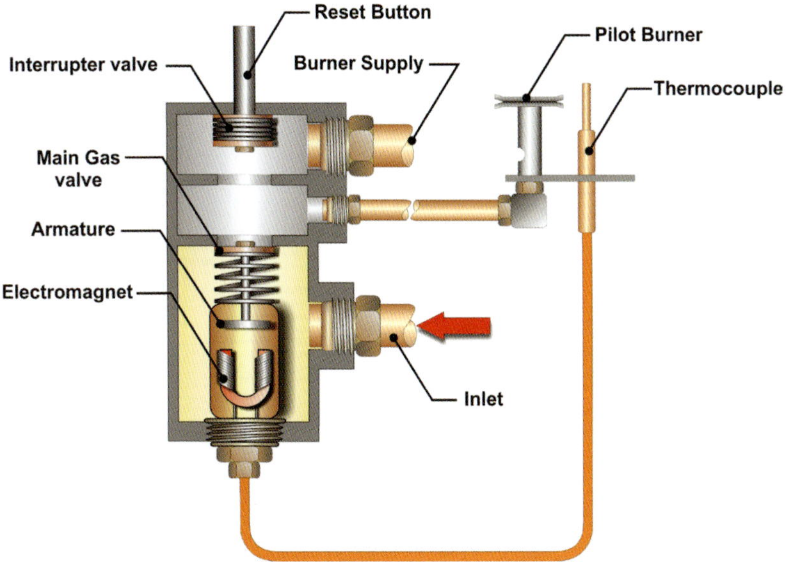

Figure 10.18 Thermoelectric valve (in closed position)

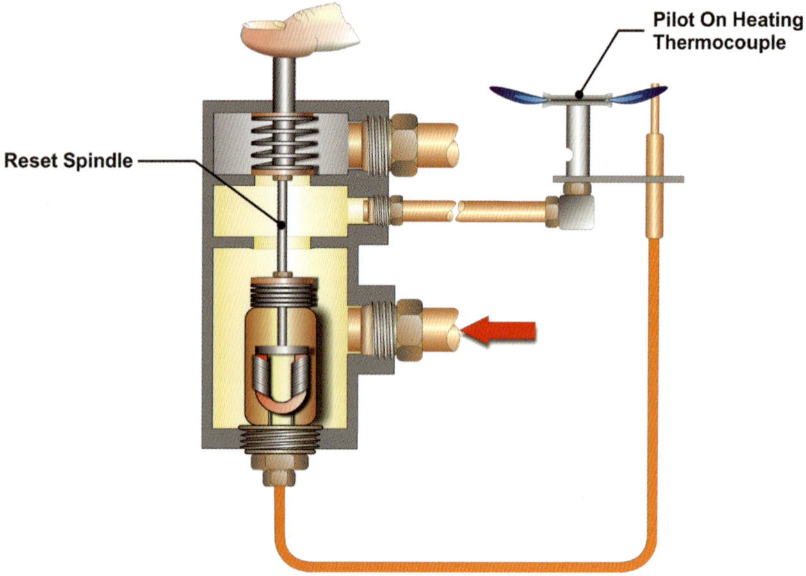

Figure 10.19 Thermoelectric valve (Valve being reset)

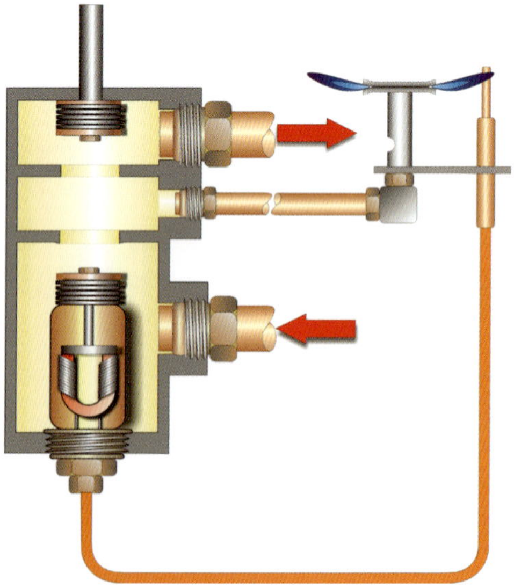

Figure 10.20 Thermoelectric valve (Valve in on position)

10.3.3 Vapour Pressure FSD Construction and Operation

As a liquid boils the vapour produced has a greater volume than the liquid. If this liquid is placed into a sealed container and allowed to boil, the resulting vapour, having no room to expand, would rapidly pressurise the container. We use this principle within a vapour pressure flame sensing device.

This control incorporates a sensing element containing a fluid (older controls used Mercury) connected to a small metal bellows within the body of the valve via a small capillary tube. As we heat the sensing element, either through a separate pilot supply or by-pass rate at the main burner, the liquid within it vaporises increasing the pressure within the sealed unit. This increase of pressure is enough to expand the bellows. This movement of the bellows is used to push open a spring loaded valve allowing gas to flow towards the main burner.

When heat is removed from the phial the vapour will start to condense. This change of state will cause the pressure within the sealed unit to decrease. The bellows will then contract allowing the valve to close through the action of the spring.

It should be noted that these valves do not normally shut off the gas supply to the burner completely, they generally only close the valve to a preset bypass rate. These valves have in the main been used on cooker ovens for a number of years.

The main fault with this type of flame supervision device is damage to the sealed unit. Any leakage will not allow the unit to pressurise therefore main flame will not be established.

Testing

Assuming this device is fitted to a gas cooker; with the main burner operating, isolate the gas supply by unplugging the bayonet and after 60 seconds restore the supply and check that the burner ignites at by-pass rate.

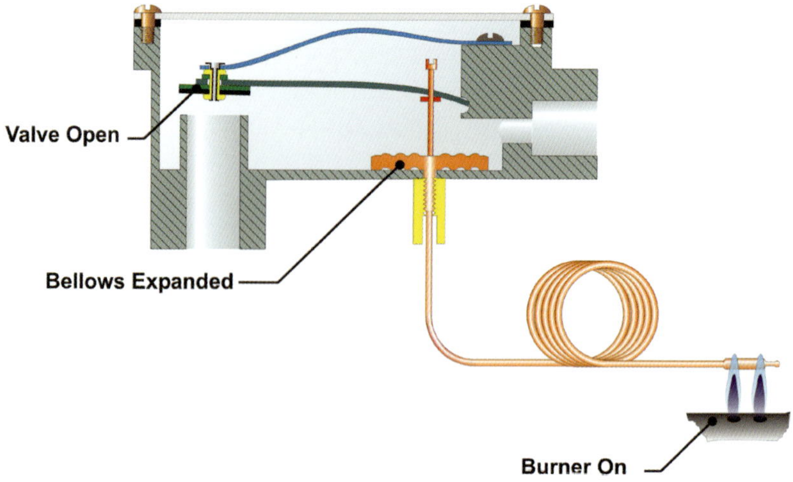

Figure 10.21 Vapour pressure valve in the closed position valve

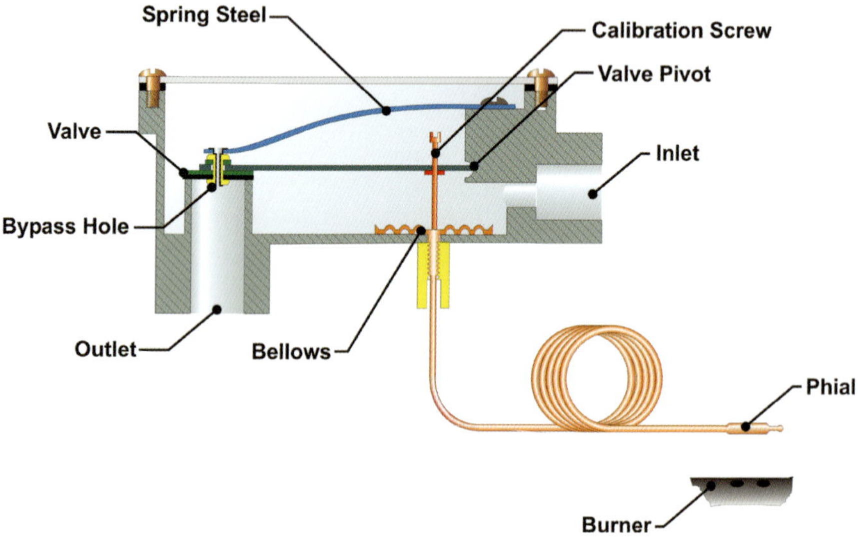

Figure 10.22 Vapour pressure valve in the open position valve

Maximum Operating Times For FSDs		
Appliance Type	**Heat Input**	**Time (seconds)**
Central Heating Boilers	70 kW_{net}	60
Cooker Oven		60
Cooker Hotplate		90
Space Heater		180
DFE		60
Warm Air Unit	60 kW_{gross}	60
Storage Water Heater	Less than 35 kW_{net}	50
Storage Water Heater	35 to 70 kW_{net}	45
Combi/Multipoint WH		60

Table 10.1

10.4 Multifuntional Controls

Control lines on gas appliances have evolved from a number of individual controls to a single multifunctional control unit. The control line in the past may have consisted of the following controls;

- Manual ON/OFF isolation valve.
- Simple type, constant pressure governor.
- Thermoelectric FSD.
- Relay valve.
- Indirect acting thermostatic valve.
- Pilot/main burners.

The control line of a present day appliance is more likely to have the following controls;

- Manual ON/OFF isolation valve.
- Multifunctional control valve.
- Liquid expansion thermostatic switch (remote sensing).
- Pilot/main burners.

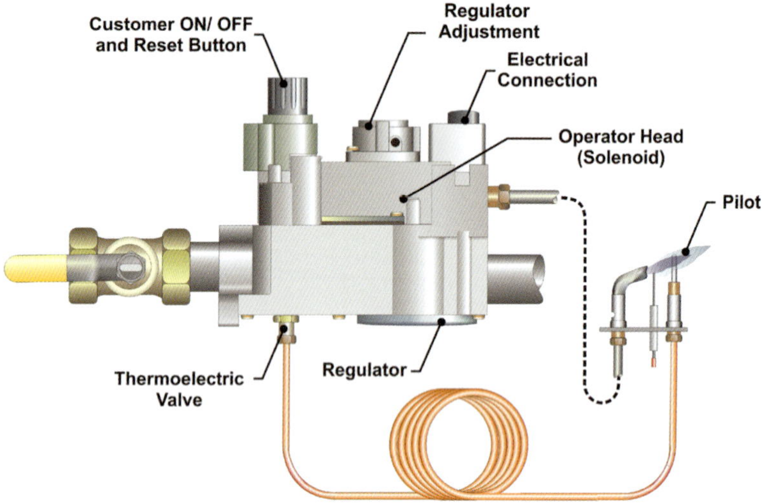

Figure 10.23 Multifunctional control valve

10.4.1 Multifunctional Controls

The use of the multifunctional control simplifies the control line. The multifunctional control will contain the following devices;

- Inlet filter.
- Inlet/outlet pressure test points.
- Manual control knob.
- Thermoelectric FSD.
- Pressure regulator (governor).
- Operator head (solenoid).

Figure 10.24 Multifunctional control valve

Figure 10.25 Multifunctional control valve

Fanned flue boilers will dispense with the thermoelectric FSD, instead they will use a pilot solenoid (in addition to the main solenoid).

10.5 Pressure and Flow Sensing

10.5.1 Pressure/Flow Sensing

Fanned, balanced flue systems are becoming more and more popular with manufacturers and installers alike. With these appliances it is imperative that the fan is checked for correct operation every time an attempt is made to light the appliance. A pressure switch is used to detect the pressure generated by the fan.

10.5.1.1 Pressure Sensing

The purpose of the pressure switch is to detect the existence of positive and negative pressure which is generated by the fan in the flue system in order to prove that the fan is operating. When the pressures above and below the diaphragm are equal it is pushed downwards by the force of the spring and the push rod operates the micro switch button proving a "no air" condition by providing continuity between Com. and NO. This condition allows the fan to run which creates positive and negative pressure within the flue system. The pos. and neg. pressures are transferred from the flue system to the pressure switch by the pressure pipes and the pressure difference across the diaphragm is sufficient to overcome the force of the spring and cause the diaphragm to flex upwards taking with it the push rod, this allows the button in micro switch to come out and the switch contacts to change over to now give continuity between Com. and NC. The switch contacts changing over permits the next part of the ignition sequence to take place. The pressure at which the switch operates is set by the manufacturers by adjusting the pressure adj. screw and is not intended to be altered. This switch will operate in the region of 1 mbar or thereabouts.

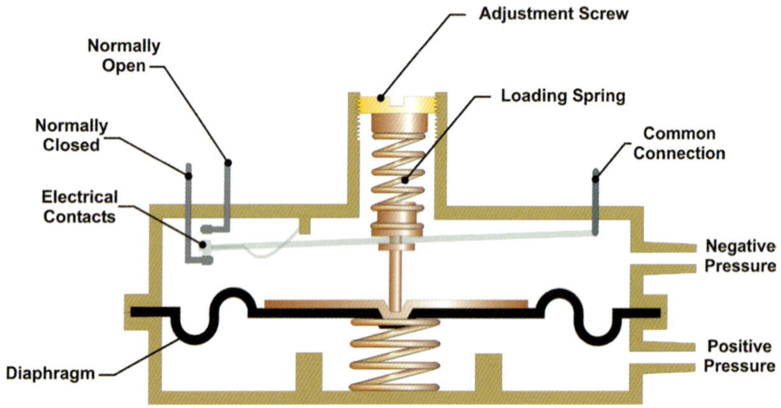

Figure 10.26 Construction of a Differential Pressure Switch.

10.5.1.2 Flow Sensing

This system utilizes a pressure switch operating in conjunction with a venturi and will detect flow as opposed to pressure. The pressure switch will detect the existence of positive and negative pressure which is generated by a venturi in the flue system only when the fan is operating. When the pressures above and below the diaphragm are equal it is pushed downwards by the force of the spring and the push rod operates the micro switch button proving a "no air" condition by providing continuity between Com. and NO. This condition allows the fan to run which creates positive and negative pressure within the venturi. The pos. and neg. pressures are transferred from the venturi to the pressure switch by the pressure pipes and the pressure difference across the diaphragm is sufficient to overcome the force of the spring and cause the diaphragm to flex upwards taking with it the push rod, this allows the button in micro switch to come out and the switch contacts to change over to now give continuity between Com. and NC. The switch contacts changing over permits the next part of the ignition sequence to take place. The pressure at which the switch operates is set by the manufacturers by adjusting the pressure adj. screw and is not intended to be altered

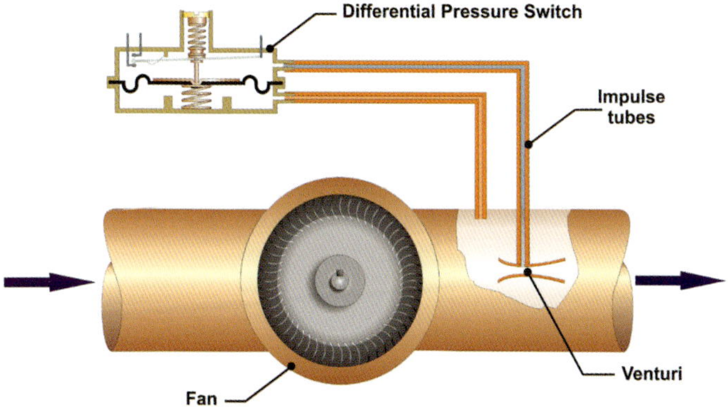

Figure 10.27 Pressure switch arrangement

Testing

Test these systems by removing the pressure sensing tubes from the switch and then attempt to ignite the boiler. All that should happen is that the fan runs, there must be no attempt at ignition. Next, replace the tubes and ensure that the appliance ignites. Then remove the tubes and ensure that the burner extinguishes. Replace the tubes and check for correct operation.

10.6 Atmosphere Sensing Device (ASD) a.k.a. Oxygen Depletion Device

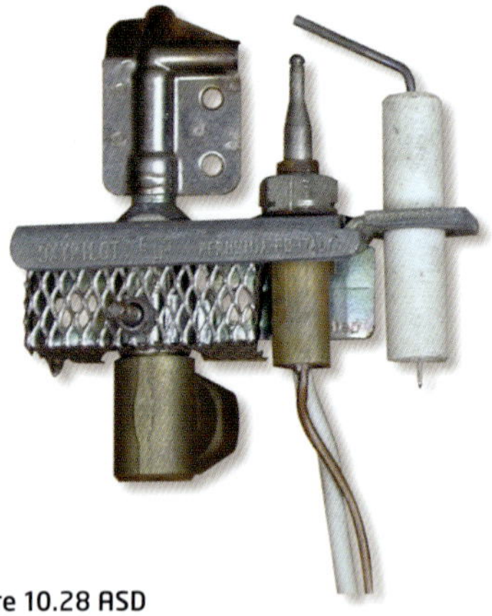

Figure 10.28 ASD

Regulation 30 (3) of the GSIUR 1998 permits the use of a non-room sealed fire, space heater or water heater in a room used or intended to be used as sleeping accommodation provided the appliance has a gross heat input of 14 kW or less and provided that *"it incorporates a safety device designed to shut down the appliance before there is a buildup of a dangerous quantity of the products of combustion in the room concerned."* This also applies to a non-room sealed instantaneous water heater installed in any location (not permitted in a bathroom or shower room). Such a device is described below.

Construction and Operation

The device consists of a specially designed pilot burner and thermocouple. Should the ambient (room) air become vitiated due to a flue or ventilation problem, the pilot flame picture will be affected in such a way that it will lift from the burner and fail to heat the thermocouple sufficiently, the thermoelectric FSD will close as though fail failure had occurred. It is not possible to test these devices (in much the same way as you have to trust that the air bag in your car will operate).

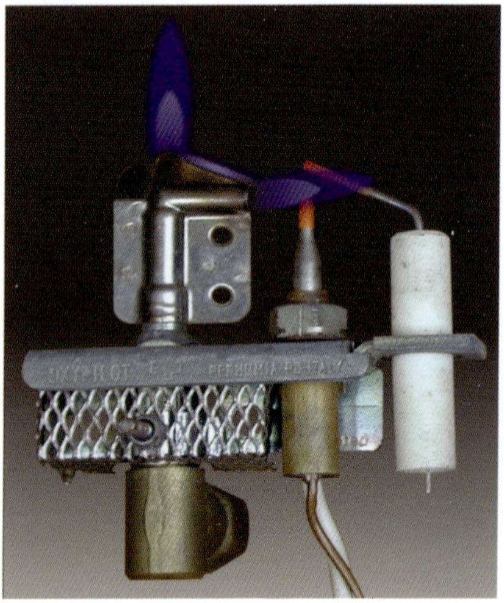

Figure 10.29 ASD flame correct

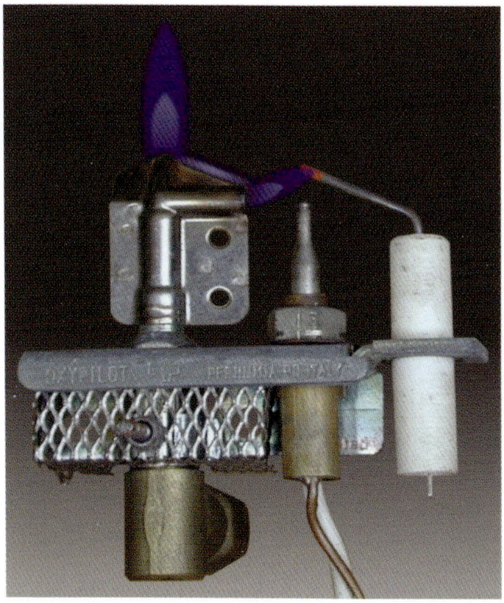

Figure 10.30 ASD flame starting to lift

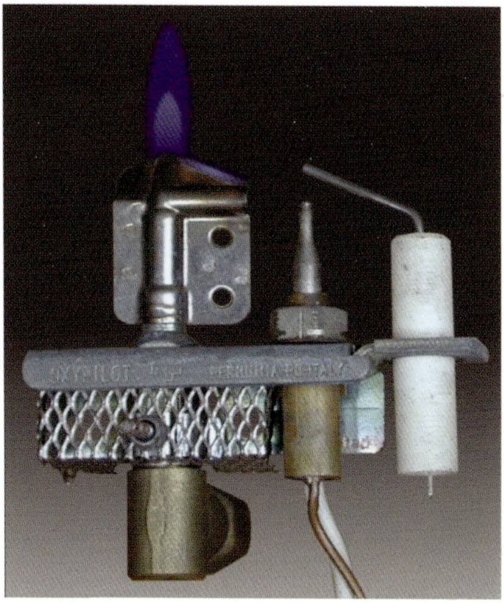

Figure 10.31 ASD flame lifted off T/couple

The engineer can only examine it for correct assembly, damage or lint build up. The unit must be exchanged as a whole, individual parts should not be exchanged. It will operate if the CO_2 concentration is in the region of 1.5 to 2% or more.

There is no practical test method for this device. All that can be done is to visually inspect it for correct assembly and location and that the flame is blue, vibrant and stable and is heating the thermocouple.

10.7 Interrupted Thermocouple Circuits

Overheat Sensing

With certain appliance/system types it is a requirement to provide overheat protection, e.g. sealed central heating boilers/systems. On appliances which have a permanent pilot, manufacturers often employ a thermo-disc 'stat wired in to interrupt the thermocouple circuit of the thermoelectric FSD. In the event of overheating occurring (e.g. due to a faulty boiler 'stat), the thermo-disc 'stat will "break", interrupting the thermocouple circuit and shutting off both main and pilot gas. The thermo-disc usually has a reset button which requires manual intervention to restore the system.

The need for a special (and more expensive) thermocouple required by this system has been dispensed with due to the use of a thermocouple interrupter facility which is part of the multifunctional control unit.

Figure 10.32 Interrupter leads

Spillage Sensing

Many open flued appliances now make use of this device to provide a greater level of safety (e.g. Johnson & Starley warm air units and Baxi Boston boilers). It will react to spillage of products of combustion at the appliance draught diverter in exactly the same way as the previous system reacted to overheat conditions. This safety feature is often referred to as a TTB (Thermische Terrugslag Beveiling).

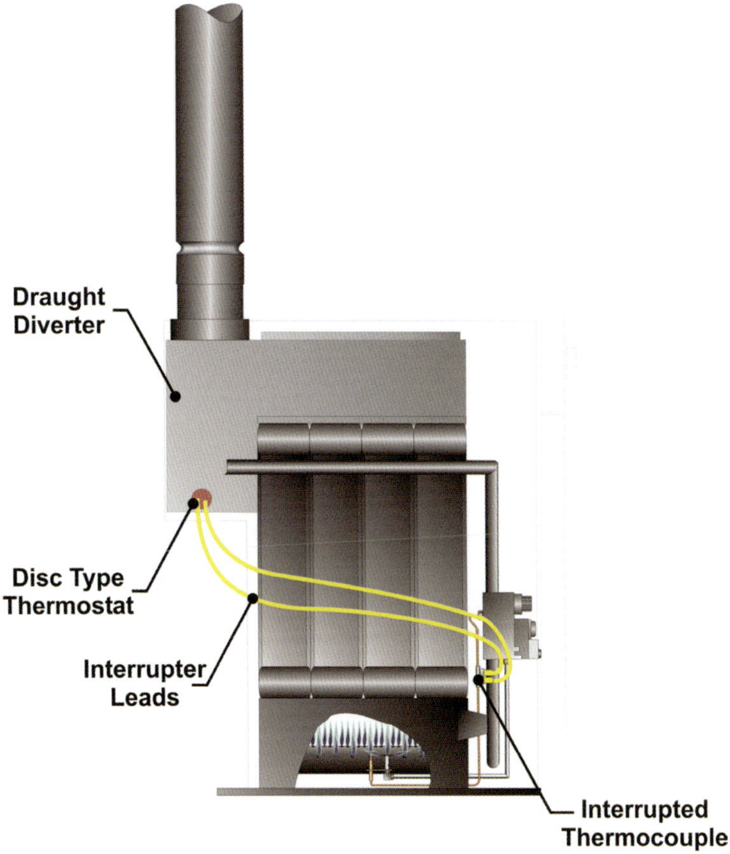

Figure 10.33 Spillage sensing device

10.8 Ignition Devices.

To allow combustion to occur we must introduce a source of ignition at a burner. This can be done by either manual or automatic means. The purest form of ignition was normally done manually by the customer using a lighted taper, match etc. This was the norm for older gas equipment, however due to the hazards associated with the likes of delayed ignition and risk of burns we normally use alternative methods to ignite the burners. Some of the common ignition devices used within the gas industry are detailed in the following paragraphs.

10.8.1 Permanent pilot

Located near the main burner these can be ignited either manually (see figure 10.34) or automatically by another ignition device. Older types of pilot did not have flame supervision however today they must have some form of supervision for example thermoelectric or flame rectification.

Figure 10.34 Pilot Burner

10.8.2 Glow coil

This device is activated by the customer turning a spring loaded gas tap. It consists of a small pilot burner which is ignited by means of a low voltage electric coil normally powered by a battery (see figure 10.35). This pilot flame would then ignite the main burner. When the customer released the gas tap it would spring back

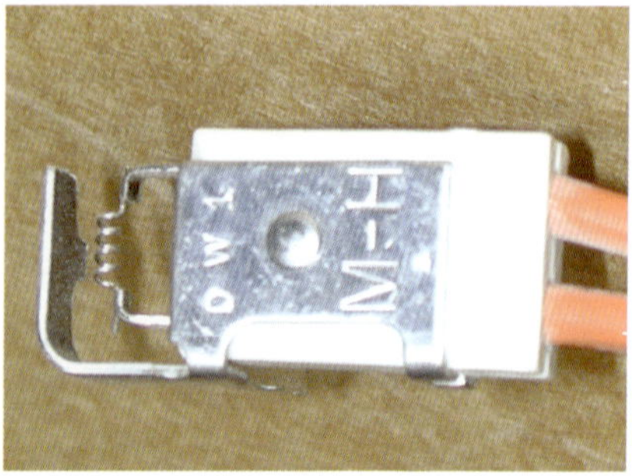

Figure 10.35 Glow Coil

turning the coil and pilot flame off. This type of ignition is normally found on older type gas fires.

10.8.3 Piezo Electric Crystal

This device consists of a sealed unit containing quartz crystals. When these crystals are compressed they store energy. When this compression is released this energy is discharged very similar to a capacitor. This discharged energy takes the form of electricity (high voltage low current) which has enough energy to jump a spark gap. The ignition unit is either located remotely at a convenient position for use by the customer or as part of a gas tap activated by the rotation of the tap. It is connected to an electrode either located above the main burner or pilot by means of a high tension electric lead. Compression of the crystals is normally by means of a spring loaded hammer incorporated in the sealed unit.

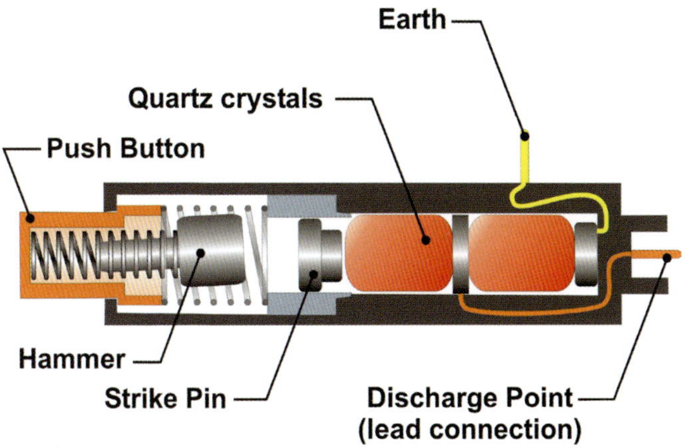

Figure 10.36 Construction of piezo ignition unit

10.8.4 Electric/ Electronic ignition

Basically these devices generate a high voltage electrical current which contains enough energy to jump a spark gap. They can be powered by either mains electricity or a battery. The high voltage can be generated using many different principles such as:

- Capacitor discharge.
- Step-up transformers.
- Electronic circuits.

10.8.5 Hot Surface Ignition (HSI)

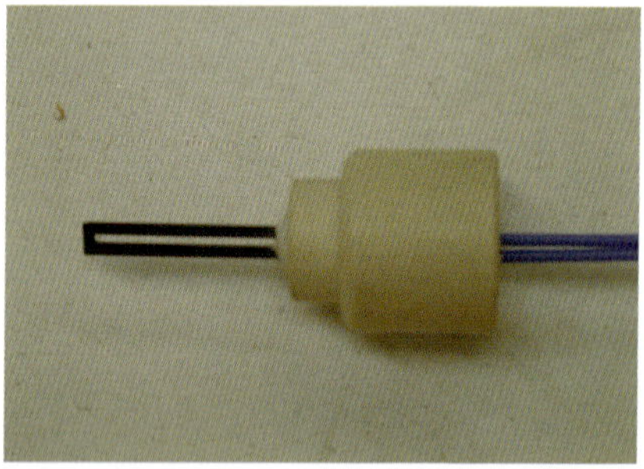

Figure 10.37 Hot Surface Ignitor

Due to the operation and burner configuration of some appliances they do not warrant the use of spark type ignition. Hot surface ignition consists of a carbon ceramic element connected to a low voltage supply. When a current is applied to the ceramic it glows white hot, very similar to the operation of an electric fire. The temperature of the ceramic is high enough to ignite any air/ gas mixture passed over the element. The benefit of this type of ignition is it is not affected by condensation, earth and earth leakage problems which are common on spark ignition systems. This is more evident with the introduction of fibrous and ceramic based burners used in high efficiency boilers. Care must be taken when cleaning or touching this element as any stress applied to the ceramic will result in failure of the component.

10.9 Sequence of Operation of Cooker FSD & Thermostatic Control

The following sequence of operation is used to explain the relationship between a liquid vapour FSD and liquid expansion thermostatic valve as used in a cooker oven. It runs through initial start up through to the oven reaching temperature and finally being turned off. The operating pressure of the appliance should be checked and confirmed as satisfactory against the manufacturers data

10.9.1 Initial start up.

When the oven is initially turned on the oven will be cold therefore the oven thermostat will be in the open position. Gas will flow through the main valve of the oven thermostat down through the supply pipe into the liquid vapour FSD. Since we are at initial start up the FSD will be in the closed position. At this point gas is allowed to flow to the burner via the FSD bypass. It can then be ignited at the burner head. Since we have a reduced flow of gas through the FSD bypass the flame will initially ignite at a reduced rate resulting in a reduced flame. This flame is used to heat the FSD phial.

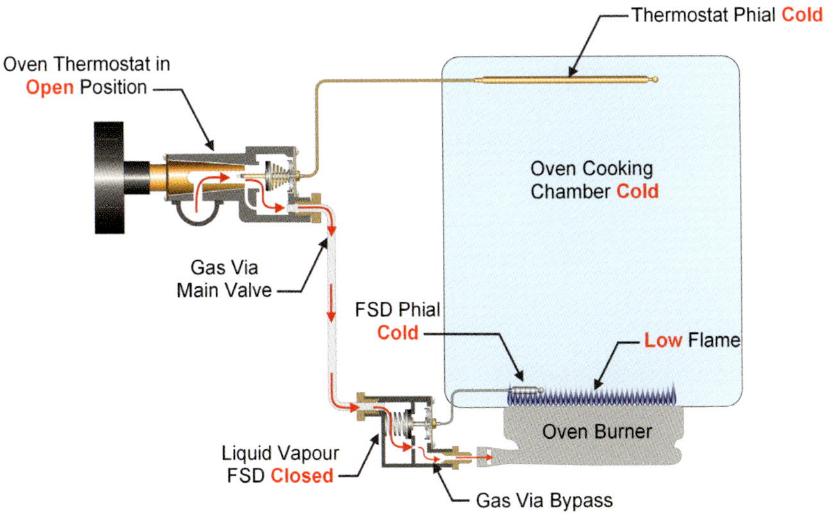

Figure 10.38 Oven initially turned on with flame established at burner

10.9.2 Main Flame Established.

As the FSD heats up the liquid within the sealed unit expands forcing open the main valve. The gas flame will then be seen to expand as more gas is allowed into the burner via the FSD. The flame will continually expand until as such time as the FSD is fully open and the full gas rate is achieved. At this point the oven is sill cold therefore the thermostatic valve will still be in the fully open position.

If the burner ignites and the flame does not expand to full rate firstly check the position of the FSD phial and for any debris on the burner. Turn of the thermostat, clean the burner and reposition the phial if necessary. Where the burner has been found clear and the phial is in the correct position the liquid expansion FSD may be regarded as faulty. Further investigation is required.

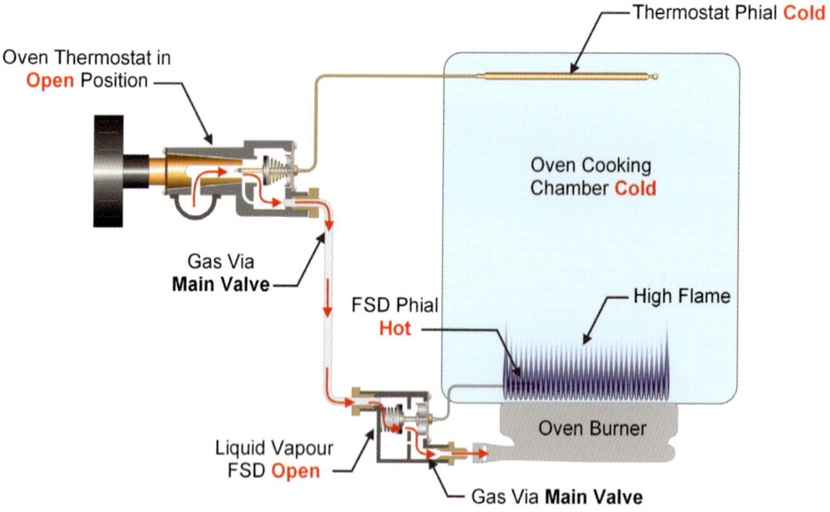

Figure 10.39 FSD heated up resulting in main flame being established

10.9.3 Oven Reaches Desired Temperature.

As the oven heats up the liquid within the phial of the thermostat starts to expand. This expansion begins to push the thermostat main valve towards it's seating. When the desired temperature within the oven is achieved the thermostat's valve will be in the closed position. When this happens a reduced gas rate is supplied to the burner via the THERMOSTAT bypass.

The flame will be seen to reduce down to the specified bypass rate. Note, since a flame is still present at the burner, the FSD will remain in the open position. This reduced rate is not due to closure of the FSD valve. The gas flame will be seen to increase and decrease during the normal operation of the oven. This is due to the thermostat opening and closing to maintain the set temperature.

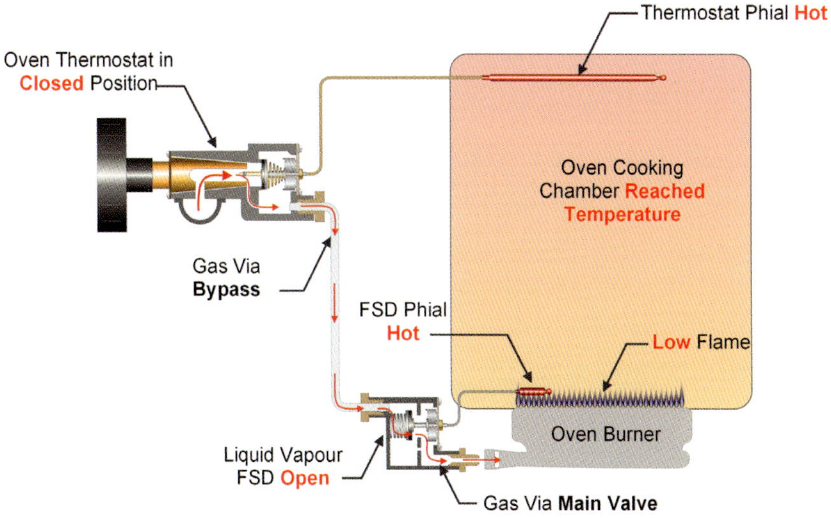

Figure 10.40 Oven temperature reached within the oven

In the event that the oven burner goes out during the normal operation of the appliance firstly check that the gas supply has not been interrupted. If the supply has been found satisfactory turn off the thermostat and open the oven door. DO NOT try and re-ignite the oven straight away as there may be a build up of gas which would result in explosive ignition. Once ventilated turn on the oven and re-ignite the burner. Wait for the FSD to open and the main flame to be established. Adjust the oven thermostat to a low setting such as gas mark 1/2 or 1. Keep checking the oven until the desired temperature has been reached. If the flame goes out suspect that the thermostat bypass is blocked. If specified by the manufacturer, clean the bypass and recheck operation. Some thermostatic valves do not facilitate strip down maintenance and as such may require to be replaced.

11. Flueing/Chimney Standards

11.0 Flueing/Chimney Standards

The correct design and installation methods for domestic flue/ chimney systems, as with ventilation, is critical for the safe operation of any gas- fired appliance. In some instances this can be a complex matter due to factors such as appliance location, building design, adjacent structures/ buildings etc. The appliance manufacturer installation instruction must be consulted in all accounts. Where these are not available or, where specific instruction is not given, we can obtain detailed guidance on the design, installation and maintenance of flue systems for appliances with a heat input not exceeding 70 kW net within BS 5440 part 1.

11.1 Classification of Flue Systems.

To ensure compliance with European Standards, appliances and flue systems have been given a classification code as specified in the *European Committee for Standardisation* document PD CEN TR 1749. Appliance classification codes relate to the methods used to evacuate the products of combustion. We can basically split gas appliances into three different types, namely:

1. Type A – Flueless.
2. Type B – Open-flued.
3. Type C – Room-sealed.

As British standards are being upgraded these designations are coming more to the fore, for example BS 5440 part 1 uses them extensively throughout the standard. Therefore it is important that the gas operative becomes familiar with these designations to ensure the correct selection, interpretation and application of all current standards pertaining to their area of work.

CEN TR 1749 uses numeric subscript with the appliance type lettering to identify each specific evacuation method. The first subscript number segregates the different individual flue configurations, where as the second number identifies whether or not the appliance has a fan, and if so, where that fan is located in relation to the heat exchanger.

The second subscript numbers are as follows:

1 – natural draught – no fan.

2 – fan located downstream of the heat exchanger (flue hood/ flue).

3 – fan located upstream of the heat exchanger (combustion chamber/ burner).

For example a B_{11} appliance is one which is open flued (B) with a draught diverter (initial 1) and natural draught (second 1) where as a B_{12} appliance is again open flued (B) with a draught diverter (initial 1) but has a fan located downstream of the heat exchanger (second 2), i.e located either on the flue hood or in the flue before the down draught diverter. Table 11.1 provides the relevant designation for specific appliance types with further diagrammatic examples of more common chimney systems.

It should be noted that Type A appliances do not have a flue system and as such the first number does not apply.

Additional supplementary suffixes are used for specific information pertaining to the safe operation of the appliances such as special evacuation methods. safety devices etc. These supplementary suffixes are listed below:

For type A and B appliances:	AS – atmosphere sensing device.
	BS – clearance monitoring device (spillage monitoring device)
For type B appliances only:	D - appliance connected to a non-metallic (third subscript) duct to evacuate hot humid air and products of combustion, for example a tumble dryer.
	P – appliance installed to a positive pressure flue system.
For type C appliances only:	R – appliances which may have either wall or roof termination.

Appliance Type	Initial Number	Description
A - Flueless	N/A	No initial number with type A appliances.
B – Open Flue	B1	Incorporates a Draught Diverter
	B2	No Draught Diverter (formally called a closed flue)
	B3	No Draught Diverter connected to a single natural draught common duct system.
	B4	Incorporates a Draught Diverter connected to the terminal by means of a flue duct.
	B5	No Draught Diverter connected to the terminal by means of a flue duct.
C – Room Sealed	C1	Horizontal balanced flue with flue and inlet ducts installed directly to outside atmosphere.
	C2	Flue and inlet air ducts are connected to a common "SE duct" system which forms part of the building construction used for multi-appliance installations.
	C3	Vertical balanced flue with flue and inlet ducts installed directly to outside atmosphere.
	C4	Flue and inlet air duct connected to a common "U" duct system which forms part of the building construction used for multi-appliance installations.
	C5	Non-balanced flue and inlet air duct system (split flue)
	C6	Flue and inlet air duct connected to a flue system not specifically designed or sold for that appliance.
	C7	Vertical flue system installed direct to outside air with the air supply taken from the loft space. The draught diverter is installed in the loft above the air inlet. (if fan assisted commonly known as a vertex system)
	C8	Non-balanced flue system where the flue is ducted direct to outside via a single or common natural draught duct system. Inlet air supply is ducted direct from outside
	C9	Vertical balanced flue system with the flue and inlet duct installed directly to outside. All or part of the air inlet uses an existing vertical duct within the building such as a chimney.

Table 11.1 - Classification of gas appliances according to flue type

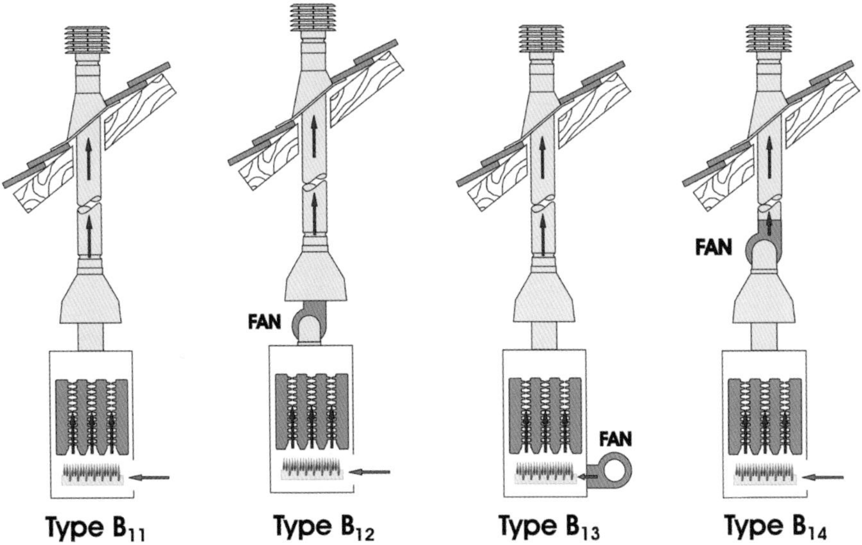

Figure 11.1 Type B1 -Open-flue appliances with Down draught diverter

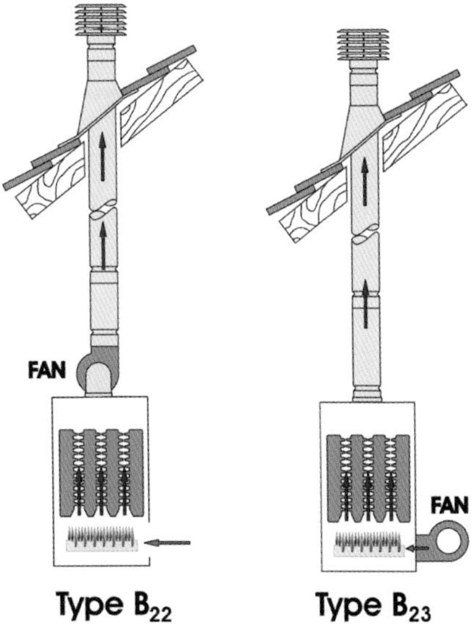

Figure 11.2 Type B2 - Open-flue appliances without a down draught diverter

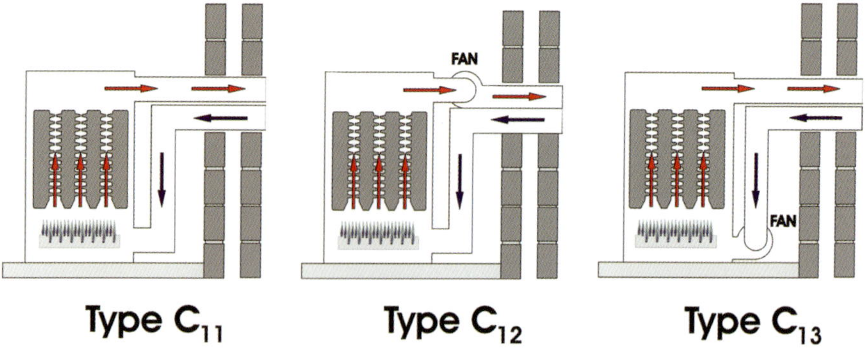

Figure 11.3 Type C - Room sealed appliances

11.1.1 European Chimney Designation

Using PD CEN TR 1749 appliances can be classified by means of their chimney/ flue configuration. In addition to this chimneys and flues themselves must be classified using a "designation string" consisting of alphanumeric coding to specify their design parameters. The coding used is based on the basic chimney designation scheme contained within BS EN 1443.

An example of a designation string is given below:

BS EN 1856 T 400 N1 D 1 G1

- Chimney Standard → BS EN 1856
- Temperature Class → T 400
- Pressure Class → N1
- Resistance to Condensate Class → D
- Corrosion Resistance Class → 1
- Sootfire Resistance Class → G1

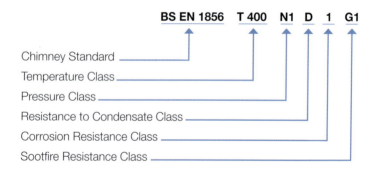

Chimney Standard - This is the manufacturing standard of the chimney in this case BS EN 1856 is for twin walled steel chimneys.

Temperature Class - The number after the 'T' designates the nominal working temperature of the chimney, in this case 400°C.

Pressure Class - This is dependant on the gas tightness achieved by the product with the number, either the number 1 or 2 (1 being the better). 'N' - negative; 'P' - positive and 'H' - diesel generator.
Resistance to condensate - 'W' wet and 'D' dry
Corrosion Resistance - This is fuel dependant and uses the numbers 1 to 3. The number three has better resistance than 1.
Sootfire resistance - This relates to the fire resistance of the material if a fire were to start in the chimney, 'G' with sootfire resistance and 'O' without.

Further guidance can be found in Approved Document J of the Building Regulations (England and Wales).

11.2 Exchange of Information and Planning

The design, installation of the chimney system, provision and installation of the gas appliance(s) may involve a number of different trades and persons. It is essential that all are involved in the decision process, especially the customer, with all necessary compatibility details documented to ensure that the chimney system is fit for purpose.

Compatibility details must include:

- type, size and route of the chimney system, and
- type and size of the intended gas appliance.

A number of factors such as cost, aesthetics and location may bear heavily on the final chimney design,The customer must be advised as to the reasons behind the chimney options and appliance selection such that an agreement can be met prior to installation.

Where the chimney system is provided as part of an appliance, for example fanned draught room sealed boiler, the installer must agree with the customer that the chimney system is compatible with the application. Any agreement must be appropriately documented.

11.3 Open Flued Natural Draught Chimneys

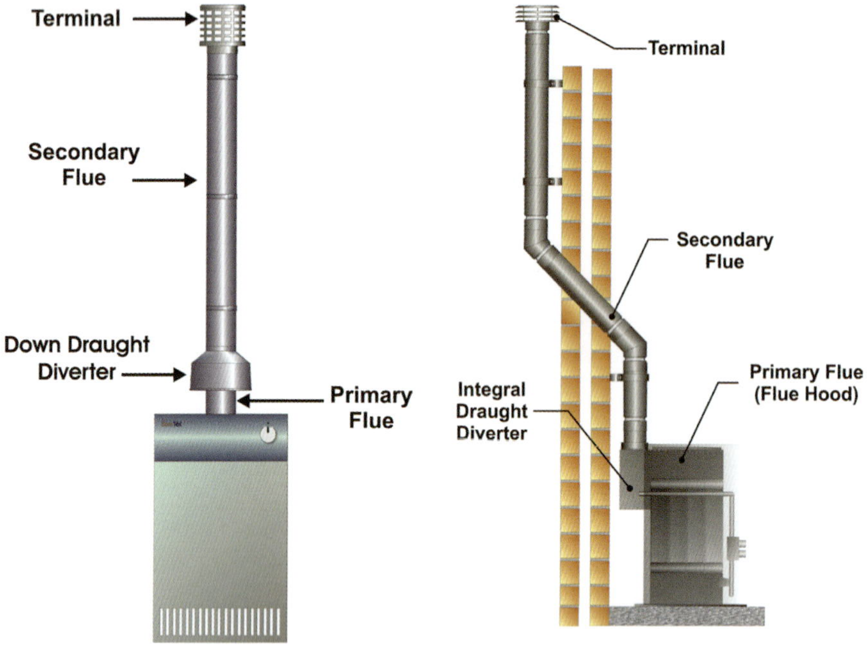

Figure 11.4 Construction of Open Flue System

An open flue consists of 4 main components;

The **primary flue**, which in most circumstances forms an integral part of the appliance and will most probably, be part of the appliance combustion chamber.

The **draught diverter,** again normally forms an integral part of the appliance, the purpose of the draught diverter is to divert any downward draught from the secondary flue away from the combustion chamber, this could be caused in certain adverse weather conditions where wind may blow down the flue, it also allows air to enter the flue system which will dilute the combustion gases, should there be an excessive "PULL" on the secondary flue the draught diverter breaks this "pull" and prevents this from affecting the combustion in the appliance.

The **secondary flue**, is the section in flue from the draught diverter to the terminal/chimney outlet.

The **terminal** or chimney outlet as it may also be referred to, although an approved terminal is not always required, fitting one can assist in preventing down draught, rain entering the flue and birds nesting in the flue. Examples of approved terminals are given in section 11.3.5.

The principle of operation of an open flue is in the different densities of the hot combustion gases within the flue and the cooler air surrounding the flue, the less dense hot flue gases (lighter) will rise through the flue system and exit via the terminal with cooler (heavier) air entering into the appliance combustion chamber, this creates the flue draught (pull), factors which may affect the flue draught are;

- **Chimney Height** - increasing the height of the chimney will increase the flue draught, however a high chimney can have an adverse affect on the safe evacuation of the products of combustion. As the chimney height increases the greater the surface area of chimney system. Depending on the material, this may result in high frictional resistance and heat loss. Both of these factors reduce the effectiveness of the chimney, therefore a high chimney or an increase in height does not necessarily mean it will operate satisfactory. Where no alternative is available, the selection of chimney pipe type and material is critical.

- **Chimney Route** - The chimney route should be as vertical and short as practical with the minimum amount of bends and elbows. Any changes in direction should be no more than 45°. Sections of chimney between bends should be as short as possible. Horizontal runs and 90° bends should be avoided unless stated otherwise by the appliance/chimney manufacturer.

- **Flue gas temperature** - As the temperature of the flue gases increases the less dense and lighter they become making it easier for them to pass through the chimney system. Alternatively as the flue gases cool they become more dense and heavier reducing the flue draught and increasing the risk of excessive condensation within the chimney. It is essential that a chimney system be designed to ensure an adequate amount of heat is retained in the products of combustion to allow their safe removal and reduce condensation. Single wall metallic chimney systems are more likely to have excessive heat loss and as such will have a greater susceptibility to flue reversal and the formation of excessive condensation. Where this is the case the chimney should be designed in such a manner that the chimney material and components used significantly reduce the overall heat loss of the chimney, for example by using twin wall insulated metallic chimney components.

- **Heat losses** - Metal chimney components conduct heat more rapidly than non-metallic components such as brick, block work etc. Long runs of chimney system expose the flue gases to a larger surface area of material increasing the risk of excessive heat loss. The chimney system should be run within the premises for as long as possible to reduce any heat losses from the system, long external runs are not recommended. Where this is unavoidable and no other alternative exists it is recommended to use twin wall insulated chimney systems to BS EN 1856 part 1. Single wall metallic chimney systems should not be used due to the high external surface temperature and excessive heat loss, especially in external locations.

- **Cross sectional area** - The cross sectional area of the chimney must be large enough to handle the total volume of the products of combustion including any dilution air. For individual appliances the chimney diameter must not be less than that specified by the appliance manufacturer. Care must be taken when installing a chimney system such that the internal surface is not damaged and any excess jointing material, if used, is removed from the inner surface. Any intrusion into the inner flue will restrict the flow of products.

11.3.1 Chimneys General

New or used appliances cannot be installed unless the appliance manufacturer's instructions are present. The route of the chimney must not impair the structural stability of the building, for example joists, roof timbers or other load bearing structures etc must not be cut unless approved measures have been employed to compensate for any structural alterations. Any openings in an individual chimney must not be in any other room other than the room in which the appliance(s) are installed. Boxing in, false chimney breasts, cladding etc around or attached to a chimney must be appropriately sealed as to prevent the products of combustion escaping and entering other parts of the premises.

Unless otherwise stated by the appliance/flue manufacturer then;

- A minimum of 600 mm vertical chimney is required directly above the appliance/draught diverter.

- The minimum size of a chimney for a gas appliance (other than for a gas fire) shall not be less than the cross-sectional area of the appliances flue spigot.

- New gas fires require the chimney to have a minimum circular cross sectional area of 12 000 mm^2 or, if the chimney is constructed with gas flue blocks, it shall have a minimum cross sectional area of 16' 500 mm^2 (no dimension that makes up the cross section area shall be less than 90 mm).

- Where a metal chimney is run outside the building it may be of the twin walled type that has an air gap separating the internal & external walls for lengths up to 3 m, for any lengths above this then it shall be of the insulated type conforming to BS EN 1856-1 to prevent condensation.

- Any existing asbestos chimney or component shall only be re-used if it is complete and no alterations are made (e.g. cut). An approved adaptor must be used when connecting to any other type of chimney component. Risk assessments must be carried out and the Asbestos (prohibition) regulations should be consulted.

- Any new gas appliance connected to an existing chimney or when a liner is being installed shall have the chimney swept unless the previous appliance was a gas appliance. Where a chimney has not been used for a long period of time then having it swept prior to installing a gas appliance will ensure that it is unobstructed.
- Where there has been a solid fuel fire previously used in the chimney, then there may have been an air supply from the under floor space ducted in to the catchment area, these existing under-grate air ducts must be permanently sealed off.
- When a chimney has been inspected and it is found to have a damper, register plate or restrictor plate fitted then these must be either removed or permanently fixed open to ensure the flue remains unobstructed.
- Only one gas appliance per chimney is permitted unless the chimney has been specifically designed to accommodate more than one appliance, for example a shared chimney systems.
- Any existing fuel burning appliances must be removed prior to connecting a gas appliance into an existing chimney. The gas appliance must be connected directly into the chimney system and not through the existing appliance.
- Where a draught diverter is required and it is not an integral part of an appliance then it must be installed in the same room/space/compartment as the appliance per the manufacturer's instructions.
- If an appliance is connected to a chimney via any other position other than at it's base, the chimney must be sealed not less than 250 mm and not more than 1 m from the point of connection. Some form of access must be made available into this void for cleaning purposes.
- An approved adaptor must be used when connecting any metal chimney to an appliance, chimney component or other make of metal chimney. The adaptor must be installed as per the manufacturers instruction. Metal chimney components or fittings must not be cut.
- Gas appliances shall never share a flue with a solid fuel fired appliance.

- Chimney/flue should be supported at 1.8 m intervals and at any bends unless otherwise specified by the chimney/flue manufacturer.
- Building regulations require when a chimney/hearth is installed that a notice is displayed detailing the suitability of the chimney and components, this notice should be attached to the fabric of the building at either the chimney/hearth that it relates to, at the electric consumer unit or at the mains water supply stopcock (see section 13).

11.3.2 Chimneys Materials

New chimneys must be constructed of a material which conforms to current standards. Existing chimneys may be constructed from materials which are no longer approved, however did meet the requirements of earlier standards, for example asbestos cement. These chimneys may still be acceptable as long as the installation is of sound construction, meets approved installation methods and has been found fit for purpose. Any defects must be rectified prior to use. The type of materials used within a chimney system will always be dictated by the chimney's purpose and location. Where doubt exists the relevant building regulations, standards and manufacturers instruction should be consulted. The following is a list of materials used in chimney construction:

- **Brick or other masonry construction** - the appliance manufacturer must be consulted as to the suitability of the appliance to be installed into an unlined brick or other masonry constructed chimney. Where an appliance is installed into this type of chimney system the method of connection into the chimney must restrict the entry of debris into the appliance spigot or connecting chimney pipe. A void must be available below the point of connection or spigot for a gas fire, to allow debris to collect without causing any restriction. Access must be available into the void either by an access plate or removal of the appliance to inspect and clean the void.
  Brick or masonry construction chimneys may be lined with:
  - Clay/ ceramic liners conforming to BS EN 1457, or
  - Concrete liners conforming to BS EN 1857, or
  - Flexible steel liner conforming to BS 715 (Revised) or BS EN 1856-2.

See section 11.3.7 for further information.

- Flue Block Systems used for gas appliances must conform to BS EN 1806 for clay or BS EN 1858 for concrete. Jointing materials may be recommended by the block manufacturer such as fire cement, high temperature silicone, hydraulically setting mortar etc. Any jointing material used must be able to withstand the operating temperatures and must not degrade with exposure to the flue products. See section 11.3.4

- Rigid Metallic chimney systems are factory made with sheet metal and may be of either single or double wall construction. Single wall must not be used externally and in general terms is not recommended. Double wall chimney pipe may be insulated by either a static air gap between the inner and outer wall or have this gap filled with an insulating material such as rock wool, perlite or vermiculite. Normally air insulated double wall metallic flue has an inner wall constructed of aluminium with a mild steel outer wall. The outer wall may be galvanised with a heavier grade metal to allow external use. Pipe designed for internal use only must not be installed externally. Insulated twin wall metallic chimney inner and outer walls are normally constructed from stainless steel. Rigid metallic chimney pipe must conform to BS 715 (revised), BS EN 1856 parts 1 and 2 as appropriate.

- Rigid Non-Metallic - asbestos cement flue systems conforming to BS 567 and BS 835 are no longer used for new gas installations, however as discussed previously may be reused as long as they are not cut or damaged. It should be noted that some fibre based cement flues conforming to BS 7435 parts 1 and 2 do not contain asbestos. Both materials look very similar, identification can only be confirmed by specialised registered companies. Where it is not know as to the asbestos content of the chimney material it should be treated as if it were asbestos with the relevant health and safety measures put in place until confirmed otherwise. Only approved adapters must be used when converting to another chimney material. Socket joints must face upwards with the gap between the socket and pipe wall sealed using an appropriate sealing material such as fibrous rope with fire cement or high temperature silicone sealant (Fig 11.5).

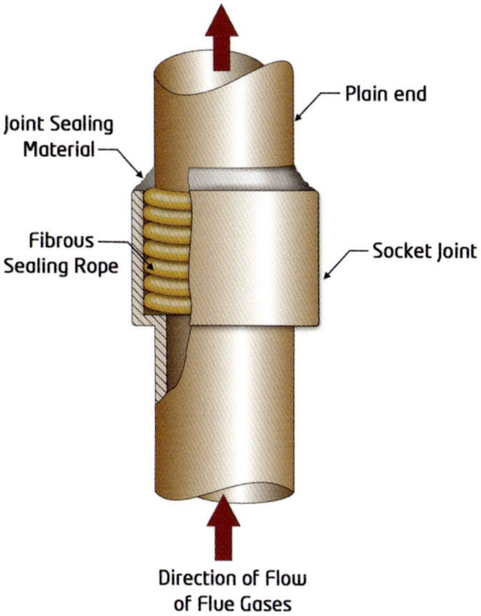

Figure 11.5 Asbestos Cement Flue System Socket Joint

- **Vitreous Enamel** chimney systems are only suitable for internal installation. Care must be taken when cutting the chimney pipe due to the shards of enamel creating a safety hazard. The installation methods are similar to those of the asbestos cement chimney system with the socket pointing upwards and appropriately sealed. This type of chimney component must meet the requirements of BS 6999.

- **Plastic flue pipe** - normally used with condensing appliances it must only be used where specified by the appliance manufacturer. Jointing must be done using approved fittings and materials strictly adhering to the manufacturers recommended installation methods. All pipe and joints must be accessible for inspection. Due to the low fire resistance of plastic flue pipe it should not be routed through any other room or internal space to outside as this will affect the fire integrity of the building. It may be permissible if encased in a suitable sealed fire resistant enclosure, further advice should be sought from the relevant local authority building control. It should be noted that if the flue pipe is encased in any enclosure there must be appropriate inspection hatches installed.

11.3.3 Temperature Effects

A chimney should be installed in such a manner to avoid the risk of igniting any adjacent combustible surfaces. The manufacturer of the chimney should give details on the separation requirements and clearances from combustible materials in their instructions. For a custom built chimney the designer is responsible for supplying details on clearances. Where no specific details are available and the flue gas temperature is likely to exceed 85°C, a single wall metal chimney shall be spaced at least 25 mm from any combustible surface measured from it's outer surface. For twin walled metal chimneys the 25 mm is measured from the outside surface of the inner liner. It is advisable to encase a metal chimney in a non-combustible sleeve as it passes through a combustible wall, floor or roof not forming part of a fire compartment with a 25 mm air gap between the chimney and sleeve. It is normal good practice to seal both sides of any opening where the chimney pipe passes through a combustible floor or wall with fire stop plates with the annular space between the chimney pipe and floor sealed with mineral wool. Any gap between the plate and pipe is normally sealed using a high temperature silicone sealant.

Where a chimney system passes through a dwelling other than the one in which it is installed it shall be encase in a non-combustible enclosure. The enclosure must be fire rated to minimum level as given in the Building Regulations.

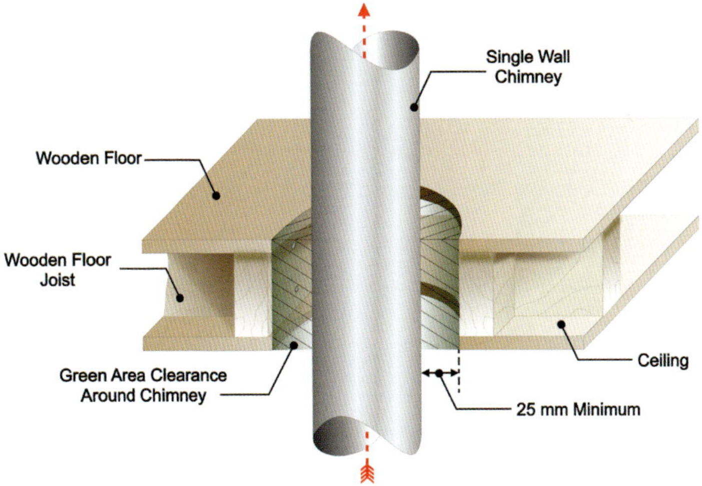

Figure 11.6 Single wall chimney - clearance from combustible surface

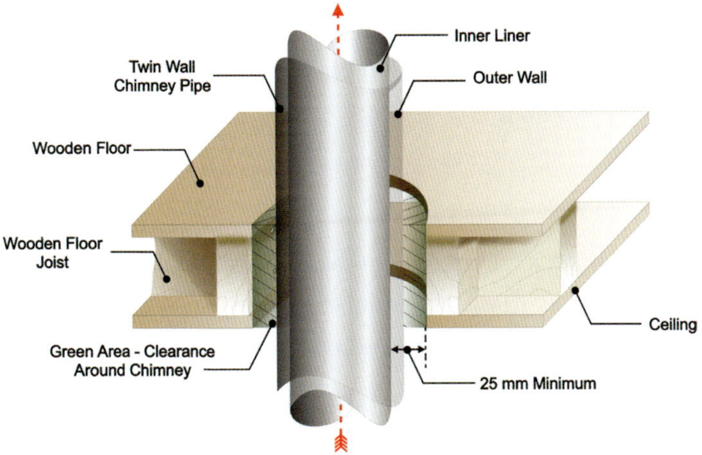

Figure 11.7 Twin wall chimney - clearance from combustible surface

11.3.4 Flue (Precast) Blocks

The following gives some guidance on the key points for the correct installation of precast block.

- New flue block installations must have a minimum cross sectional area no less than 16 500 mm^2 with no internal dimension less than 90 mm
- Precast blocks that are not built in to the building shall be secured to the building as per the flue block manufacture instructions, any fixing shall not penetrate the blocks.
- Any blocks that are broken or cracked shall not be used.
- Offset blocks shall have a maximum offset of 30°.
- A minimum of 600 mm vertical flue is required directly above where the appliance connects to the flue.
- It is vital during construction of the blocks that any surplus jointing material (snotters) is removed from the internal edges of the flue, if this is not done then it may reduce the cross sectional area of flue and could reduce the flow of the products of combustion exiting through the flue which may in turn lead to the appliance spilling.
- Appliances must be approved by the appliance manufacturer for use with a precast block flue system.
- A chimney that has been constructed from gas flue blocks should not have plaster applied directly to the flue blocks as the possible operating temperature of the flue may cause any directly applied plaster to crack.
- Where a flue system is required to extend the flue blocks through a roof space, then the flue should be a minimum of 125 mm in diameter double walled flue (single walled metal or flexible flue lines should not be used for this purpose).
- When connecting a block to metal chimney then the correct adaptors as specified by the chimney manufactures shall be used.
- When installing a gas fire to a block chimney then there shall be a space provided below the spigot of the fire for the collection of any debris that may fall down.

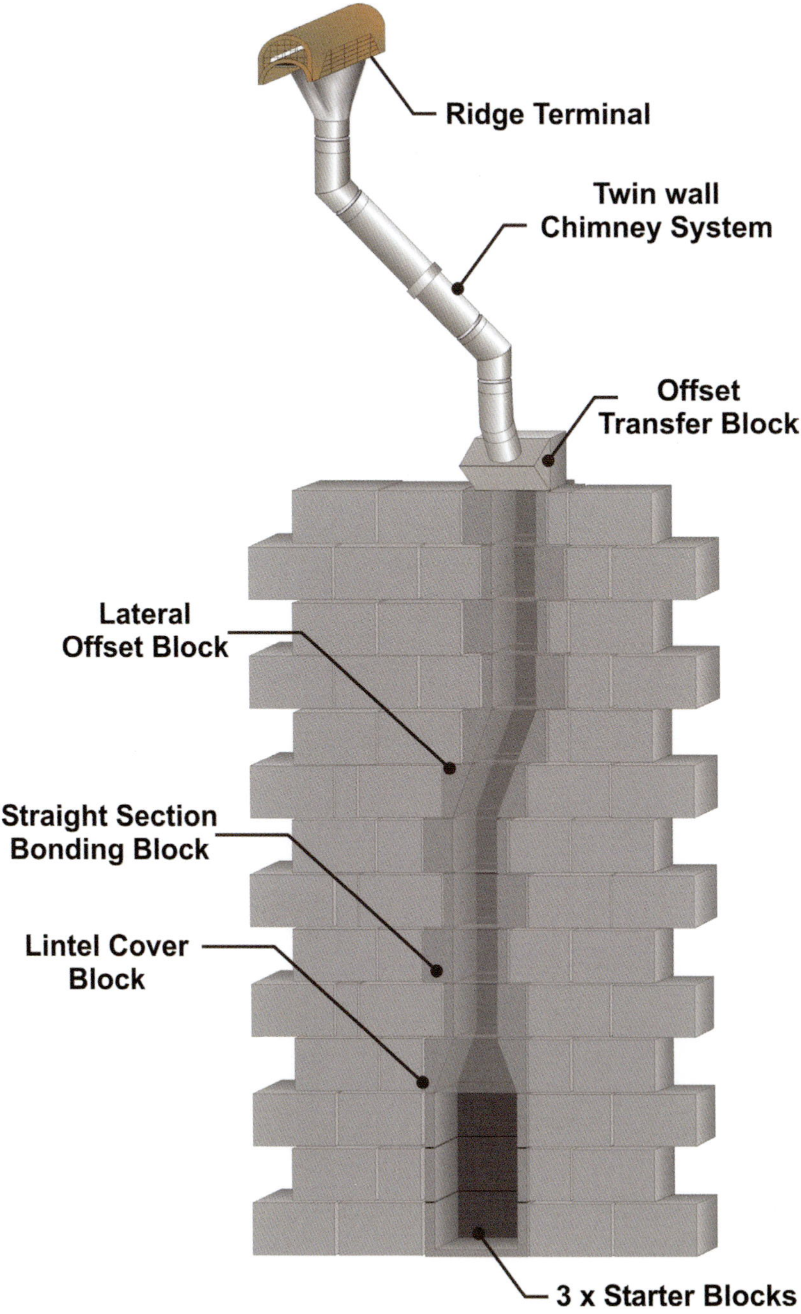

Figure 11.8 Block Chimney construction

11.3.5 Chimney Outlets (Terminals)

Terminals play an important part in the safe operation of the chimney system and must be positioned correctly. They are mainly designed to:

- aid in the evacuation of the flue gases to outside atmosphere, even under extreme weather conditions,
- prevent entry of rain and any foreign matter into the chimney system such as leaves, snow, small animals and birds etc which may block the chimney.
- reduce down draught.

Approved terminals must be designed such that any opening must allow entry of a 6 mm ball but prevent entry of a 16 mm ball. Where the chimney has a cross sectional area dimension of 170 mm or less they must have an approved terminal, however chimneys fitted with a pot and above this size which were built for solid fuel appliances do not require any other terminal when they serve a gas fire or circulator. A suitable guard may be required when a terminal is not fitted on a chimney outlet where there is the likelihood of birds nesting or other forms of wildlife entering the chimney, this guard should have a maximum size of the minor dimension of any opening of 20 mm (e.g. an opening of 15 mm x 30 mm would be acceptable).

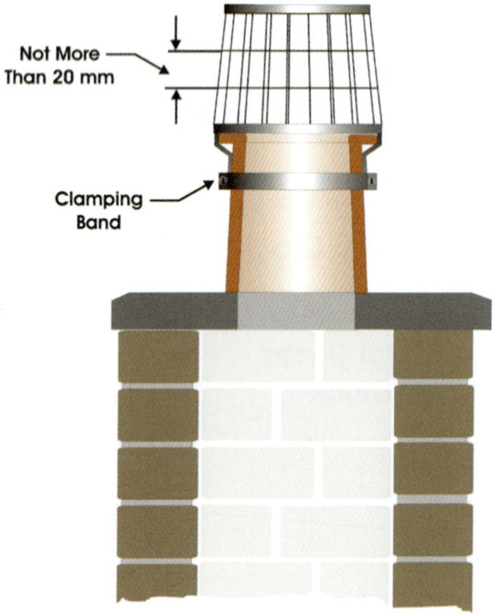

Figure 11.9 Bird Guard

Terminals are constructed from a number of different materials such as aluminium, stainless steel, mild steel, clay, ceramics etc and come in many different designs. The type and size of terminal used must be suitable for the appliance(s) installed. Only specific terminals are suitable for use with DFE gas fires (unless stated otherwise by the appliance manufacturer the minimum chimney dimension is 175 mm) and care must be given to ensure that any existing terminal complies with the appliance manufacturers requirements. The terminal manufacturer should state whether or not their terminal is suitable for this application. Clay chimney inserts which are used to ventilate redundant chimneys are not approved for use with any fuel burning appliances and must be removed prior to installing a gas-fired appliance (see figure 11.12).

Figure 11.10 Approved terminals which may also be suitable for use with DFE fires

Figure 11.11 Unsuitable Terminals for a DFE fire as the chimney outlet may be less than 175 mm

Figure 11.12 Non-approved chimney inserts

11.3.6 Chimney outlet positions for open flue, natural draught installations

Where a chimney passes through a tiled/slated roof the joint shall be weatherproofed by the use of a flashing that has a minimum upstand of 150 mm at any point where the flue passes through the roof.

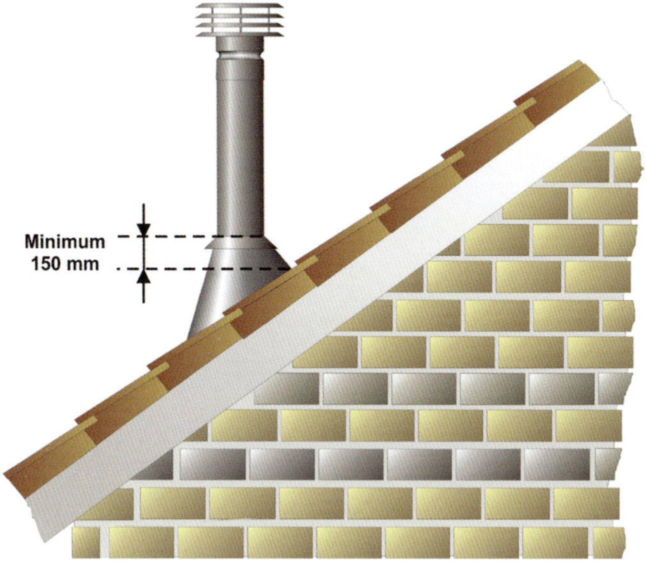

Figure 11.13 Minimum upstand of chimney flashing

To prevent down draught occurring when terminating the chimney outlet on steeply pitched roofs it is recommended that the outlet should be located at the highest point of the roof e.g. at or above the ridge. Should a slabbed over chimney outlet be used then there should be side outlets on opposite sides with free areas of at least 12 000 mm^2.

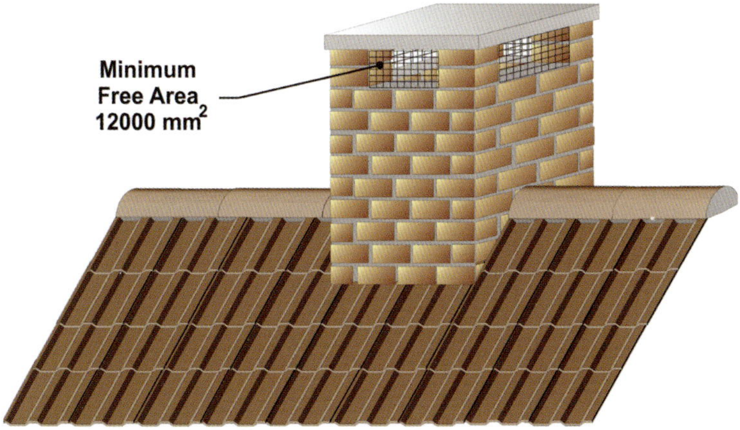

Figure 11.14 Slabbed over chimney

When you have multiple chimneys terminating in close proximity (within 300 mm) of each other then the following conditions shall be met:

- The terminals shall be at least 50 mm apart.
- All operational chimney outlets shall terminate at the same height.
- Ridge terminals which are open on all 4 sides shall be at least 300 mm apart.

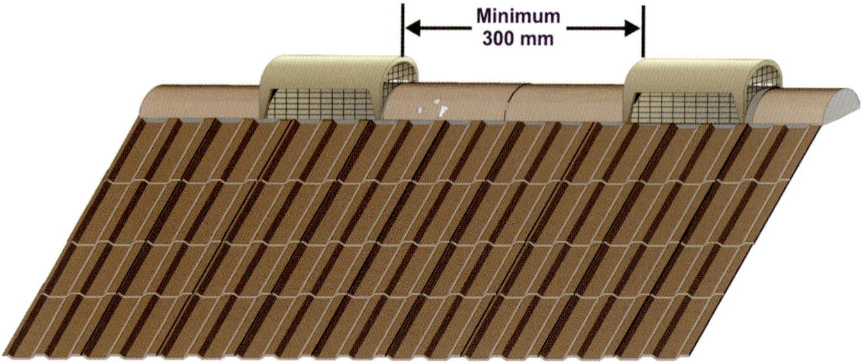

Figure 11.15 Distance between chimney outlets located on ridge

Where a passive stack ventilation (PSV) system is installed in a dwelling that also contains an open flued appliance, then where possible, the outlets for both should terminate on the same face of the building to ensure both outlets are subjected to the same external wind conditions. The open-flue chimney should terminate at the same height or above that of the PSV terminal to minimise the risk of down-draught.

The position for the chimney outlets are given in the following diagrams.

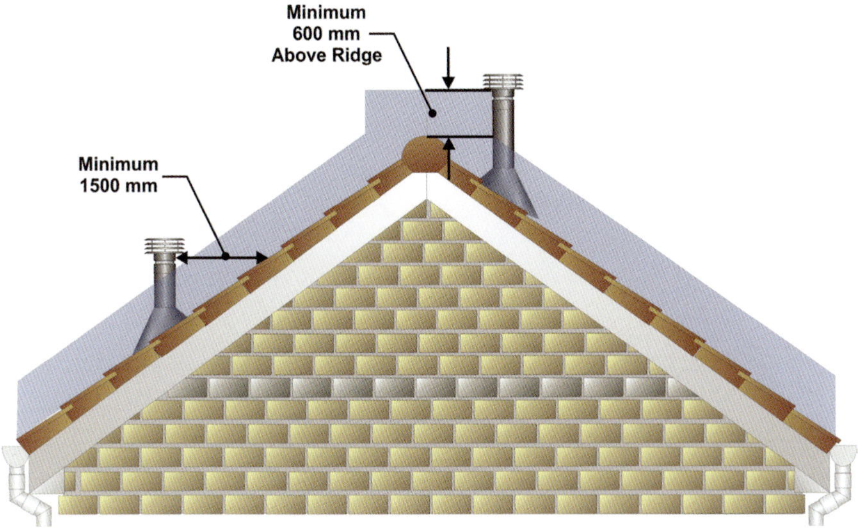

Figure 11.16 Open flue, Natural Draught Chimney termination on pitched roof

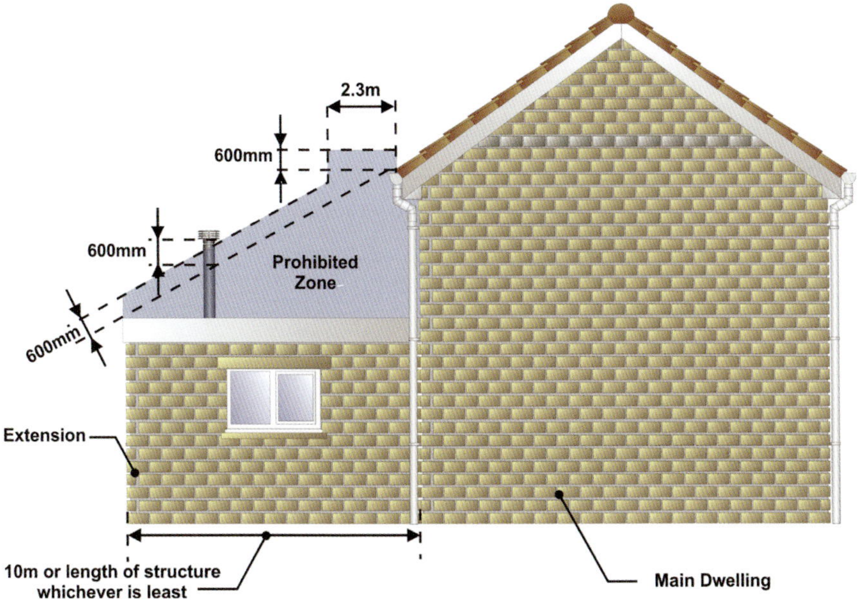

Figure 11.17 Termination of open flue, natural draught chimney near adjacent structure or building

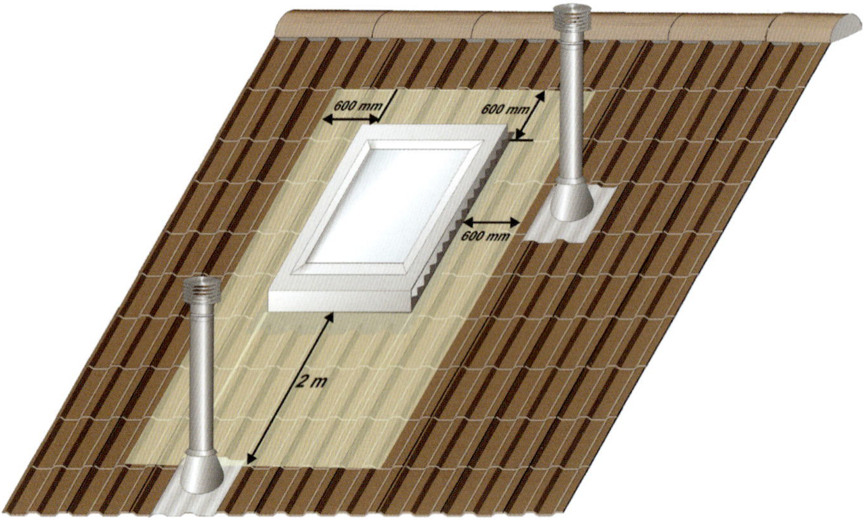

Figure 11.18 Open flue or room sealed, natural or fanned draught chimney termination adjacent to window or any other opening on pitched roof

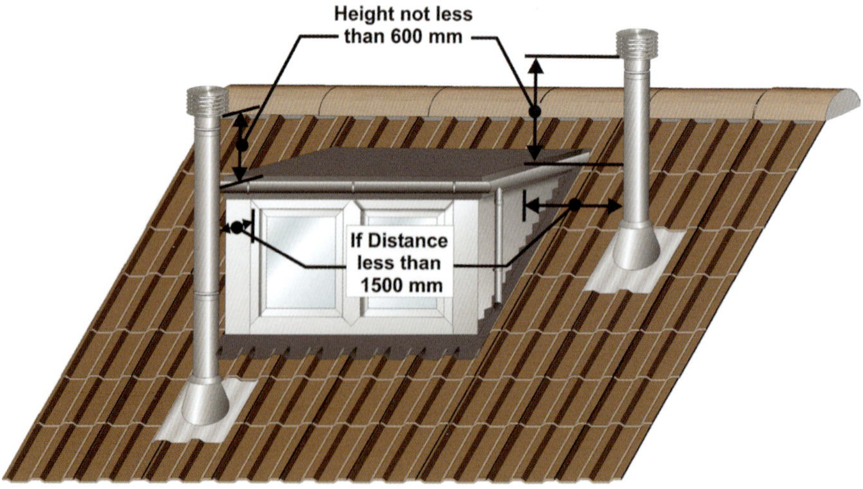

Figure 11.19 Open flue, natural draught chimney termination adjacent to window or any other opening on pitched roof

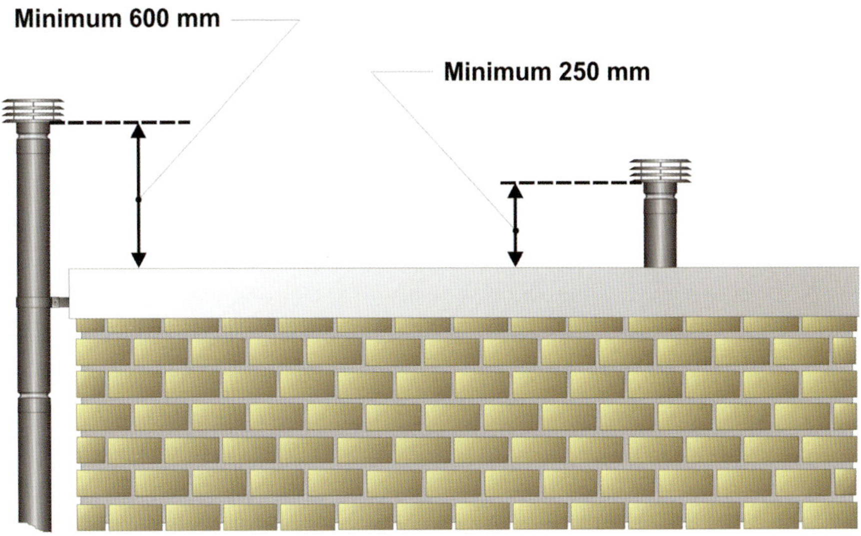

Figure 11.20 Open flue, natural draught termination on flat roof no parapet or structure

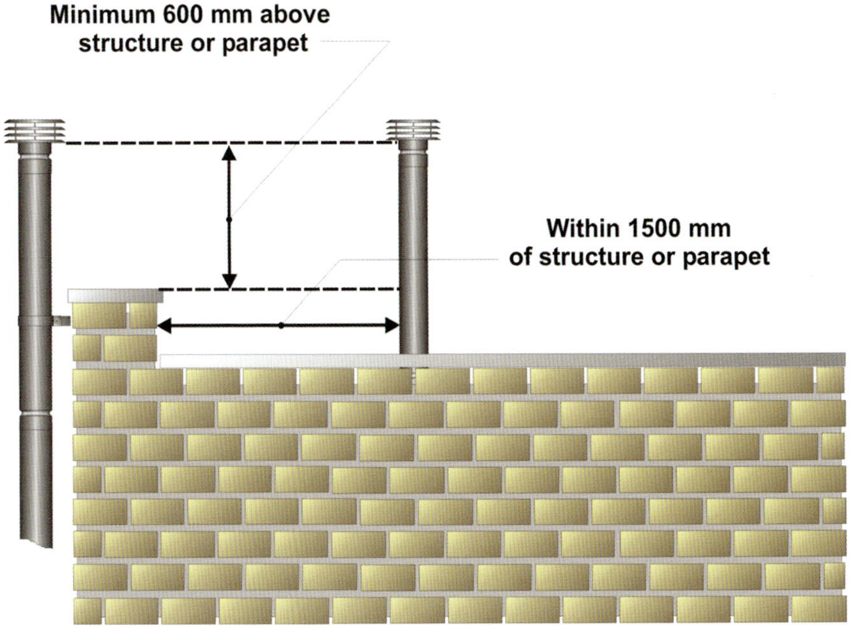

Figure 11.21 Open flue, natural draught termination on flat roof next to parapet or structure

11.3.7 Lining chimneys

New chimneys of brick or masonry construction shall be lined at the time they are built with either clay or concrete flue liners.

An existing chimney will normally be lined with a metal stainless steel liner, although an alternative method would be a poured concrete liner. This involves inserting an inflatable tube down the chimney then pouring concrete into the annular space between the tube and chimney wall. When the concrete has set the tube is then deflated and removed. Poured concrete liners must only be installed by competent approved contractors and independently certified as compliant and fit for it's intended purpose. HETAS provides guidance on poured concrete liners which are suitable for solid fuel appliances. These types of liner are also approved for use with gas appliances. Poured concrete liners are not suitable for use in new chimney systems or where high levels of condensation may be present, especially chimney's which have previously been used for another fuel.

Where a metal liner is to be installer then the chimney must be swept prior to the installation to ensure that any soot deposits are removed as these may cause the liner to corrode, the liner should be capable of lasting the life span of the appliance (10 to 15 years).

When an appliance is to be replaced and the chimney has previously been lined with a metallic liner, then unless the existing liner can be assured to continue to operate for the full life span of the new appliance, the liner shall be replaced.

After lining the chimney then the annular space between the liner and the chimney shall be sealed at the top and bottom, the liner shall be supported at the top of the chimney, at the base of the liner the annular space must be sealed in such away that any seal cannot fall out.

Where a back boiler is to be installed into an existing chimney that was lined during construction with a clay or concrete lining then flue from the appliance shall be connected to the chimney liner with either a short length of rigid or flexible flue pipe. The rigid or flexible flue pipe must protrude into the existing liner by a minimum of 150 mm with the annular space between the liner and the flue pipe appropriately sealed.

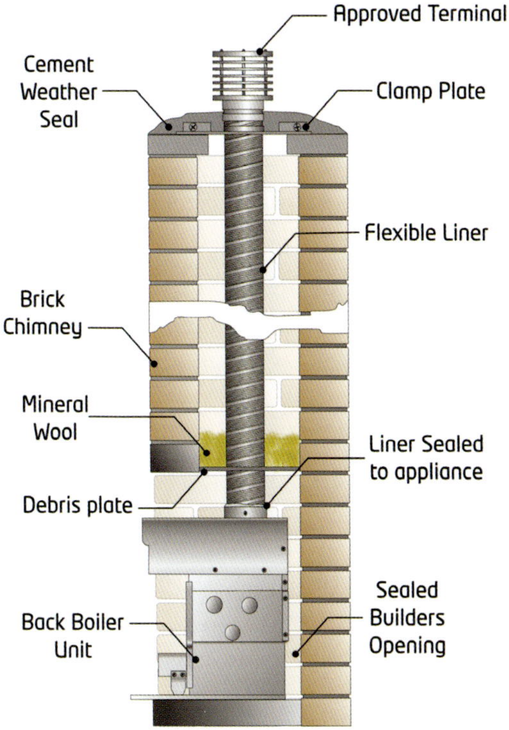

Figure 11.22 Flue liner installation onto a back boiler unit (fire removed for clarity)

Appliance type/ combination	Chimney length
Gas fire or a gas fire with a circulator	Greater than 10 m (external wall)
	Greater than 12 m (internal wall)
Gas fire with back boiler unit	All lengths
Circulator	Greater than 6 m (external wall)
	Greater than 1.5 m external and total length greater than 9 m

Table 11.2 Appliance/chimney combinations which require the chimney to be lined

When installing an appliance to a chimney there should be sufficient space for any build up of debris, access shall be provided for the removal of debris from the void.

Where any appliance is;	Depth mm	Volume dm^3
Fitted to an unlined brick chimney	250	12
Fitted to a lined brick chimney that has been previously used with solid fuel or oil		
Fitted to a flue block or metal chimney that has been previously used with solid fuel or oil		
Fitted to a flue block/metal/lined brick chimney where the chimney is new, unused or has been previously used with gas	75	2

Table 11.3 Minimum Void Dimensions below an Appliance Connection

11.3.8 Condensation in open flue, natural draught chimneys

The following steps shall be taken to ensure problems of excessive condensation forming in chimneys are minimized.

- Single walled chimneys shall not be routed externally for gas appliances other than for the final part of the flue as it passes through the roof to its termination.
- As stated prevoiusly twin walled flue which has only an air gap for insulation shall not be installed externally for a length of more than 3 m. Where lengths in excess of this are unavoidable insulated chimney conforming to BS EN 1856 part 1 must be used.
- Where condensation within the chimney is unavoidable, for example when attached to high efficiency appliances, the chimney must be designed for "wet" use. This type of chimney should incorporate sealed joints which will prevent condensation leaking from the chimney. These types of chimney products are identified by having a "W" marked on them.

- Where it is known or suspected that condensation is or likely to form in the chimney suitable means for the removal and disposal of condensate must be employed. The condensate pipe should be installed at the lowest part of the vertical chimney. To ensure products of combustion do not leak out of the condensate pipe a water trap should be installed as near the point of connection to the chimney as practicable.
- All materials that are used on a chimney/appliance where condensed products of combustion are produced should be resistant to the mildly acidic condensation produced. Materials such as copper, copper based alloys, mild steel and certain grades of stainless steel are not suitable. Non metallic components such as plastic, GRP etc may only be used when the manufacturer specifies it's suitability.

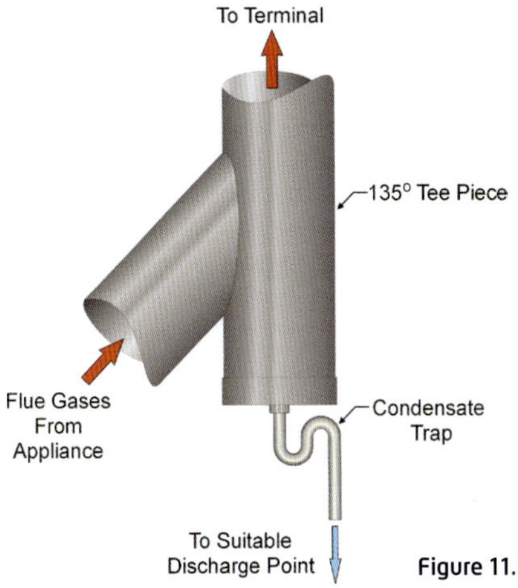

Figure 11.23 Condensate removal from chimney

11.3.9 Thermal Inversion

Thermal inversion or spillage can be caused by a number of different factors either due to faults on the appliance or it's chimney system or other influences such as extract fans, paddle fans, cooker hoods, tumble dryers etc. The less commonly identified cause is due to the passive stack effect. Passive stack ventilation (PSV) is described in detail in section 4.3.4. In addition to the actual PSV system the passive stack effect can be generated by other open-flue appliances such as a gas-fire in the same or connecting room as the open-flue appliance. Where this chimney system terminates above that of the open-flue appliance there is a possibility that it may affect it's operation resulting in "flue reversal". Where a number of different open-flue appliances are installed either in the same room or in connecting rooms it is advisable that they terminate at the same height to minimise this problem. This also applies to PSV which should terminate either at or below the height of the open-flue terminal and on the same face of the building.

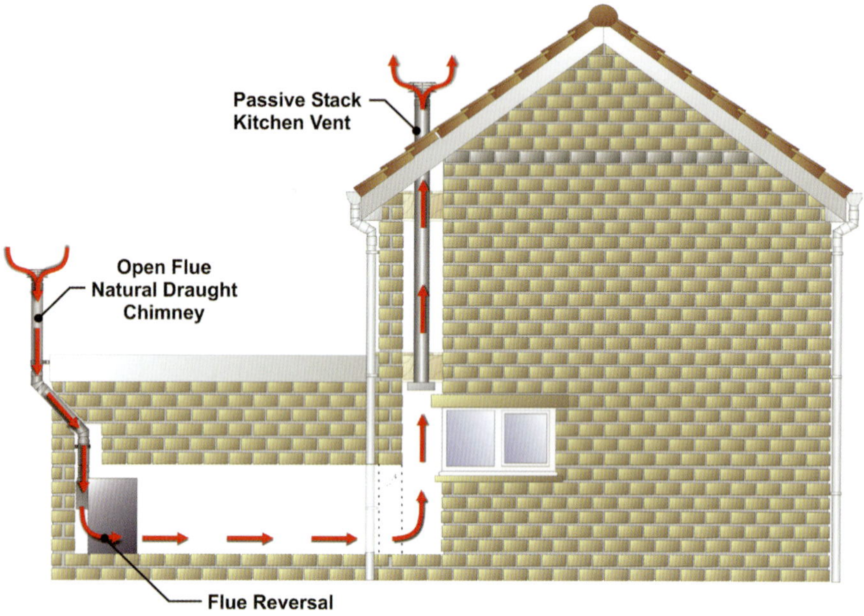

Figure 11.24 Thermal Inversion

11.3.10 Fanned Draught Open Flue Chimney Systems

Where a open flue chimney requires the installation of a fan to assist flue performance this can be achieved by either the appliance manufacturer or retrofitting a fan on the existing chimney system. Fans may be installed inline or at the chimney termination point. As stated by the Gas Safety (Installation and Use) Regulations, where a fan is used for the purpose of evacuating the products of combustion, a safety interlock must be fitted such that the appliance will not operate if the fan were to fail. Some manufacturers of chimney fans incorporate all the necessary safety features in their design with no requirement to install any additional safety devices. The fan duty, chimney route and size are critical to ensure the safe evacuation of the flue products even in adverse weather conditions. It should be noted that any chimney system downstream of the fan is pressurised above atmospheric pressure and as such any joints must be proved leak tight. It is advisable either to fit a fan on the termination point which will maintain the secondary chimney at a pressure less than atmospheric or minimising the length of chimney from the fan to the termination point. When fitting a retro fit fan to the chimney system the draught diverter, if installed, must not be removed, The fan and appliance manufacturers instructions must be adhered to at all times.

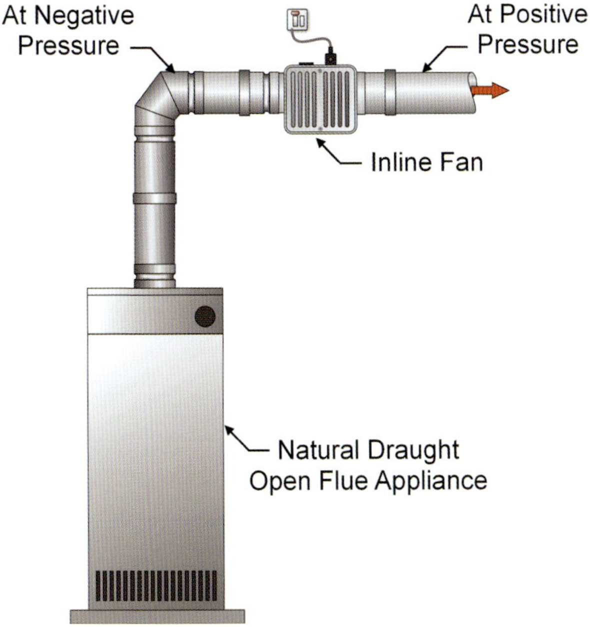

Figure 11.25 Fanned draught, open-flue chimney system with in line fan

Part of the commissioning process of this type of chimney system may include setting the fan to the correct speed for the specific flue/appliance arrangement. Safety controls shall be incorporated into the chimney system to ensure that any flow sensor proves in the "no flow"position before the fan starts, then the sensor should prove "flow" before the appliance can be operated. Should the sensor detect "no flow" during normal operation for more than 6 secs then the gas supply to the main burner should be cut off. If this were to happen a form of manual intervention is required before the gas supply can be re-established unless the appliance incorporates a flame supervision device. Any valve used as part of the safety system to isolate the gas supply must conform to BS 7461 or BS EN 161.

Where a fan-powered chimney system has been installed in a dwelling, any other open flued appliances in the dwelling shall be tested for spillage with the fan-powered chimney in operation and any interconnecting doors open where applicable.

11.3.11 Shared Natural Draught Open Flue Chimney Systems

A shared flue is when 2 or more appliances are connected into the same flue. In this circumstance then each appliance shall be:

- of the natural draught type with a draught diverter,
- fitted with a flame supervision device, and
- incorporate a safety device that will shut the appliance down before there is a dangerous build up of products of combustion in the room.

The chimney shall be designed to ensure the complete evacuation of all combustion products from the connected appliances. Access must be made available for inspection/ maintenance. There must be no discharge of combustion products through any other connected appliance to the flue system when they are not in use.

Where the appliances are installed on different floors of a building each appliance must be appropriately labelled stating that it is part of a shared chimney system and must not be removed or replaced without first consulting

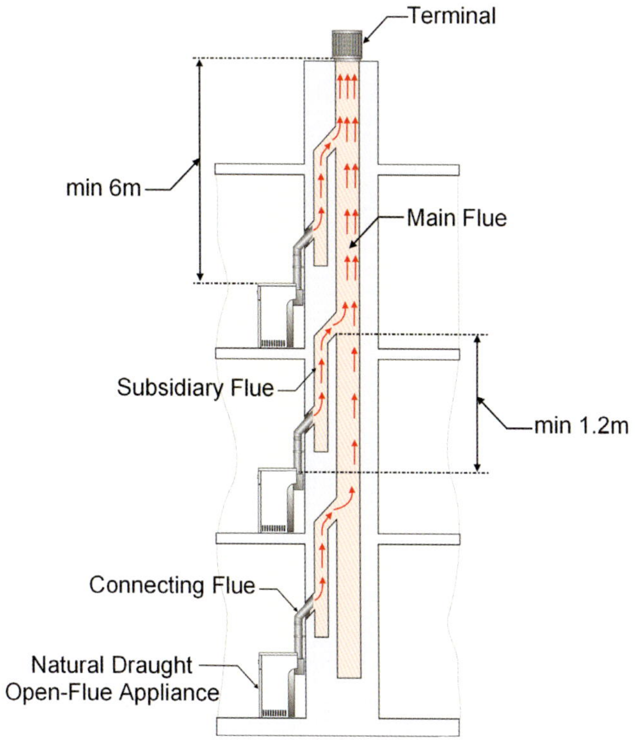

Figure 11.26 Shared chimney system

the responsible person for the building. Replacement appliances which are installed into an existing chimney must be of the same type and no greater rating than the appliance which was removed. The connecting pipe between the appliance and chimney system must rise at least 1.2 m above the appliance outlet before connection into the main chimney system (this increases to 3 m for a gas fire).

The chimney must not be run externally or be encased in a duct or building structure of an external wall due to the high possibility of unacceptable heat loss from the chimney system.

The minimum cross sectional area of a shared chimney is 40 000 mm^2 and must be sized as per BS 5440 part 1 depending appliance type and rating.

11.4 Room-sealed Natural Draught (Balanced Flue) Chimney Systems

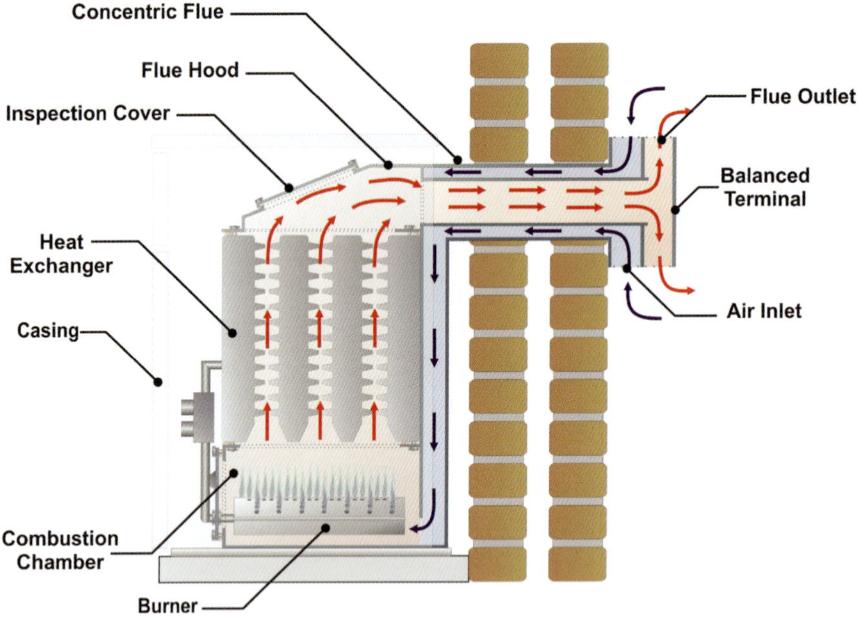

Figure 11.27 Room Sealed, natural draught chimney system.

This type of balanced flue systems have benefits over traditional open flued systems in such that they are sealed from the room containing the appliance, the down side being that they normally require to be installed on an outside wall. The appliance itself forms an integral part of this flue system therefore it is vital that all seals/components are intact, other parts of the flue include the terminal and a flue duct which will normally itself have an inner duct, air for combustion is admitted through the outer of the two ducts into the appliance and flue gases exit from the appliance through the inner duct to the terminal.

The principal of operation of the natural draught balanced flue is that both the air inlet and the flue outlet are normally located together at the same point on an external wall, therefore they are subjected to the same wind or outside pressure conditions, the motive force in the flue is similar to that of the open flue in that the hot less dense (lighter) flue gases rising out of the appliance and the cooler more dense (heavier) incoming air entering the appliance. Terminal guards shall be provided where persons could come in to contact with the terminal, in the absence of manufacture instructions then a guard shall be fitted where a terminal is fitted less than 2.1 m above ground including any balcony or flat roof that people have access to. The guard shall be fitted so that any part of the guard has at least a 50 mm clearance from the terminal is achieved, the guard shall have no sharp edges and shall not allow the passage of a 16 mm ball through any opening.

Room sealed chimneys shall be sealed on assembly and weather sealed to the structure as recommended by the appliance manufacturer. The ingress of water across a cavity wall can be prevented by fitting a drip ring to the flue in the cavity.

Room sealed chimneys passing through combustible walls shall be per appliance manufacturer instructions, where no specific instructions are given or required then the flue passing through the wall shall be contained in a sleeve which should be made from non-combustible material and be sized to provide at least a 25 mm air gap.

11.5 Room-sealed Fanned Draught Chimney Systems

Room sealed fanned draught operate in a similar principal to the natural draught system, the main difference being a fan providing the motive force in the flue which in turn increases the available length of the flue allowing more flexibility in sitting the appliance.

Room sealed fanned draught appliances will normally have the flue system (including plume management kits) supplied by the appliance manufacturer, where this is not the case then the installer shall ensure that, all components are as specified by the manufacturer and installed per their instructions.

Terminal guards shall be provided where persons could come in to contact with the terminal, in the absence of manufacture instructions then a guard shall be fitted where a terminal is fitted less than 2.0 m above ground including any balcony or flat roof that people have access to.

The guard shall be fitted so that any part so that at least a 50 mm clearance is achieved from the terminal, the guard shall have no sharp edges and shall not allow the passage of a 16 mm ball through any opening.

Room sealed fanned draught chimneys passing through combustible walls shall be per appliance manufacturer instructions, where no specific instructions are given or required then the flue passing through the wall shall be contained in a sleeve which should be made from non-combustible material and be sized to provide at least a 10 mm air gap.

Where the flue system is located in enclosed spaces (ceiling voids etc) then they shall be installed per manufacturers instructions and provisions made to ensure that they can be visually inspected.

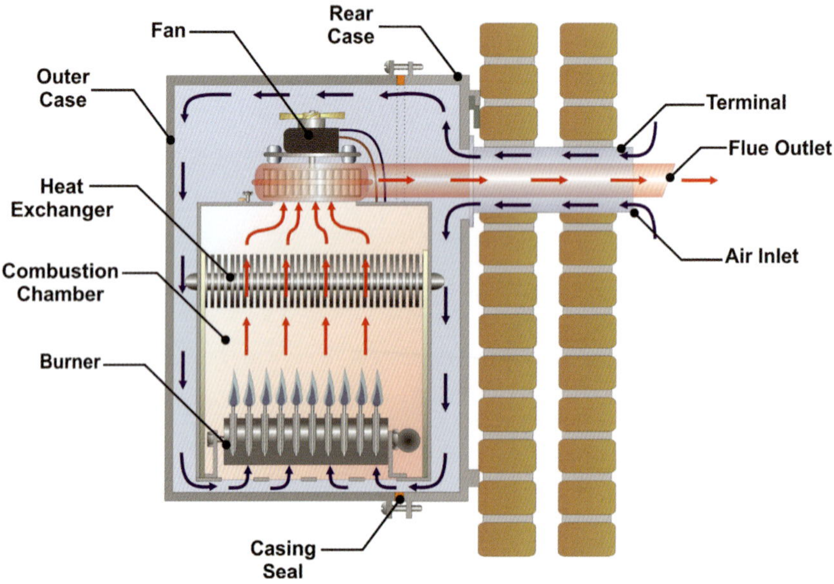

Figure 11.28 Room-sealed, horizontal fanned draught chimney system

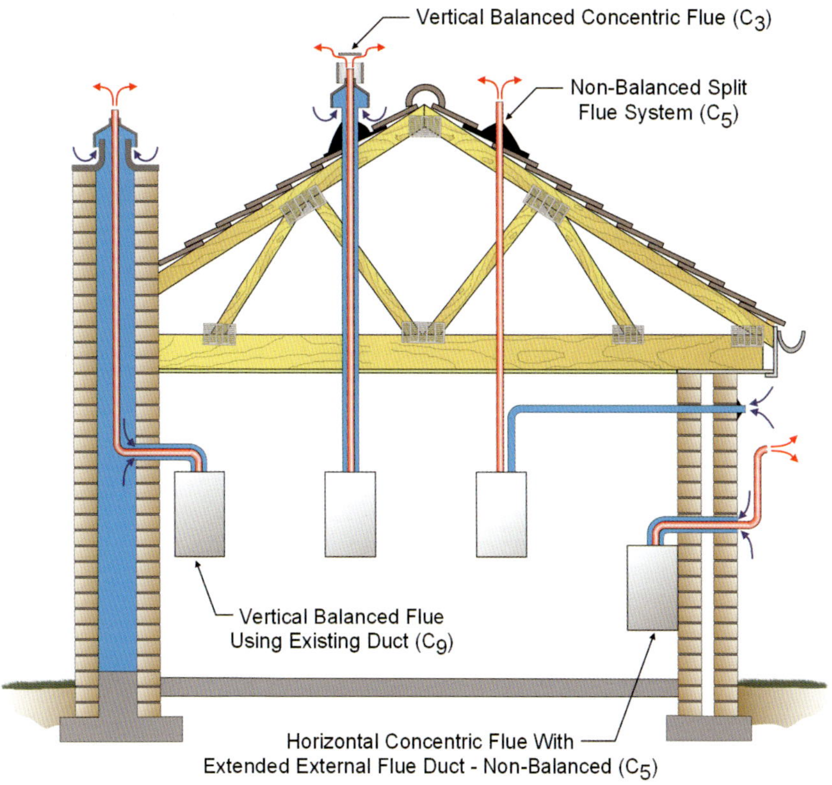

Figure 11.29 Alternative Room-sealed fanned draught chimney configurations

11.5.1 Room Sealed Natural & Fanned Draught Chimney Maintenance Checks

The following checks shall be carried out during routine maintenance:

- The seal between the appliance combustion chamber and the room is complete and in good condition, this may include the case seal/grommets/ sight glasses and that there are no signs of corrosion/distortion on the combustion circuit.
- Ensure that internal equipment (cables, capillary tubes etc) are secured so that they cannot become trapped interfering with the sealing of the combustion circuit when any casing is fitted.
- Ensure that the flue duct is continuous throughout the wall.
- The chimney configuration is free from debris.

11.6 Balanced Compartments

A balanced compartment is similar in operation to a balanced flued appliance The balanced compartment however uses the compartment structure itself as a functional part of the installation therefore it is critical that the compartment is constructed correctly and maintained to ensure safe operation. There shall be no other openings into the compartment other than for the flue and ventilation arrangements.

The compartment door or access cover must meet the following requirements:

- A notice shall be attached stating that the door must be kept closed at all times.
- The door shall be fitted with a self closing mechanism.
- There shall be a draught sealing strip fitted to the door frame.
- There shall be an electrical interlock that shuts down the appliance when the door is opened.
- The door cannot open into any room that contains a bath or a shower or when the appliance has rated net heat input of greater than 12.7 kW, then the door cannot open in to any room that may be intended to be used for sleeping accommodation.

The air supply duct inlet shall be no more than 150 mm below the chimney outlet, this may then be ducted to low level (300 mm or less from floor level) within the compartment. The duct shall have a minimum cross-sectional area of 7.5 cm^2 per kW net of the appliances maximum rated input. This equates to 1.5 times the high level ventilation for a compartment. Where the ceiling is greater than 300 mm above the bottom of the draught diverter an additional high level opening should be provided in the air duct of the same size as the duct (see figure 11.30). Where the air supply is ducted to high level only then the cross-sectional area shall not be less than 12.5 cm^2 per kW net (This equates to 2.5 x the high level ventilation for a compartment) of the appliances maximum rated input (see figure 11.31)

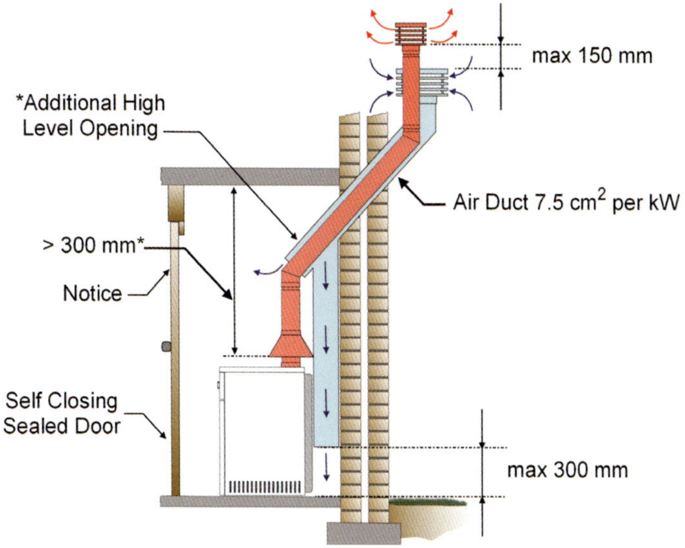

Figure 11.30 Balanced Compartment - Low level ducted ventilation

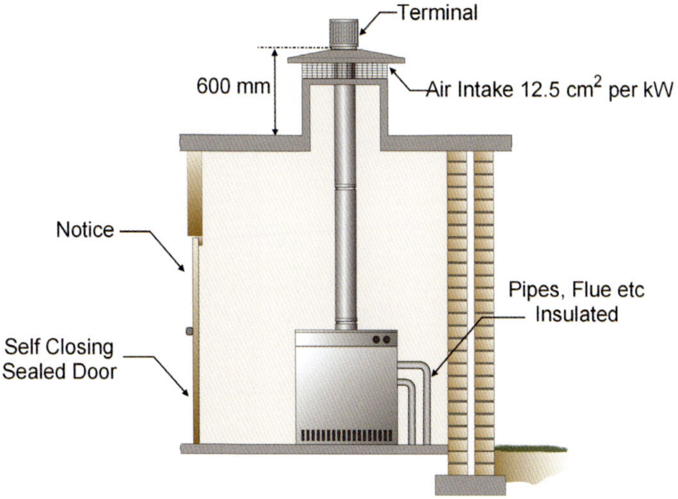

Figure 11.31 Balanced Compartment - High level only ventilation

11.7 SE-duct, U-Duct and System Chimneys

A SE-duct, U-duct and system chimneys are common shared chimney's which allow multiple room sealed appliances on different floors of a building to discharge the products of combustion through a common point of termination. The SE-duct and U-duct are built into the building structure using masonry components such as concrete blocks. Originally these chimney systems where designed for non condensing appliances and with their design may not be appropriate for condensing appliances. A system chimney may be designed as part of the building structure or added at a later date to an existing building. This type of chimney system, if the design criteria permits , allow the connection of high efficiency condensing appliances. Condensate removal is facilitated at the base of the chimney.

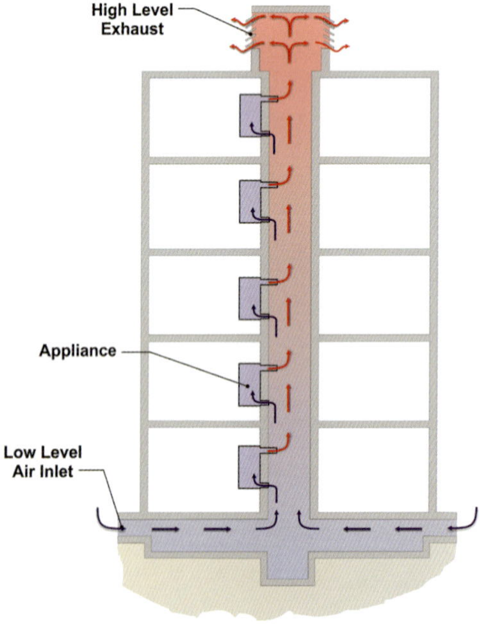

Fig 11.32 SE Duct - Shared Chimney System

A SE-duct is a chimney system designed to rise vertically through the building, discharging at a point above roof level. The air inlet is at low level and may be either a single inlet taken from a neutral pressure zone (e.g. an underground space) or via a horizontal duct run from one side of the building to another. The inlet and outlet shall be open to atmosphere.

Where the air inlet duct is located at or below ground level suitable measures must be taken to ensure that inlet ducts are position such that they do not get flooded or blocked by debris such as leaves, snow etc. They must have removable grilles fitted that have openings that would allow entry of a 10 mm diameter ball but not of a 16 mm diameter ball. The inlet ducts at low level must be labelled detailing the purpose of the duct and contain details of the responsible person for the building (Local authority, landlord etc). Specialist advice must be obtained when confirming the suitability of the size of the SE-duct, however guidance can be found in BS 5440 part 1.

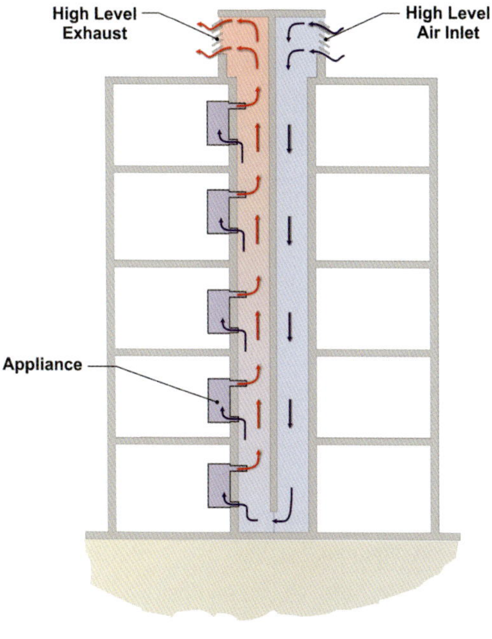

Fig 11.33 U Duct - Shared Chimney System

A U-duct will be constructed in a similar manner but the key difference is that both discharge outlet and the air inlet will be above roof level adjacent to each other.

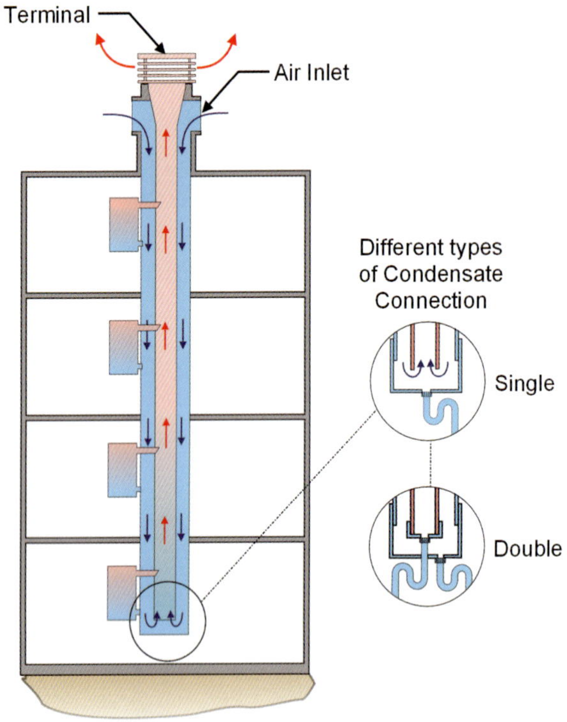

Fig 11.34 System Chimney

A system chimney may be constructed as a concentric or separate twin pipe system. Concentric systems may be used for room-sealed fanned and non-fanned draught appliances which may be condensing or non-condensing whereas the separate twin pipe system is designed to be used on fanned draught only. These types of system rise vertically through the building and terminate at a balanced chimney outlet above roof level. The discharge and air inlet point are adjacent to one another. Shared systems are sized in accordance with BS EN 13384 part 2.

11.7.1 General Criteria

- The inlet/outlet ducts shall be at least 250 mm above the roof and at least 1.5 m form any walls or parapets. Where this is not practical the outlet must be raised such that the base of the opening is above the structure.

- Only appliances designed and approved by the appliance manufacturer may be installed into these types of chimney system.

- Any appliances fitted to these chimney systems should be labelled to indicate that the chimney system is shared.

- Replacement appliances shall not be greater in heat input than the original appliance.

- The ducts and appliances shall be regularly inspected for safe operation as far as it is reasonably practical.

- The installer of the chimney system shall inform the owner or occupier of the premises for the need for regular checks to ensure that they can be used safely.

11.8 Vertex Chimney system

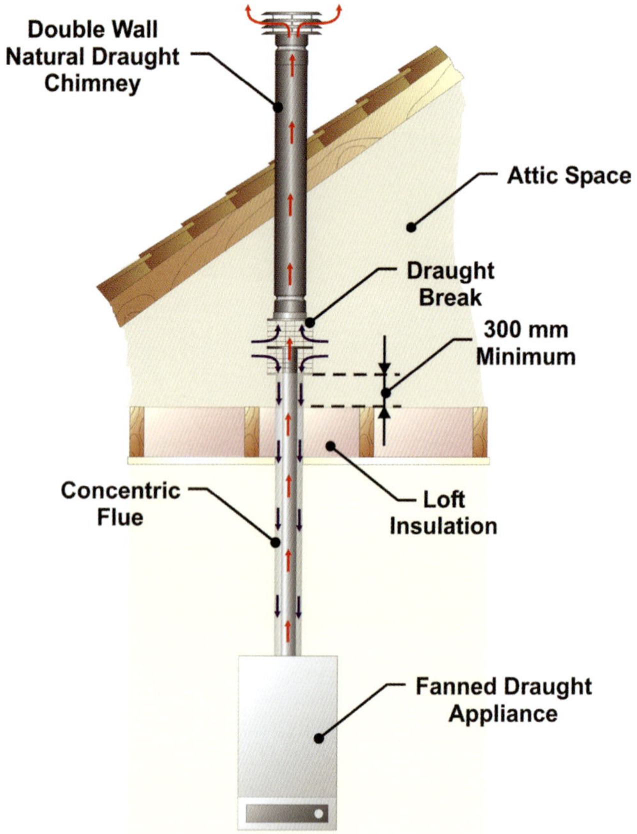

Figure 11.35 Vertex Chimney System

Vertex flues were developed to allow more flexibility with the location of boilers, where there is no suitable outside wall available then a vertical flue system may be the solution, although with a vertical room sealed fanned flue system there will be limitations to the length of the flue, with the vertex flue this may allow greater flexibility to be achieved as this type of flue system utilizes a room sealed appliance then they can be fitted in locations such as bedrooms that may have be unsuitable for the equivalent size of open flued boiler.

The vertex flue normally comprises of a room sealed fanned boiler with a vertical flue duct comprising of an outer duct in which air is drawn from the attic space through the duct in to the appliance and an inner duct that carries the combustion gases from the appliance to the draught break in the attic, the draught break should be at least 300 mm above any flooring or insulation in the attic, the flue above the draught break (secondary flue) can be compared with operation of an open flue and should be installed in a similar fashion per the appliance manufacturer instructions, should there be down draught or a blockage in the secondary flue then spillage may occur at the upper section of the draught break, therefore a spillage test at this point should be carried out when any "work" is performed on the appliance per the manufacturers instructions.

As the appliance takes its air from the attic space then the attic space must be adequately ventilated, if the appliance is installed in a compartment then it should also be ventilated as required per the appliance manufacturer.

11.9 Fan Diluted Flue system

In this type of installation a fan introduces fresh air in to the flue duct in order to dilute the flue gases to a safe concentration at their point of discharge, normally used when two or more boilers are connected to a flue system, due to the flue gases being diluted this allows the flue outlet to be located at points that would otherwise be unacceptable or undesirable.

In all cases the design and installation of fan diluted systems is a specialist matter and must only be carried out by persons competent to do so in accordance with the flue and appliance manufacturer's instructions.

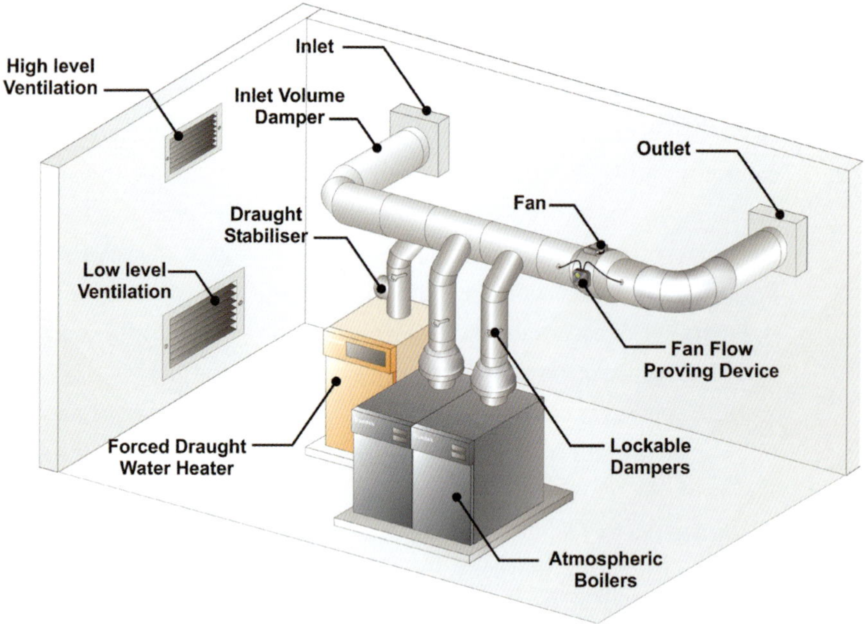

Figure 11.36 Fan Dilution flue system

11.10 Condensing Appliances

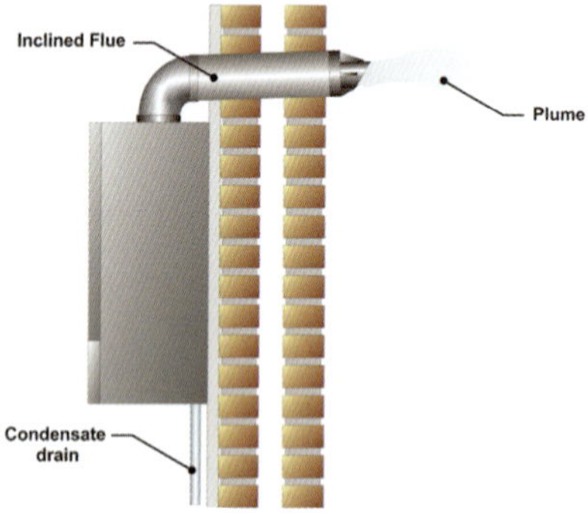

Figure 11.37 Condensing Appliance

In an effort to conserve energy and reduce harmful emissions, appliance manufacturers have developed appliances (HE; higher efficiency) which recover the latent heat of condensation liberated by the water vapour in the products of combustion. The flue will normally rise from the boiler to the terminal so that any condensation formed runs back in to the appliance where it can drain through the appliance condensate drain pipe. The condensate drain pipe must be made from a material that will resist the corrosive properties of the condensate which may be mildly acidic, Mild steel, copper and copper based alloys are not permitted. The condensate drain pipe may connect into the soil or rainwater drainage system or directly into a soak away pit. Basement locations may utilize a condensate pump. At all times the design and installation of condensate drain shall be in accordance with the specific appliance manufacturer's instructions.

The flue may be, depending on the appliance manufacturer, made of plastic due to the lower flue gas temperature from this type of appliance.

The flue outlet shall at all times be sited in such a manner that the plume (wet combustion products) will not cause damage or a nuisance. Consideration should be given to neighbouring properties and the effects of wind conditions. Any discharging horizontal outlet shall be at least 2.5 m from a facing wall/fence/building or property boundary.

Where the plume may be a nuisance, when provided and permitted by the appliance manufacturer, plume kits may be used. In some instances this allows the repositioning of the flue outlet at the terminal to direct the flue gases away from the building either upwards or to the side. This type of system does not require additional flue pipe.

Alternatively the manufacturers provide an extended length of flue duct which can raise and reposition the flue outlet. This type of plume kit is manufacturer and appliance specific. When extending the flue duct the position of the outlet must be such that it is on the safe face of the building as the air inlet to minimise pressure differences between the two ducts. Where the flue outlet duct terminates less than 2 m above ground level, as with any room sealed terminal, a suitable guard must be fitted even though the temperature of the flue gases are less than that of a normal appliance.

Small appliances (those rated at 4 kW net or less) may, provided that the manufacturers specify, have a combined flue and condensate discharge which does not require the installation of a specific condensate pipe directed into a drain. The flue/condensate terminal must protrude by at least 75 mm beyond the face of the external wall and not be be sited where the condensate can drain onto a footpath etc where it could freeze creating a slipping hazard. These flues will drop towards the terminal unlike those which have a condensate pipe.

11.11 Room sealed chimney outlets

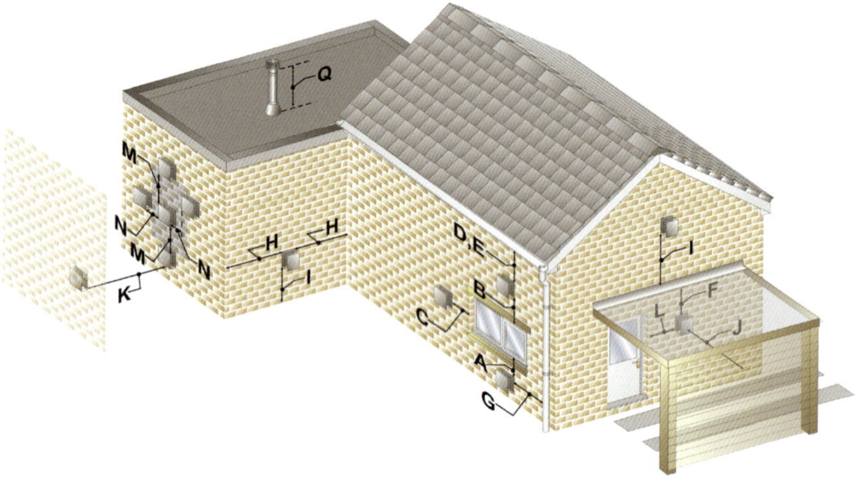

Figure 11.38 Termination positions for Room Sealed, Fanned Draught & Natural Draught Outlets

Where a terminal is to be located within a car port or building extension, then the following recommendations apply;

- There should be two open and unobstructed sides.
- If the roof is made of a plastic material then the installation should be treated with great care as there may be no simple way of protecting the roof.
- In table 11.4 dimension F is then the minimum size measured between the lowest part of the roof and the highest part of the flue terminal.

	Location of room sealed chimney outlet positions (kW inputs are expressed in net)		Minimum clearances	
			Natural draught	Fanned draught
A	Directly below an opening (air brick/openable window etc)	Up to 7 kW	300 mm	300 mm
		Above 7 kW up to 14 kW	600 mm	
		Above 14 kW up to 32 kW	1500 mm	
		Above 32 kW up to 70 kW	2000 mm	
B	Above an opening (air brick/openable window etc)	Up to 7 kW	300 mm	
		Above 7 kW up to 14 kW	300 mm	
		Above 14 kW up to 32 kW	300 mm	
		Above 32 kW up to 70 kW	600 mm	
C	Horizontally to an opening (air brick/openable window etc)	Up to 7 kW	300 mm	
		Above 7 kW up to 14 kW	400 mm	
		Above 14 kW up to 32 kW	600 mm	
		Above 32 kW up to 70 kW	600 mm	
D	Below temperature-sensitive building components, e.g. plastic gutters, soil pipes or drain pipes		300 mm	75 mm
E	Below eaves		300 mm	200 mm
F	Below balconies or a car port roof		600 mm	200 mm
G	From a vertical drain/soil pipe		300 mm	150 mm*
H	From an external or internal corner		600 mm	300 mm
I	Above ground/roof/balcony level		300 mm	300 mm
J	From a surface facing the terminal		600 mm	600 mm
K	From another terminal facing the terminal		600 mm	1200 mm
L	From an opening in a car port into the dwelling (e.g. door or openable window)		1200 mm	1200 mm
M	Vertically from a terminal on the same wall		1500 mm	1500 mm
N	Horizontally from a terminal on the same wall		300 mm	300 mm
Q	Above the intersection with a roof		N/A	300 mm

*This dimension may be reduced to 75 mm for appliances up to 5 kW input.

Table 11.4 Room sealed chimney outlet positions

11.11.1 Proximity of Flue Outlets to Boundaries

The plume from a room sealed terminal can cause a nuisance to neighbouring properties, especially if it is a condensing appliance (see section 11.10). The minimum distances away from a boundary line when the flue outlet is discharging horizontally on to the boundary, runs parallel to the boundary or discharges at an angle are given in Figure 11.39. Additional care must be given when discharging towards a property such that any flue products do not enter into any openings in the adjacent property or re-enter into the property in which the appliance is installed. Note: condensing appliances will require greater distances due to the discharge plume (see 11.10).

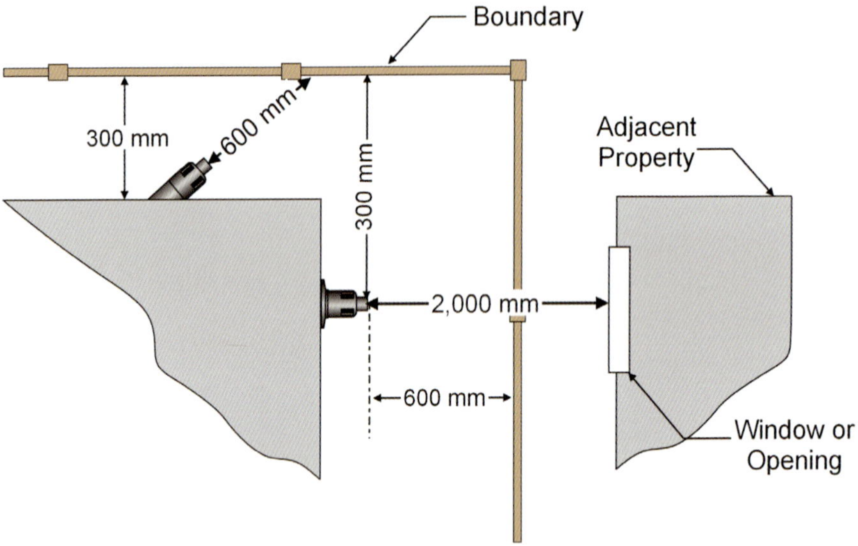

Figure 11.39 Flue Outlet positions in proximity to Boundaries

11.11.2 Termination within basement areas, light wells and external spaces formed by retaining walls.

Chimney outlets must not terminate or discharge into enclosed external areas such as basements, light wells or spaces formed by retaining walls or passages unless specific criteria is met to ensure the safe dispersal of the flue gases. In all accounts natural draught non-room sealed appliances must not terminate into these areas, however room sealed and fanned draught non-room-sealed appliances if discharging into these areas must meet the following criteria:

(a) The chimney outlet must be located not more than 1 m below the top level of the basement area, light well or retaining wall.

(b) The basement area or light well must be formed by a single retaining wall creating an uncovered passageway at least 1.5 m wide. This passageway must terminate at or above ground level with no obstructions at either end such as to restrict the circulation of free air beyond and around the retaining wall and structure.

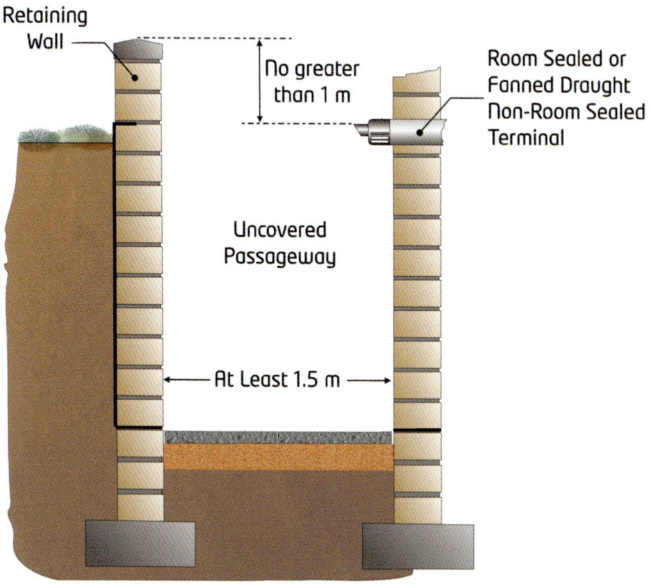

Figure 11.40 Chimney Outlet Discharge into a Basement Area, Light Well or External Space Formed by a Retaining Wall

11.12 Concealed Chimneys and Flues

Where a chimney or flue is routed through a void such as a ceiling space or enclosure, suitable means or access must be provided to allow inspection of the system throughout it's length.

Chimneys or flue systems must not pass through any other dwelling as access for inspection may not be available. They can pass through communal areas including purpose provided ducts where access for inspection should be available.

All inspection hatches must not impair the fire integrity, thermal and acoustic properties of the duct as required by the relevant building regulations. Inspection panels must be sealed in such a manner that the same fire, thermal and acoustic properties of the surrounding structure are maintained. There must be at least one inspection hatch for all voids in which the chimney/ flue passes through, with each hatch measuring at least 300 mm x 300 mm

An inspection hatch is required to be fitted at not more than 1.5 m from any joint. It is also preferable that a hatch be positioned next to any change in direction. Where this is not possible then the bends should be visible from both directions as viewed from the hatches.

As from the 1st of January 2013 installations without inspection hatches will be classified as at risk. Up until this time a visual risk assessment must be carried out to ensure the chimney/ flue is found to comply with current standards and that no obvious defects are apparent. In addition suitable CO alarm(s) must be installed. If these criterion are met the appliance may be left in operation until this date.

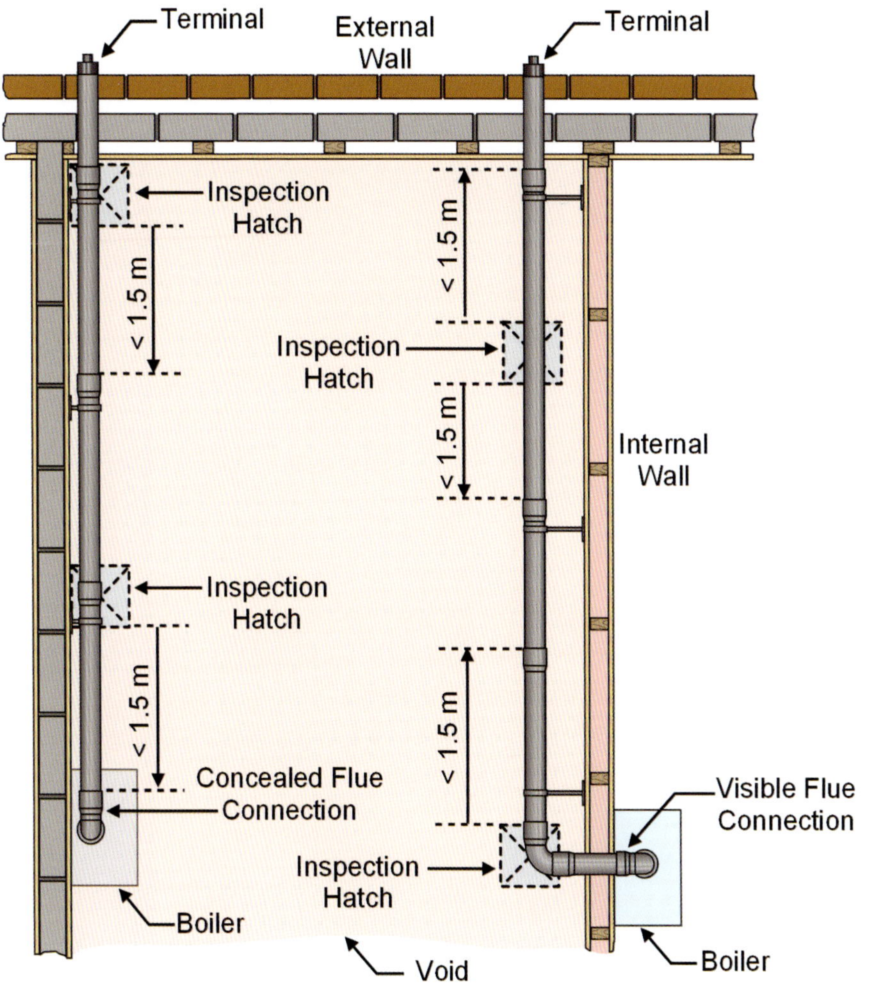

Figure 11.41 Inspection Hatch Positions for a Horizontal, Room Sealed, Fan Assisted Flue Routed in a Void

11.13 Positive Pressure Case Appliances

Historically, fanned draught room-sealed boilers were of the positive pressure type (See Figure 11.42, which shows the differences between positive and negative pressure appliances). For a positive pressure appliance, it is essential to ensure that the combustion chamber casing is firmly secured to the boiler, as the manufacturer intended, with the correct seal in a good condition. If this is not achieved, there is a real risk that products of combustion may escape into the room and due to the poor combustion that is likely to occur, high levels of carbon monoxide (CO) could be produced creating a dangerous environment. A list of these types of appliances is given in table 11.5.

Regulation 26(9) of the Gas Safety (Installation and Use) Regulations (GSIUR) requires an examination of the effectiveness of any flue following work on a gas appliance.

A test method to help ensure that case seals of positive pressure gas appliances comply with the requirements of the GSIUR, has been developed by the gas industry and is described below.

Step 1

Before the case is put back on the appliance the following checks should be carried out:

- Are any water leaks evident?
- Is the backplate or case corroded?
- Where corrosion is evident, is it likely to affect the integrity of the case, backplate, or seal?

Note: The extent of the corrosion should be carefully checked with a sharp instrument e.g. a screwdriver. If the instrument does not perforate the corroded area, this should be deemed acceptable, but the gas user should be advised of the problem and potential consequences if a repair is not made.

- Are the combustion chamber insulation linings intact?
- Is the backplate or the case distorted or damaged? Pay particular attention to the area where the case and seal meet. This may have been caused by explosive ignition of the main burner.
- Is the case sealing material intact and in good condition? (e.g. pliable, free from discolouration, trapped debris, etc.). Will it continue to form an adequate seal between the case and the backplate?
- Is anything trapped or likely to be trapped when the case is put back on (e.g. wires, thermocouple capillaries, tubes, etc.)?
- Are other gaskets and seals intact?
- Is the pilot inspection glass undamaged?
- Are the case fastenings and fixings (including fixing lugs) in good condition? (e.g. screws/nuts stripped).
- Are there any signs of discolouration on or around the appliance, which may have been caused by leaks of products of combustion from the appliance?

Rectify any defects identified in Step 1 as necessary and proceed to Step 2.

Note: Where defects are identified they should be classified using the following criteria in accordance with the current Gas Industry Unsafe Situations Procedure.

Where there are inappropriate or missing case fittings or defective seals, which cannot be remedied, but there is no evidence of leakage, the appliance should be classified as At Risk (AR). If there is evidence of actual leakage, then the appliance should be deemed Immediately Dangerous (ID). Where suitable replacement seals are no longer available the appliance should be classed as ID and regarded as obsolete.

Step 2

When the case has been put on the appliance the following checks should be carried out:

- Is the case fitted correctly?
- Is a "mark" visible showing that the case had previously been fitted closer to the backplate?
- Are all the case screws adequately tightened?
- Is a bright area visible on the screw thread of any of the case securing screws, indicating that the screw was previously secured more tightly?
- Is anything trapped and showing through the case seal?

Rectify any defects identified in Step 2 as necessary. Proceed to Step 3.

Step 3

- Operate/light the appliance
- Ensure that the main burner remains lit (i.e. set the appliance and room thermostats to their highest settings).
- Check for possible leakage; initially this can be done by running your hands around the boiler casing and backplate.
- Then check for possible leakage etc. as in Step 4 where practicable.

Step 4

- Check for possible leakage of combustion products from the appliance
- Where joints have been disturbed, check with leak detection fluid to confirm that there are no gas escapes.
- Check for possible leakage of combustion products from the appliance using a taper, an ordinary match, or similar. (A taper can be used to get into less accessible locations).

Note: Whilst smoke tubes and smoke matches can be used, the results may require further interpretation and these methods are currently being validated.

- Light the taper/match and allow the flame to establish. Position the flame very close to the case seal or any possible leakage point (e.g. back panel).
- The flame will be blown quite easily by the draught caused by a leak. Move the taper around the entire seal, using fresh tapers as required.
- To investigate the seal at the bottom of the case – hold the lit taper between the bottom of the case and the appliance control panel. Does the flame flicker slowly or is it disturbed by leakage flowing from the case? Try the taper in several positions.

Attention: DO NOT confuse natural convection with leakage. DO NOT look for a gas escape with this method.

Rectify any defects as necessary and re-check. If still unsure seek expert advice.

Note: When using this method, be careful not to set fire to surrounding fixtures/furnishings.

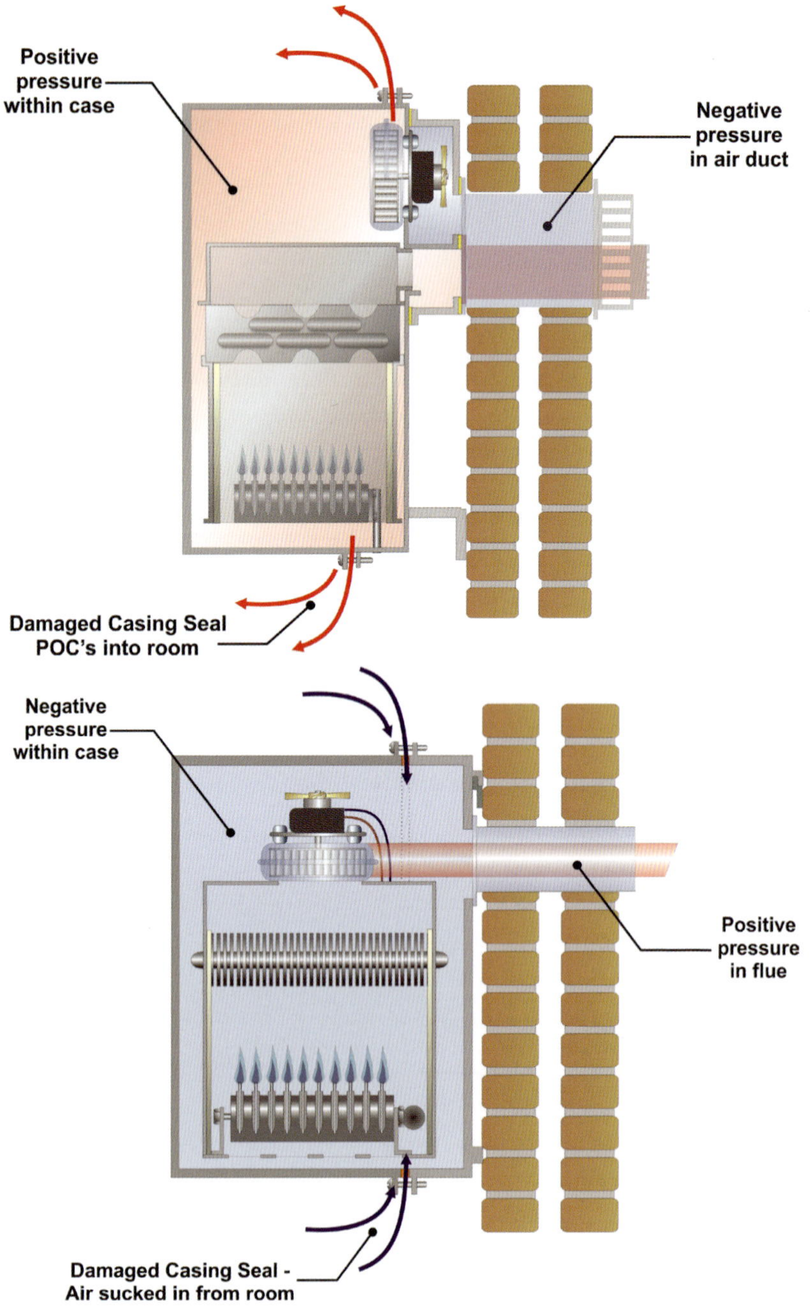

Figure 11.42 Positive and Negative pressure boilers

Table 11.5 contains a list of room-sealed fan assisted positive pressure gas appliances. This list is not exhaustive, but may be used as guidance to appliances that are believed to operate under positive pressure.

Manufacturer and Model	Manufacturer and Model	Manufacturer and Model
Alde International (UK) Ltd	Halstead Heating & Engineering	Stelrad Group Ltd
Alde 2927 Slimline	Ltd	Ideal Elan 2 40 F*
	Halstead 45F*	Ideal Elan 2 50 F *
Brassware Sales Ltd	Halstead 55F *	Ideal Elan 2 60 F*
Ferrolli 76 FF *	Halstead 65F*	Ideal Elan 2 80 F*
Ferrolli 77 FF *	Wickes 45F*	Ideal Excel 30 F *
	Wickes 65F*	Ideal Excel 40 F*
Crosslee (JLB) (Pyrocraft)	Barlo Balmoral 45F*	Ideal Excel 50 F *
AWB 23. 09 WT Combi	Barlo Balmoral 55F *	Ideal Excel 60 F*
Crosslee (Trisave Boilers Ltd)	Barlo Balmoral 65F*	Ideal Sprint 80 F*
Trisave Turbo T45*		Ideal W2000 30 F *
Trisave Turbo T60*	Harvey Habridge Ltd	Ideal W2000 40 F*
Trisave Turbo 30 *	Impala MK 11	Ideal W2000 50 F *
Trisave Turbo 22 *	Impala MK 11 Ridgeseal	Ideal W2000 60 F*
	Impala Super 2 (HF)	
Glow Worm Ltd	Impala Super 2 (VF)	Worcester Bosch
Economy 30 F *		Heatslave 9.24 RS F *
Economy 40F*	Potterton Myson Ltd	Worcester 9.24 Electronic RSF *
Economy 50 F *	Myson (Thorn) Olympic 20/35F ‡	Worcester 9.24 Electronic RSF
Glow Worm Fuelsaver 35 F *	Myson (Thorn) Olympic 38/50F ‡	'S'*
Glow Worm Fuelsaver 45F*	Myson (Thorn) Apollo Fanfare	
Glow Worm Fuelsaver 55 F *	15/30	
Glow Worm Fuelsaver 65F*	Myson (Thorn) Apollo Fanfare	
Glow Worm Fuelsaver 80F*	30/50	
Glow Worm Fuelsaver 100 F *	Supaheat 50/15 with 'A' control	
	Supaheat GC 50/15	
Glynwed Domestic & Heating	Netaheat MK I 10/16	
Appliances Ltd	Netaheat MK I 16/22 BF	
AGA A50	Netaheat MK II 10/16 BF	
AGA A50 A	Netaheat MK II 16/22 BF	
AGA A50 NG	Netaheat MK II F 10-16 BF	
AGA A50 SS	Netaheat MK II F 16-22 BF	
AGA A50 ANG	Netaheat Electronic 6/10	
AGA A60	Netaheat Electronic 10/16	
AGA A60 NG	Netaheat Electronic 16/22	
AGA A75 NG	Netaheat Electronic 10/16 e	

Hi-light P50 Hi-light P50A SC Hi-light P50 S Hi-light P50 SS Hi-light P50 S/A Hi-light P50S/A GLC Hi-light P50S/A SC Hi-light P50/A Hi-light P70 Hi-light P70 S Hi-light P70 SS	Netaheat Electronic 16/22 e Netaheat Profile 30e Netaheat Profile 40e Netaheat Profile 50e Netaheat Profile 60e Netaheat Profile 80e Netaheat Profile 100e	
‡ A safety enhancement kit has been designed for these appliances and is available from Potterton Myson Ltd. * Boilers where spares relevant to case seal problems are still available, based on information provided by manufacturers.		

Table 11.5 Room sealed, fan assisted, positive pressure gas appliances

11.14 Open Flue Inspection & Testing

Testing the open flues on appliances can be separated into three areas:

1. Visual inspection.
2. Flue Flow Test (smoke test).
3. Spillage testing.

Taking each one in turn the following procedures should be administered and only an acceptable pass in each section will allow you to proceed to the next.

11.14.1 Visual Inspection

An inspection of the whole flue is required to ascertain that the flue is constructed and is suitable for the appliance that is connected. Particular attention should be given to the following points:

- Are there signs of spillage.
- Is there adequate ventilation.
- Check the flue route/length/size and that it only serves one room or appliance.
- Is the catchment space is sealed/clear of debris/correct size.

- Is the chimney suitable for the appliance that is to be connected to it.
- Is the down draught diverter in the same room as the appliance.
- Have the correct adaptor and correct method of jointing to the appliance been used.
- Is there at least 600 mm vertical rise from the appliance before the first bend.
- Are any bends a maximum 45° from the vertical.
- Ensure all joints are correctly made (no excessive jointing materials).
- Are there the correct clearances from combustible materials (25 mm).
- Are fire stops fitted where applicable.
- Is the flue correctly supported.
- Ensure that there are no dampers or obstructions unless secured in the open position.
- Is the chimney outlet the correct type, size and positioned correctly.
- Is the chimney weatherproofed as it exits from building.

Part of the inspection may involve gaining access to any loft spaces and other properties that the flue passes through as far as is practical to do so.

Should a masonry chimney fail the inspection a solution may be to install a suitable approved liner.

After you have satisfied yourself that the flue conforms to the standards and has proved to be satisfactory on the visual inspection can you proceed to the Flue Flow Test.

11.14.2 Flue Flow Testing (smoke test)

The purpose of this test is to detect leakage from the flue. A successful flue flow test will be demonstrated by the smoke from the pellet issuing from the correct terminal only.

The flue flow test should be carried out in the following manner.

- Turn off the appliance which is connected to the chimney that is being tested.
- Turn off any fans or appliances in the room that may affect the test.
- Close all doors and windows to the room.
- Prepare the flue/appliance for the test, this may require that a fire which is designed to be installed with a closure plate has the closure plate installed for the test.
- Offer a smoke match up to the testing position, this is to determine if the flue has natural "PULL" when cold.
- It the flue has little or no "PULL" heat up the flue for 10 minutes minimum (may require up to 30mins if using a blowtorch).
- Re-check with a smoke match if heating was required to ensure that the chimney now has a "PULL" and if it has not then suspend the test and investigate as to the possible causes.

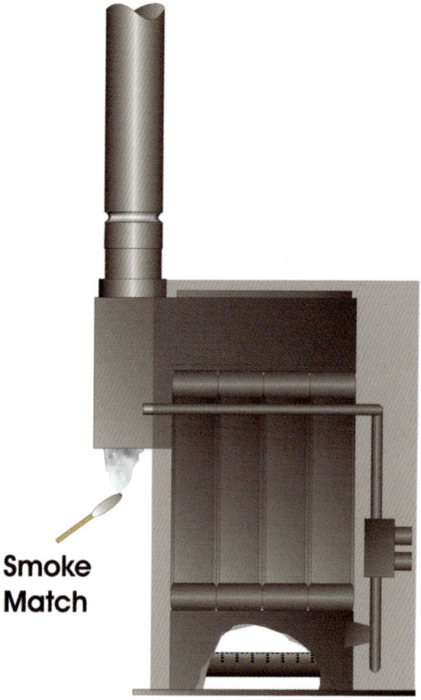

Figure 11.43 Heating Chimney using gas bottle

Figure 11.44 Heating Chimney using gas bottle

- Position the smoke pellet (one that generates 5m^3 of smoke in a 30s burn time) in a safe position at the start of the flue then ignite the pellet.
- Inspect the chimney/flue for leakage as the smoke flows through it. Check for leakage of smoke throughout its length as far as practical including:
  - Any room where the chimney/flue is located or passes through.
  - Any cupboard or attic that it may pass through.
  - Any External part of the chimney/flue (cracks in mortar).
  - Any other dwellings that the chimney/flue may be routed.
  - You may require more than one smoke pellet to carry out the test.
  - Confirm that smoke only exits from the correct outlet and though no other.

After you have satisfied yourself that the flue has passed the Flue Flow Test then the appliance may be installed and a Spillage Test as follows must be carried out.

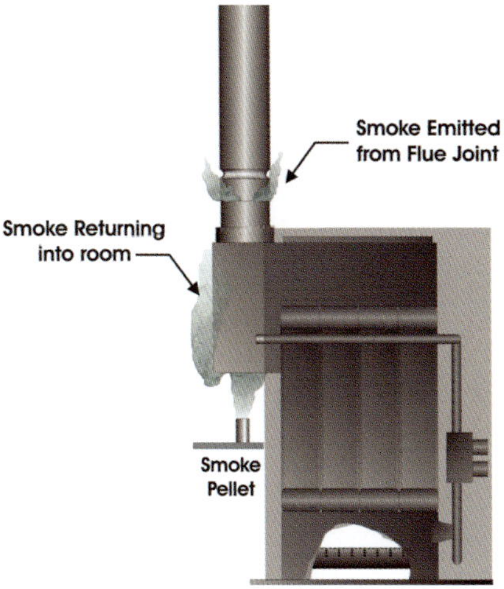

Figure 11.45 Flue Flow - fail

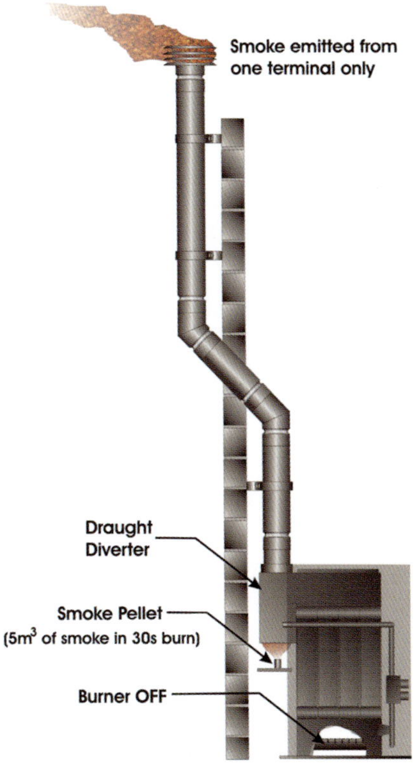

Figure 11.46 Flue Flow Test - Pass

New or used appliances cannot be installed unless the appliance manufacture instructions are present (if they are not present then manufacturer shall be consulted).

11.14.3 Spillage Test

Using the manufacturer's specific instructions

- Consult the manufacturer's instructions.
- Close all doors and windows and adjustable vents.
- Operate any extraction/circulation fans at there maximum settings within the room including any/all of the following:
  - Expel air type.
  - Cooker hood.
  - Tumble dryer.
  - Warm air unit if the return air is taken from the room.
  - Any other open flued appliance with a power flue.
  - De-stratification fan.
  - Radon gas extract system.
- Open any Passive Stack Ventilation (PSV).
- Turn OFF any mechanical air SUPPLY systems (unless they are interlocked to the appliance).
- With the appliance operating at full load, check that it clears the POC using the method specified by the manufacturer. If required, switch off, disconnect and the appliance and rectify any faults.
- Close any PSV and repeat the test. If required, switch off, disconnect and the appliance and rectify any faults.

When the manufacturer does not provide specific instructions

- Close all doors and windows and adjustable vents.
- Operate any extraction/ circulation fans within the room as detailed above.
- Turn OFF any mechanical air SUPPLY systems (unless they are interlocked to the appliance).
- Open any Passive Stack Ventilation (PSV).
- Using a smoke match tube where possible offer the smoke match to the draught diverter or gas fire canopy within 5 minutes of operating the appliance at full rate.
- Observe the flow of smoke, for the test to pass all the smoke should be drawn into the flue (BS 5440: 1 states that "an odd wisp of smoke" can be ignored).
- Close any PSV and repeat the test.
- If spillage occurs leave the appliance operating for a further ten minutes and re-test.

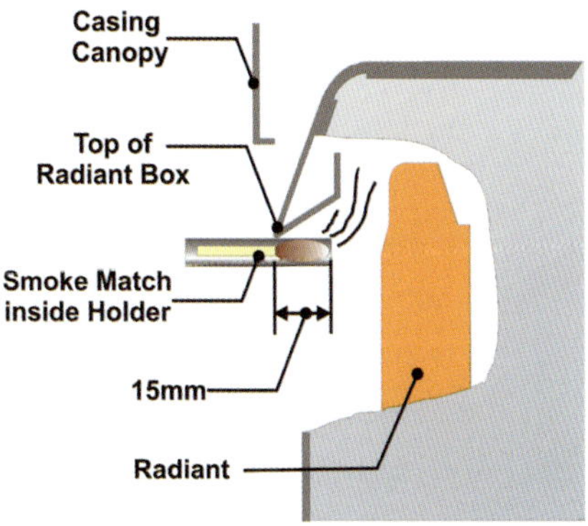

Figure 11.47 Manufacturers specific spillage test on fire

Figure 11.48 Spillage test fail - smoke emitting from down draught diverter.

- If required, switch off, disconnect and the appliance and rectify any faults.

- If there are any extraction fans in other rooms, repeat the tests with internal doors open, all windows, external doors and adjustable vents closed and fans running.

If the appliance should fail the spillage test, then the test should be repeated with a window slightly open, where the appliance now passes the spillage test(s) then purpose provided permanent ventilation should be installed (to determine the size of the vent required, measure the size of the area of opening when the window was opened), where the appliance fails the spillage test again then it should be treated as Immediately Dangerous and investigations carried out as to possible causes.

Routine maintenance checks should be carried out on all chimneys used for gas appliances to ensure their continued safe operation.

12. Re-Establishing Gas Supplies

12.1 Introduction

When the gas supply has been turned off at the emergency control, or there has been a failure of the gas supply, the gas supply will have to be re-established and operatives will be required to perform a visual risk assessment of all appliances on the installation.

This does **NOT** mean that the operative will "work" on the appliance's, indeed, the operative may not hold a certificate of competence for a particular appliance category, but he can still re-establish the gas supply to it and perform a visual risk assessment.

If for however during re-establishing a gas supply work is carried out on an appliance (i.e. burner has to be removed to replace a faulty ignition), then the operative would be required to undertake all checks as per the Gas Safety (Installation & Use) regulation 26(9).

IGE/UP/1B 2nd Edition stipulates that where there has been a **COMPLETE** loss of supply pressure or installation pressure, then the installation will require to be tested for tightness and purged. This requirement applies to competent engineers but is not extended to consumers who, for example, have an electronic token meter, which will cause a pressure loss in the event of no credit.

If the installation pipework has not been depressurised and there is no possibility of air entering the pipework, then there is no requirement to test or purge.

Regulation 6(6) of the Gas Safety (Installation and Use) Regulations states *"Where a person carries out any work in relation to a gas fitting which might affect the gas tightness of the gas installation he shall immediately thereafter test the installation for gas tightness at least as far as the nearest valves upstream and downstream in the installation."*

As a competent person, the engineer has a duty of care to inform the responsible person of any unsafe situations, which the engineer would reasonably be expected to identify when the appliance is visually inspected. The inspection would be limited to aspects of the appliance installation in the immediate vicinity of the appliance. For example, the engineer would not be expected to gain access under suspended floors to inspect installation pipework but he would be expected to identify any issues with visible pipework at the appliance location. Likewise, it would be unreasonable to expect the engineer to enter loft spaces or cupboards to inspect flue systems but it would be reasonable to expect the engineer to identify any flue problems either at the appliance location or with any external part of the flue system which is visible.

Any problems identified must be dealt with in accordance with the "Gas Industry Unsafe Situations Procedure".

12.2 Risk Assessment

When there is no possibility of air having entered the system, the visual risk assessment must consist of the following aspects:

12.2.1 Location

Is the room type suitable for the appliance type?
Is the room volume sufficient?
Compartment or room installation?
Clearances from combustibles and obstructions?

12.2.2 Flue

Termination?
Signs of spillage?
Correct use of bends?
Correctly jointed?
Proximity to combustibles?
Ceiling/floor penetration?
Provision for inspection?

12.2.3 Ventilation

Room and/or compartment?

Size (effective free area)?

Correctly installed?

Direct or indirect?

12.2.4 Signs of Distress

Heat stress at appliance or scorching of adjacent surfaces?

Corrosion?

Damage to gas or electrical components?

Soot deposits?

Evidence of Carbon Monoxide?

12.2.5 Stable & Secure

Will the stability of the appliance affect safety?

e.g. Cast iron heat exchanger appliance fixed using cavity fixings.
Cooker without stability bracket.
Cooker which is unstable.
Outset fire where the spigot is not engaging the closure plate.
Inset fire not sealed to opening.

When there is a possibility of air having entered the system the visual risk assessment must consist of the following additional aspects:

12.2.6 Flame Picture

Is the ignition and cross lighting smooth or is there explosive ignition?

Is the flame blue, vibrant and stable (some burners are designed to burn with a yellow flame)?

12.2.7 User Controls

These controls will normally be gas taps but any gas control operated by the customer must be checked for safe and correct operation.

Are gas taps easy to operate?

Does the burner remain lit at simmer or low setting?

Does the cooker lid SSOV extinguish the hotplate burners?

Are FSDs operating correctly (in terms of user operation)?

The appliances examined and any results of the visual risk assessments performed should be noted by the engineer on their work report.

13. Labels and Notices

Labels, notices and forms are used within the gas industry to identify specific important gas fittings; instruct a customer on the safe operation of an installation, warn them of any dangers which might exist within that installation or provide relevant safety information when work has been performed. The following diagrams show examples of these labels, notices and forms. Companies may use their own specific products or buy from another firm, although they may differ from company to company the information provided remains the same. It should be noted that some labels and notice design, colour and layout is stated by industry regulations and standards and cannot be reproduced in any other format.

13.1 Industry Unsafe Situations Warning Labels & Notices

Figure 13.1 - Immediately Dangerous Warning Label

SAFETY WARNING

You are warned that this gas appliance/ installation has been classified:

AT RISK

The gas /appliance/ installation is UNSAFE and has been turned off for YOUR SAFETY. It must not be turned back on until an engineer has carried out remedial work on the gas appliance/ installation to render it safe to use.
It is an offence to continue using an unsafe gas appliance/ installation under THE GAS SAFETY (INSTALLATION AND USE) REGULATIONS.

DO NOT REMOVE THIS LABEL

Engineers Name:	Registration No:
Brief Description of Fault:	Date:

GAS safe REGISTER

Figure 13.2 - At Risk Warning label

Serial No: WARN/0045681

WARNING/ADVICE NOTICE

GAS safe REGISTER

This form should be completed in accordance with the requirements of the current Gas Industry Unsafe Situations Procedure

Registered Business Details:

Company Name:
Address:
Post Code:
Telephone No:
Gas Engineer :
Licence No:

Customer Details:

Customer Name:
Address:
Post Code:
Telephone No:
Owner: Responsible Person:
Occupier: Tenant:

THIS NOTICE IS ISSUED FOR YOUR SAFETY

Escape of Gas:

An escape has been detected on the installation outwith the tolerances of a tightness test and the supply of gas has been: Turned Off Disconnected

Gas Appliance / Installation Pipework:

Appliance: Installation Pipework:
Type: Make:
Model: Serial No:
Location (Position/room):

Unsafe Situation:

Immediately Dangerous: At Risk: Not to Current Standards *see overleaf for details
Reason for notice:

With your permission it has been DISCONNECTED from the gas supply and a WARNING LABEL attached:
With your permission it has been TURNED OFF from the gas supply and a WARNING LABEL attached:
You have refused to allow it to be made safe and a warning label has been attached: *see overleaf for details
The appliance/installation has been left in operation and DOES NOT constitute an IMMEDIATELY DANGEROUS or AT RISK situation:

I confirm that I have received this warning notice concerning the safety of the gas installation. I understand that the use of an appliance/installation which has been deemed IMMEDIATELY DANGEROUS or AT RISK could present a hazard and could place me in breach of the Gas Safety (Installation and Use) Regulations:

Gas Engineers Signature:	Print Name:	Date:
Responsible Persons Signature:	Print Name:	Date:

 Copies: White – Gas User/ Responsible person Yellow - Gas Engineer

Figure 13.3 - Warning/ Advice Composite Notice - May be used for ID, AR and NCS situations

13.1.1 Emergency Service Provider Warning Labels

Due to their limited scope of activities, Emergency Service Providers normally use specific labels to identify particular unsafe situations which are not within their scope of competence to rectify. Where an ID or AR situation has been identified, either on the gas installation or appliance(s) a "Do Not Use" label is applied to either the installation or appliance(s). This label is different from the industry labels used by gas operatives as it instructs the customer that an unsafe situation exists or may exist and the installation/ appliance(s) must not be used until as such time as they have been checked and any fault rectified by a suitably competent Gas Safe Registered engineer. The industry unsafe situations procedure is still applied with the installation/ appliance made safe by turning off or disconnecting from the gas supply.

Where the ESP operative has been called to a reported smell of fumes and the installation has been found gas tight, a "Concern for safety" label is applied to the appliance(s) to warn against use until as such time as it has been confirmed safe to use by a competent Gas Safe Registered operative. The ESP operative again, due to their limited scope of activities, cannot confirm the safe operation of the appliance and always err on the side of safety by leaving the appliance turned off.

Figure 13.4 - ESP Unsafe Installation Warning Label

Figure 13.5 - ESP Unsafe Appliance Warning Label

Figure 13.6 -ESP Concern for Safety Label

13.2 RIDDOR F250G2 Form

It is a statutory requirement for all Gas Safe registered engineers to report directly to the HSE any unsafe situation which they have reason to believe has caused or may cause a danger to any person. RIDDOR form F250G2 is used for this purpose. This form may be filled in as a paper copy and posted or on line via the HSE web site.

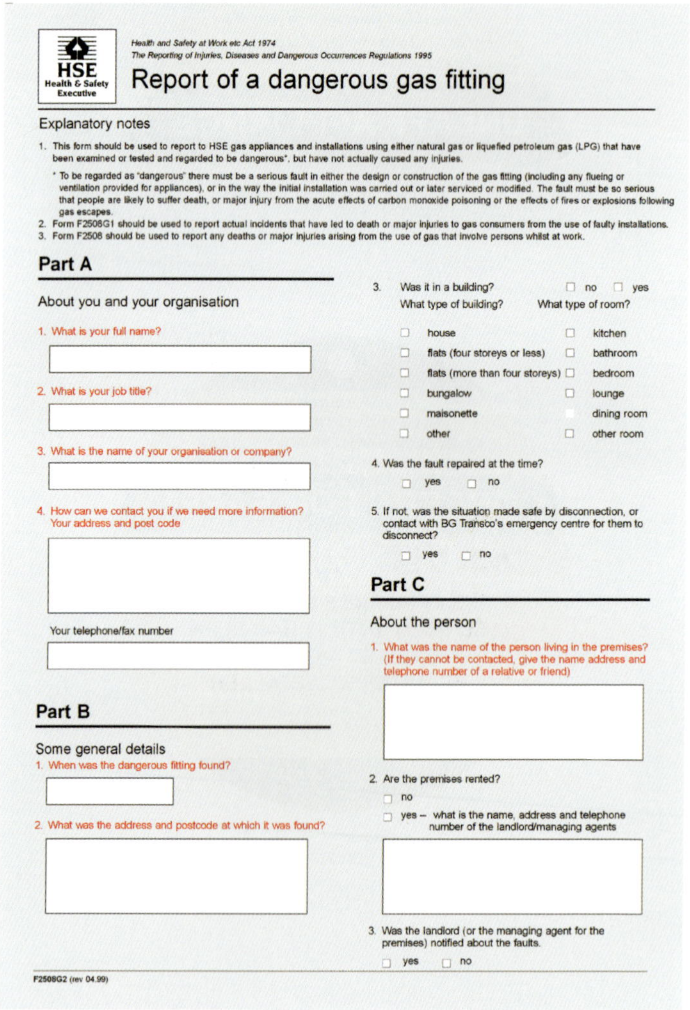

HSE Health & Safety Executive

Health and Safety at Work etc Act 1974
The Reporting of Injuries, Diseases and Dangerous Occurrences Regulations 1995

Report of a dangerous gas fitting

Explanatory notes

1. This form should be used to report to HSE gas appliances and installations using either natural gas or liquefied petroleum gas (LPG) that have been examined or tested and regarded to be dangerous*, but have not actually caused any injuries.
   * To be regarded as "dangerous" there must be a serious fault in either the design or construction of the gas fitting (including any flueing or ventilation provided for appliances), or in the way the initial installation was carried out or later serviced or modified. The fault must be so serious that people are likely to suffer death, or major injury from the acute effects of carbon monoxide poisoning or the effects of fires or explosions following gas escapes.
2. Form F2508G1 should be used to report actual incidents that have led to death or major injuries to gas consumers from the use of faulty installations.
3. Form F2508 should be used to report any deaths or major injuries arising from the use of gas that involve persons whilst at work.

Part A

About you and your organisation

1. What is your full name?
2. What is your job title?
3. What is the name of your organisation or company?
4. How can we contact you if we need more information? Your address and post code

Your telephone/fax number

Part B

Some general details

1. When was the dangerous fitting found?
2. What was the address and postcode at which it was found?
3. Was it in a building? ☐ no ☐ yes

What type of building?	What type of room?
☐ house	☐ kitchen
☐ flats (four storeys or less)	☐ bathroom
☐ flats (more than four storeys)	☐ bedroom
☐ bungalow	☐ lounge
☐ maisonette	☐ dining room
☐ other	☐ other room

4. Was the fault repaired at the time? ☐ yes ☐ no
5. If not, was the situation made safe by disconnection, or contact with BG Transco's emergency centre for them to disconnect? ☐ yes ☐ no

Part C

About the person

1. What was the name of the person living in the premises? (If they cannot be contacted, give the name address and telephone number of a relative or friend)
2. Are the premises rented?
   ☐ no
   ☐ yes – what is the name, address and telephone number of the landlord/managing agents
3. Was the landlord (or the managing agent for the premises) notified about the faults. ☐ yes ☐ no

F2508G2 (rev 04.99)

Figure 13.7 RIDDOR FORM - F250G2 Front Page

Part D

About the dangerous gas fitting

1. What was the main fault?
   - ☐ gas leak
   - ☐ inadequate flue
   - ☐ inadequate ventilation
   - ☐ other

2. What type of appliance was involved?
   - ☐ boiler
   - ☐ instant water heater
   - ☐ combined fire and boiler
   - ☐ warm air unit
   - ☐ decorative fire
   - ☐ non-decorative fire
   - ☐ convector
   - ☐ cooking appliance
   - ☐ other appliance

3. What type of gas was involved?
   - ☐ natural gas
   - ☐ liquid petroleum gas (LPG)
   - ☐ LPG/air
   - ☐ other gas

4. Was the appliance:
   - ☐ flueless
   - ☐ open-flued
   - ☐ room-sealed
   - ☐ other (eg closed flue)

5. Who last serviced the appliance (if known)?

6. What date was the appliance installed (if known)?

7. Was the appliance bought second hand (if known)?

   ☐ no ☐ yes ☐ don't know

8. What is the name of the installer (if known)?

9. What is their address and postcode?

10. What is their telephone number?

Part E

Summary of the dangerous gas fitting

Please say how dangerous you consider it to be, and why, and what action you have taken to make things safe by repairing faults at the time, disconnecting the gas supply, or advising occupiers (or the landlord or managing agent for the property) of the faults you are reporting.

Part F

Your signature

Signature

Date

Where to send the form

Incident Contact Centre, Caerphilly Business Centre, Caerphilly Business Park, Caerphilly, CF83 3GG.
or email to riddor@natbrit.com or fax to 0845 300 99 24

For official use

Client number	Location number	Event number	
			☐ INV REP ☐ Y ☐ N

Figure 13.8 RIDDOR FORM - F250G2 Reverse Page

13.3 Additional Warning/ Advisory Labels & Notices

These Labels and notices are used to warn or advise the customer or any person within the household of situations which may have a bearing on gas safety within their premises.

13.3.1 Uncommissioned Appliance/ Installation

Where an appliance/ Installation has been installed and as of yet not been commissioned the appliance/ installation must be disconnected from the gas supply and the following label affixed.

WARNING
UNCOMMISSIONED APPLIANCE/INSTALLATION
This appliance/ installation has NOT been fully commissioned and MUST NOT be used until it has been connected to the gas supply by a competent gas operative who must ensure that the appliance is fully commissioned before use.
Gas Operative's Name
Registration No
Date
safe

Figure 13.9 Uncommissioned Appliance Label

13.3.2 Electrical Bonding Label

To meet the requirements of regulation 18 (2) where main equipotential bonding is not fitted this notice informs the responsible person of the safety requirements and their responsibility to have this bonding carried out by a suitably competent person.

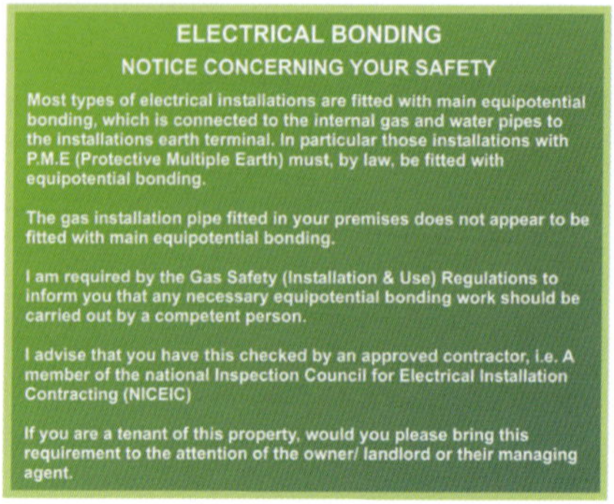

ELECTRICAL BONDING

NOTICE CONCERNING YOUR SAFETY

Most types of electrical installations are fitted with main equipotential bonding, which is connected to the internal gas and water pipes to the installations earth terminal. In particular those installations with P.M.E (Protective Multiple Earth) must, by law, be fitted with equipotential bonding.

The gas installation pipe fitted in your premises does not appear to be fitted with main equipotential bonding.

I am required by the Gas Safety (Installation & Use) Regulations to inform you that any necessary equipotential bonding work should be carried out by a competent person.

I advise that you have this checked by an approved contractor, i.e. A member of the national Inspection Council for Electrical Installation Contracting (NICEIC)

If you are a tenant of this property, would you please bring this requirement to the attention of the owner/ landlord or their managing agent.

Figure 13.10 Electrical Bonding Notice

13.3.3 Hearth Plate

A hearth plate is a legal requirement imposed by the Building Regulations and must be fitted when any new fireplace, hearth, flue or chimney system is installed or where the existing chimney has been extended, altered or refurbished. The label must be robust, indelibly marked and securely attached to the fabric of the building in an unobtrusive but obvious location such as the chimney or hearth it relates to, adjacent to the electric consumer unit, etc.

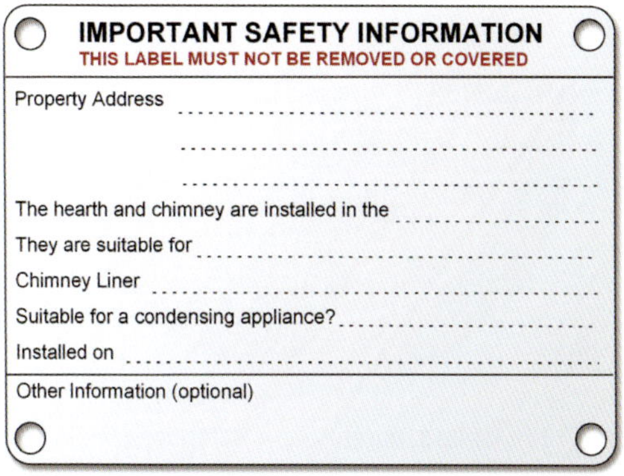

Figure 13.11 Hearth Plate/ Notice

13.3.4 Compartment Label

Figure 13.12 is a typical label affixed to the inside with a compartment which houses a gas appliance. It provides the customer with important safety information relating to the safe use of the appliance.

Figure 13.12 Appliance Compartment Label

13.3.5 Flueless instantaneous Water Heater

Flueless water heaters must have a label attached in a prominent position on the heater stating the maximum time the appliance can be operated continuously. The time limit being 5 minutes.

Figure 13.13 Flueless Water Heater 5 Minute Warning Label

13.3.6 Balanced Compartment

It is an industry requirement that a notice be displayed on the outside of any access door(s) into a balanced compartment to instruct the responsible person for the premises to keep the door closed at all times except where access is required to check and/or reset any controls.

Figure 13.12 Appliance Compartment Label

13.3.7 Fireguards

It is a requirement of BS 5871 that the Manufacturers instructions for the appliance/fireguard be left with the owner or occupier of the premises in which the appliance is installed. Within these instructions reference is made to the provision of a suitable fireguard in accordance with BS 6539 or BS 6778 where particularly vulnerable persons may be exposed to the hot surfaces or naked flame of the fire, for example the young, elderly or infirm.

This label may be included in the manufacturers pack or more likely attached to a suitable point on the fire. It must only be removed by the customer or occupier.

Figure 13.15 Fireguard Notice

13.4 Meter Labels and Notices

13.4.1 Suitably Worded Notice

This label must be provided on or near the meter. This is essential in order that the appropriate person has information relating to the procedure to be followed in the event of a gas escape.

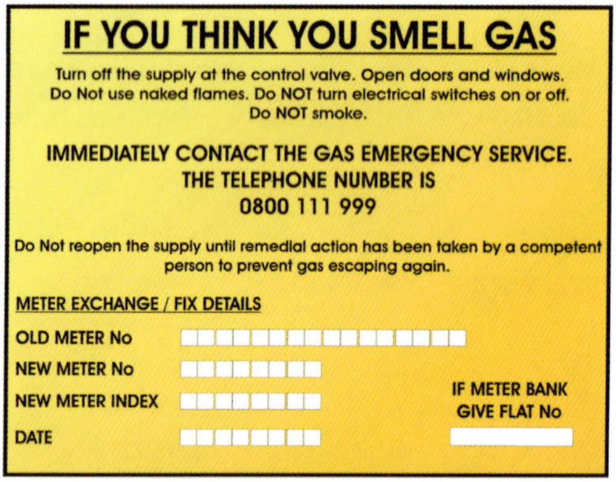

Figure 13.16 Meter Label (suitably worded notice)

13.4.2 Gas Emergency Control

If the Emergency Control Valve is not adjacent to the primary meter (more than 2m from or separated by a wall or partition), the ECV must have this label fixed on or near to the ECV.

In addition a notice specifying the location of the ECV shall be fitted on or near the meter.

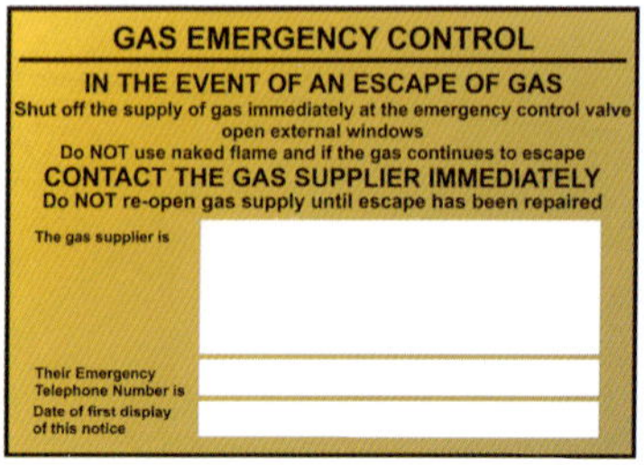

Figure 13.17 ECV Label

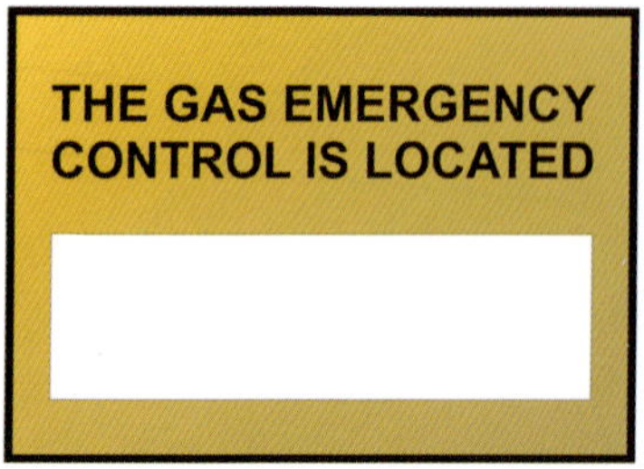

Figure 13.18 ECV Location Label

13.4.3 Gas Valve method of operation tape

The means of operating the key or lever (handle) of the ECV must be indicated. This is satisfied by the use of ON/OFF tape.

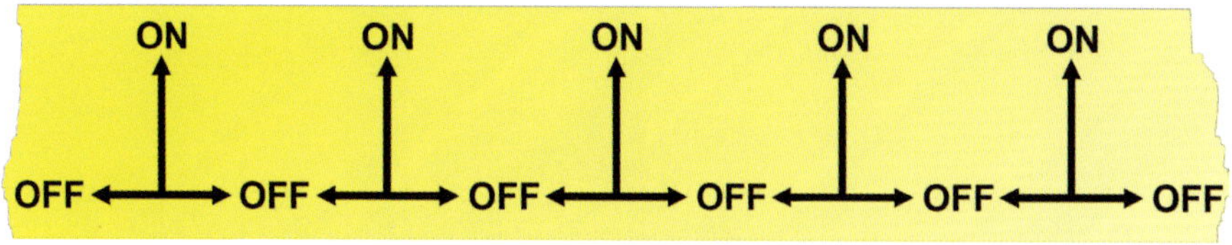

Figure 13.19 On/Off tape

13.4.4 Secondary Meter

If there is/are secondary meters served by the primary meter, a notice shall be fixed on or near the primary meter indicating the number of secondary meters so connected. In addition, every secondary meter shall be labelled "SECONDARY METER".

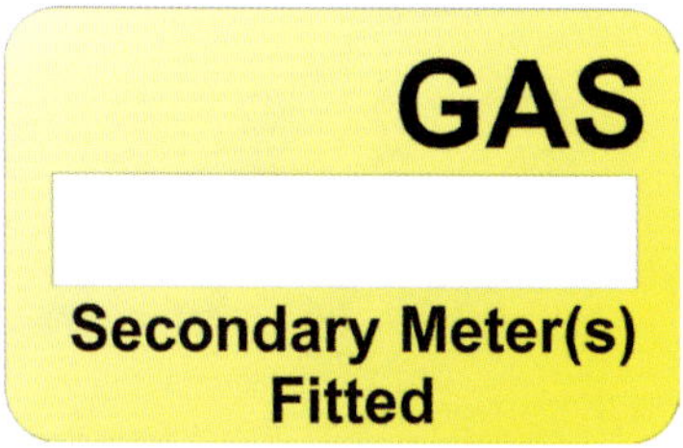

Figure 13.20 Secondary Meter

13.4.5 Joint Service

Where a service pipe serves more than one primary meter a notice shall be displayed on or near each primary meter indicating such.

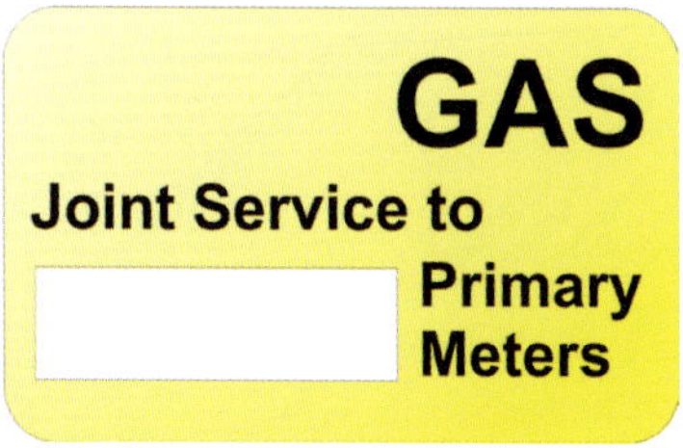

Figure 13.21 Joint Service Label

13.4.6 Gas Service "Live Gas" Tag

The gas service tag is affixed to the service pipe below the emergency control valve. It is used as a visual indicator that the service is live and contains gas. This tag meets the requirements of regulation 16 (3) by showing the service is still live albeit that the meter has been removed. This can also be met by the application of gas identification tape.

Figure 13.22 - Gas Service "LIVE GAS" Tag

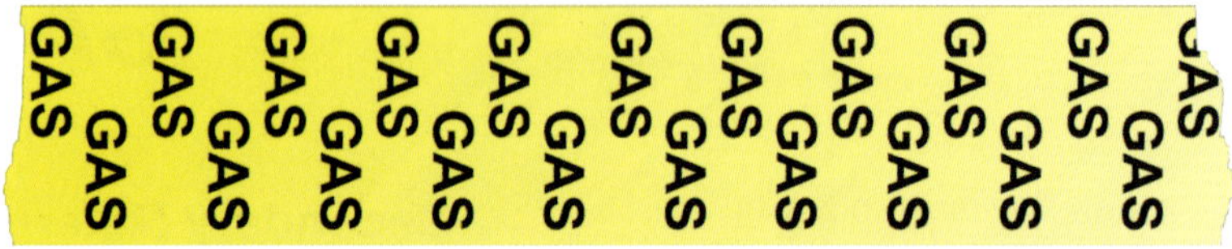

Figure 13.23 - Identification Tape

13.4.7 Meter outlet sealing disc

Where a sealing disc has been installed either on a new meter installation or to seal the gas supply in an existing installation this label is attached to the outlet of the meter installation to inform both the responsible person and the gas safe registered engineer of it's presence.

Figure 13.24 - Disc Label

13.4.8 Commercial Meter Labels

Commercial meter installations require additional labels which are usually in a composite form (A3 paper size) and include a meter line diagram and EX (hazardous area) indication.

Figure 13.25 - EX Label

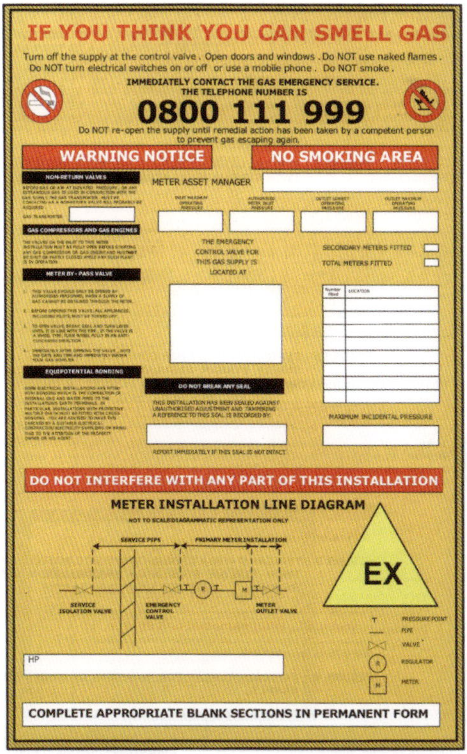

Figure 13.26 - Composite Form

13.5 Medium Pressure Supply Labels and Notices

Additional notices and labels are required for medium pressure fed meter installations over and above those required for low pressure fed meters.

13.5.1 Medium Pressure Supply

Due to the hazards associated with medium pressure fed installation this visually distinct label is affixed at the meter installation above the meter bar to warn that the supply pressure may be up to 2 bar and additional and additional due care and attention must be given.

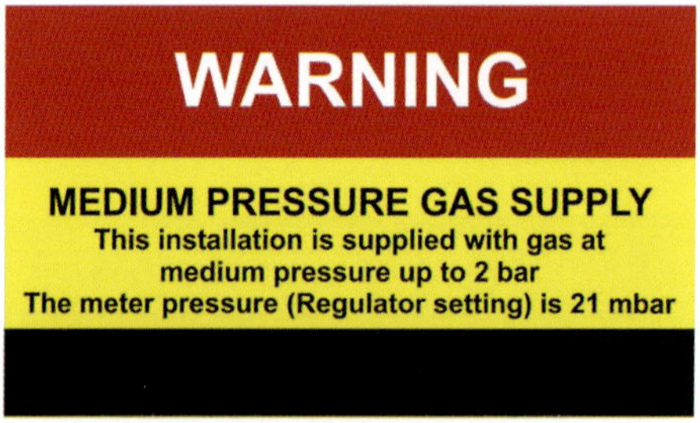

Figure 13.27 Standard Medium Pressure Supply Label

13.5.2 Medium Pressure Regulator Operating Details.

When a medium pressure regulator is commissioned or has a service check labels are affixed at the meter installation to indicate the actual operational parameters of the regulator, for example operating pressure, relief setting, slam-shut setting etc. There are two different labels for the different regulator types, two stage or single stage.

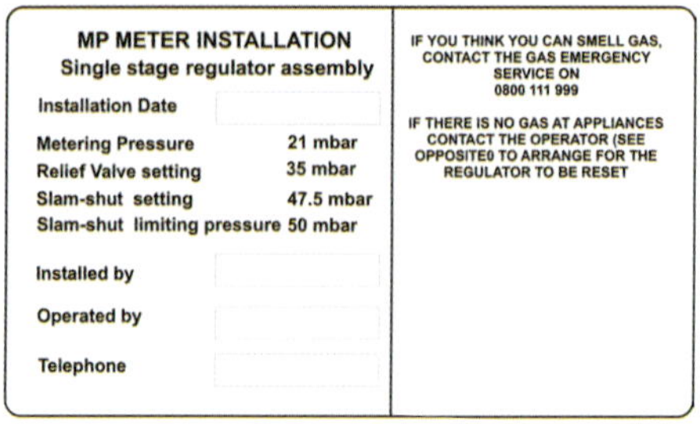

Figure 13.27 Standard Medium Pressure Supply Label

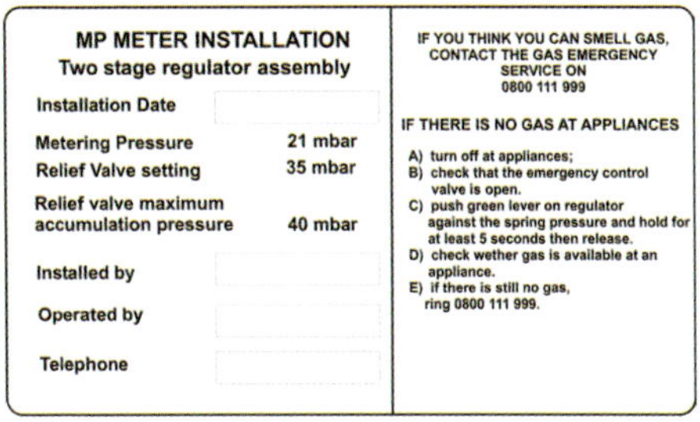

Figure 13.29 Two Stage Regulator Label

13.5.3 Meter Box Advisory Labels

Additional labels are applied to the meter box at strategic points to specify further information which is vital for the safe operation of the medium pressure fed meter installation.

Figure 13.30 Outlet Pipework and Vent Exit Location Label to be affixed to RHS of meter box

Figure 13.31 Meter Box Rear Knock Out Label

Figure 13.32 MCV Operation Label

13.6 Landlord/ Gas Safety Certificate

Landlords are required by Law to ensure that appliance(s), including the chimney/flue associated with that appliance(s), and installation pipework installed in any part of a premises owned by them or under their control is maintained in a safe working condition such that it will not pose a risk to any person who lawfully occupies the premises.

As stated in Regulation 36 of the GSIUR, a safety check must be carried out on each appliance and it's associated chimney/ flue system for which they have responsibility at intervals not exceeding 12 months. This also includes a tightness test of the installation.

All safety checks must be be carried out by a suitably competent Gas Safe Registered engineer. All results from the safety check must be recorded on a suitable certificate and must include the following information:

- the date of the safety check.
- the address of the premises in which the safety check was carried out.
- name and address of the landlord or, where appropriate, their agent.
- description of the location of each appliance and associated chimney/flue.
- a record on any defects identified.
- any remedial action taken.
- the results of any safety checks as required by Regulation 26(9)
- name, signature and licence/ registration number of the engineer or company carrying out the safety check. .

A copy of the safety check must be available to not only the landlord and where applicable their agent, but also the tenant. These certificates normally come with three sheets where the original top sheet is given to the landlord with copies retained by the tenant and engineer. This record must be retained by the landlord for a minimum of 2 years.

This certificate is not valid if the serial number has been defaced or altered. **Serial No: LGSC1/ 0123456**

This Landlords/Gas safety Certificate should be retained for a minimum of 2 years

LANDLORD/GAS SAFETY CERTIFICATE

This Landlord/Gas Safety Certificate records the outcome of tests and visual inspection as required by the Gas Safety (Installation and Use) Regulations

Next Safety Check Due Within Next 12 Months:

Only for use by Gas Safe Registered Engineers

REGISTERED BUSINESS DETAILS

Gas Engineer:

Gas Safe Register™ No:

Company:

Address:

Postcode:

Tel:

ADDRESS (PREMISES OF WORK UNDERTAKEN)

Name:

Address:

Postcode:

Tel:

OWNER/LANDLORD (OR WHERE APPROPRIATE THEIR AGENT)

Name:

Address:

Postcode:

Tel:

Rented accommodation Yes or No | No. of appliances tested

DETAILS OF WORK CARRIED OUT

Visual inspection of installation (Pass/Fail/N/A) | Gas tightness test (Pass/Fail/N/A) | Equipotential bonding (Yes/No) | Emergency Control Valve (ECV) accessible and operable: (Yes/No)

APPLIANCE DETAIL

	LOCATION (eg Kitchen)	TYPE	MAKE	MODEL	LANDLORD'S YES/NO	INSPECTED YES/NO	CHIMNEY/ FLUE OF/RS/FL
1							
2							
3							
4							

INSPECTION DETAILS

	Operating Pressure (mbar) or Heat Input (kW)	Combustion Analysis Initial reading (if applicable)	Safety Devices Operating correctly Yes/No/NA	Ventilation satisfactory Yes/No	Chimney termination & condition satisfactory Yes/No/NA	Chimney/ Flue performance check		Appliance serviced Yes/No	Combustion Analysis Final Reading (if applicable)	Appliance Safe to use Yes/No
						Flue Flow Pass/Fail/NA	Spillage Test Pass/Fail/NA			
1										
2										
3										
4										

	DEFECT(S) IDENTIFIED	Warning/Advice notice serial No (If applicable)*		ACTION TAKEN
1			1	
2			2	
3			3	
4			4	

Safety certificate issued by: Engineers signature | Print name: | Date:

Safety certificate issued by: Responsible person signature | Print name: | Date: | Tenant/Landlord/Agent

Original (to the person ordering the work)

Figure 13.33 - Example of a Landlords/ Gas Safety Certificate

Glossary and Appendices

Glossary

Appropriate fitting means a fitting which -
(a) has been designed for the purpose of effecting a gas tight seal in a pipe or other gasway.
(b) achieves that purpose when fitted; and
(c) is secure, so far as is reasonably practicable, against unauthorised opening or removal.

The responsible person
In relation to any premises, means the occupier of the premises or, where there is no occupier or the occupier is away, the owner of the premises or any person with authority for the time being to take appropriate action in relation to any gas fitting therein.

Distribution main
Means any main through which a transporter is for the time being distributing gas and which is not being used only for the purpose of conveying gas in bulk.

Cyclic volume
The volume of gas contained in each revolution of a diaphragm meter.

Emergency control
Means a valve for shutting off the supply of gas in an emergency, being a valve intended for use by a consumer of gas.

Fire stop
A non combustible seal which is designed to prevent the transmission of smoke or fire.

Flue
Means a passage for conveying the products of combustion from a gas appliance to the external air and includes any part of the passage in a gas appliance duct which serves the purpose of a flue.

Gas
Means any substance which is or (if it were in a gaseous state) would be gas within the meaning of the Gas Act 1986 except that it does not include gas consisting wholly or mainly of hydrogen when used in non-domestic premise.

Gas appliance
Means an appliance designed for use by a consumer of gas for heating, lighting, cooking.

Gas fittings

Means gas pipework, valves (other than emergency controls), regulators and meters, and fittings, apparatus and appliances designed for use by consumers of gas for heating, lighting, cooking or other purposes for which gas can be used.

Gas storage vessel

Means a storage container designed to be filled or re-filled with gas at the place where it is connected for use or a re-fillable cylinder designed to store gas.

Gas water heater

Includes a gas fired central heating boiler.

Installation pipework

Any pipework for conveying gas for a particular consumer and any associated valve or other gas fitting including any pipework used to connect a gas appliance to other installation pipework and any shut off device at the inlet to the appliance.

LPG

Liquefied petroleum gas.

Primary meter

Means the meter nearest to and downstream of a service pipe or service pipework for ascertaining the quantity of gas supplied through that pipe or pipework by a supplier.

Purge

The use of gas to displace air.

Operating pressure

In relation to a gas appliance, means the gas pressure which it is designed to operate.

Room sealed appliance

Means an appliance whose combustion system is sealed from the room in which the appliance is located and which obtains air for combustion from a ventilated uninhabited space within the premises or directly from the open air outside the premises and which vents the products of combustion directly to open air outside the premises.

Service pipe

Means a pipe for distributing gas to premises from a distribution main, being any pipe between the distribution main and the outlet of the first emergency control, downstream from the distribution main.

Service pipework

Means a pipe for supplying gas to premises from a gas storage vessel, being any pipe between the gas storage vessel and the outlet of the emergency control.

Service valve

Means a valve (other than an emergency control) for controlling a supply of gas, being a valve -

(a) incorporated in a service pipe; and
(b) intended for use by a transporter of gas; and
(c) not situated inside a building.

Supplier in relation to gas means -

(a) a person who supplies gas to any premises through a primary meter; or
(b) a person who provides a supply of gas to a consumer by means of the filling or re-filling of a storage container
(c) a person who provides gas in re-fillable cylinders for use by a consumer.

Transporter

In relation to gas means a person who conveys gas through a distribution main.

Work

In relation to a gas fitting includes any of the following activities carried out by any person, whether an employee or not, that is to say -

(a) installing or re-connecting the fitting;
(b) maintaining, servicing, permanently adjusting, disconnecting, repairing, altering or renewing the fitting or purging it of air or gas;
(c) where the fitting is not readily movable, changing its position; and
(d) removing the fitting;

but the expression does not include the connection or disconnection of a bayonet fitting or other self-sealing connector.

Appendix I

SI Units

The SI metric system (Systems Internationals d'unites) is extensively used throughout most parts of the world and has widely replaced our more conventional British imperial system of measurement. However, within the gas industry we still use the imperial system in some of our measurements due to the age of equipment still in circulation such as meters reading in ft^3 and appliances with gross heat inputs in Btu's/hr.

SI system uses seven primary units, from which our other important units are derived.

Primary Units	Unit of measurement	Symbol
Length	metre	m
Mass	gram	g
Temperature	Kelvin	K
Electric current	ampere	A
Time	second	s
Quantity of substance	mole	mol
Luminous intensity	candela	cd

Table 1 - Primary SI Units

Appendix 2

Conversion Tables

Length					
1 in	=	25.4 mm	1 mm	=	0.03937 in
1 ft	=	304.8 mm	1m	=	39.37 in
1 yd	=	914.4 mm	1m	=	3.281 ft
1 mile	=	1.609 km	1km	=	0.624 mile
Area					
1 in²	=	645.2 mm²	1 mm²	=	0.001550 in²
1 in²	=	6.452 cm²	1 cm²	=	0.1550 in²
1 ft²	=	929 cm²	1 m²	=	10.76 ft³
1 acre	=	4047 m²	1 acre	=	0.0247 acre
1 acre	=	0.4047 ha	1 ha	=	2.471 acre
Volume (space)					
1 in³	=	16390 mm³	1 mm³	=	0.000061 in³
1 in³	=	16.39 cm³	1 dm³	=	61.02 in³
1 ft³	=	0.02832 m³	1 dm³	=	0.03531 ft³
1 ft³	=	28.32 dm³	1 m³	=	35.31 ft³
Volume (Liquid/ gas)					
1 pint	=	0.5683 litre	1 mm³	=	0.000061 in³
1 gallon	=	4.546 litre	1 litre	=	61.02 in³
1 ft³	=	28.32 litre	1 litre	=	0.03531 ft³
1 ft³	=	0.02832 m³	1 litre	=	0.22 gal
			1 m³	=	35.31 ft³
Note: The volume conversion factor for gas changes dependant on temperature pressure and water vapour content. To ensure consistency we always refer to the volume of gas under standard reference conditions (st) which is 15 °C, 1013.25 mbar and dry					
Mass					
1 oz	=	28.35 g	1 g	=	0.03527 oz
1 lb	=	453.6 g	1 kg	=	2.205 lb
1 lb	=	0.4536 kg	1 tonne	=	2205 lb
1 ton	=	1016 kg	1 tonne	=	0.9842 ton
1 ton	=	1.016 tonne			
Pressure					
1 in wg	=	2.5 mbar	1 mbar	=	100 pa
1 lbf/in²	=	68.95 mbar	1 mbar	=	0.4 in wg
1 lbf/in²	=	0.06895 bar	1 bar	=	14.50 lbf/in²
1 ft water	=	30.48 mbar	1 bar	=	100,000 pa
1 ft water	=	0.3048 m water	1m water	=	3.281 ft water
1 atmosphere	=	1013.25 mbar (st)	1m water	=	98.07 mbar
Heat Energy					
1 Btu	=	1055 J	1 kWh	=	3.6 MJ
1000 Btu	=	1.055 MJ	1 cal	=	4.1868 J
1 Therm	=	100 000 btu	1 J	=	0.000 9478 Btu
1 Therm	=	105.5 MJ	1 MJ	=	0.009478 therm
Heat Rate					
1000 Btu/h	=	0.2931 kW	1 W	=	1 J/s
1000 Btu/h	=	1.055 MJ/h	1 kW	=	3.6 MJ/h
1 HP	=	0.7457 kW	1 kW	=	3412 Btu/h
1 HP	=	2.685 MJ/h	1 kW	=	1.341 HP
			1 MJ/h	=	0.2778 kW
			1 MJ/h	=	947.8 BTU/h
Calorific Value					
1 Btu/ft³	=	0.03723 MJ/ m³(st)	1 MJ/m³	=	26.86 Btu/ft³ (st)
Flow Rate					
1 ft³/h	=	0.02832 m³/h	1 m³/h	=	35.31 ft³/h
1 gallon/h	=	4.546 litres/h	1 litre/h	=	0.22 gallon/h